Royal Confinements

Royal Confinements:

A Gynaecological History of Britain's Royal Family

Jack Dewhurst

St. Martin's Press

New York

Library of Congress Catalog Card Number: 80–52921
ISBN 0–312–69466–0

First Edition

To my parents-in-law,
Eileen and Roland Atkin,
with affection

Contents

Acknowledgements

Writing this book has given me enormous pleasure but I could not have accomplished it without the help of many people. I am delighted to record my indebtedness to them: to my wife for encouragement throughout the whole of its gestation and for her patient proof-reading; to my secretary, Mrs Patricia Hawkins, for typing the manuscript, correcting my errors and providing additional details for some sections; to Miss Olwen Hedley and Mrs Lira Winston for their help with historical research; to Mrs Georgina Going for tracing many references; Mrs Rosamund Brodie, Mrs Sally Josephson and Mr Frank Moore for their assistance in uncovering obscure details; to Dr David Harvey, Dr John Pryse-Davies and Dr Michael de Swiet for their advice on the illnesses of William, Duke of Gloucester, and Queen Anne; to Professor Cedric Carter and Professor Mogens Ingerslev for genetic advice regarding the Prince and Princess of Denmark; to Mr Geoffrey Chamberlain, Professor Paul Polani, Mr Robert Perceval, Mr O. V. Jones, Mr John L. Thornton and Miss Patricia Want for their willing help at various times in various chapters; to Mrs Una Bloch for her help with the early history of George Rex and Mrs Gila Falkus for much textual improvement.

Introduction

This story of royal births spans two hundred years, a period which saw tremendous changes in the knowledge and practice of midwifery in Britain. Indeed, perhaps the only two generalizations possible are that at no point during this period was childbearing remotely like it is today, and that throughout these years there was an appalling loss of mother and child life.

How great this wastage was can scarcely be evaluated now, for not until the middle of the eighteenth century, half-way through our story, do records of maternal mortality begin to appear. These show great variation, but even the most favourable indicate that childbirth carried a risk a hundred times greater than it does today. The earliest records are from the Dublin Lying-in Hospital, where one mother in every hundred died – and Dublin had a high reputation for the quality of its midwifery; one of the earliest textbooks on the subject was written there by Fielding Ould in 1742. Elsewhere the risks were even higher. In Vienna three per cent of mothers died, and in Paris the figure was four per cent.

Delivery at home was in one respect safer, for the risk of infection – childbed fever – was far less. In the first part of the nineteenth century the death-rate of mothers delivered at home, under the care of the Westminster General Dispensary, was only 0.2 per cent whilst among patients in the London Lying-in Hospital it was 2.9 per cent. Childbed fever devastated maternity hospitals, and as numbers rose, overcrowding occurred and even simple cleanliness was lacking. Le Fort, a famous French gynaecologist, describing conditions in the Maternité in Paris in the nineteenth century, tells of floors washed once a month, midwives attending fever cases and normal cases alike, and of childbed fever, measles, bronchitis and infectious fevers all nursed together; the toll on mothers' lives was 12.4 deaths in every hundred.

How many more women died in pregnancy and labour during the first part of our story we do not know. There were no maternity hospitals before 1730, so they were spared the scourge of epidemics of puerperal fever, but with knowledge of the process of childbearing little more than elementary, death and serious injury must have been commonplace. Nor are there any records of how many babies died at birth or soon afterwards, so we can only guess at this and probably few of us would put the figure high enough.

Most confinements were conducted by self-styled midwives with no knowledge or qualifications and often with little humanity. The only claim to be considered midwives at all rested in their own fecundity and seniority – 'as if a woman were more expert in that art for her dotage or old age'. Only a minority appear to have made any attempt to improve their skill or to treat their patients with compassion.

Some of the earliest recorded midwives were employed and rewarded by the royal family. One Margaret Cobbe attended Elizabeth Woodville, wife of Edward IV, when she gave birth to the future Edward V on 1 November 1470; Mrs Cobbe received £10 a year for the rest of her life. Alice Massey received a similar sum as royal midwife to Elizabeth of York, wife of Henry VII. Alice Dennis received £100 for each of her attendances on Anne of Denmark, wife of James I, when Anne gave birth to her daughter Mary in 1605 and to Sophia the following year. Alice was only selected at the last moment for the Queen was reluctant to decide which of the various midwives assembled she would have 'until the easiness or hardness of her travail doth urge her to it'.

These leading ladies of their profession helped greatly to raise standards. Moreover by the seventeenth century the midwives' cause was also being championed by three distinguished male practitioners of the art who also served the royal family – Peter Chamberlen the Elder, physician to the queens of James I and Charles I; Dr William Harvey, physician to the same two sovereigns and author of the first original text on midwifery in English; and Dr William Sermon, physician to Charles II.

Peter Chamberlen the Elder, a most distinguished member of the very complicated Chamberlen family which we will meet again shortly, presented a petition to James I in 1616 'that some order may be settled by the state for the instruction and civil government of midwives'. The proposal never obtained approval and it was many years before any such governing body was to be formed. The more reputable man-midwives, of course, did all they could to improve the skill and practice of their female counterparts, though in one case, at least, the motivation may not have been entirely altruistic. Dr Peter Chamberlen, nephew to his namesake who had petitioned James I, proposed to the Royal College of Physicians in 1634 that a Corporation for training and licensing midwives be set up, with himself as its head. Such a scheme would have given him strong influence over nearly all the midwifery practice in London and it was not approved.

For many years there was bitter feuding between midwives and man-midwives, the latter teaching and practising under extraordinary difficulties. They were on the one hand vilified by their female counterparts, who resented their intrusion into what they regarded as a woman's province, and on the other they were treated with contumely by physicians who refused them admission to their college. Some man-midwives even had to enter the birth-room stealthily so that the patient would not be aware that they had been called in. Percival Willughby – a most distinguished man-midwife of the seventeenth century – tells how, when summoned by his daughter who wanted his advice on a difficult case, not wishing to alarm the patient, he 'crept into the chamber on my hands and knees and returned and it was not perceived by the lady'.

At the root of the trouble between male and female practitioners of midwifery was the use of obstetric instruments which was almost exclusively a male preserve. The midwife could only await the natural outcome of the labour, or try, as many did, to expedite it by the crudest methods. Midwives of the ignorant sort, who were much in evidence, were prone to resort to astonishing barbarities to attempt to hasten delivery, instead of allowing nature to take its course.

Willughby defined the midwife's duty in these terms: 'The midwife's duty, in a natural birth, is no more but to attend, and wait on nature, and to receive the child; and (if need require) to help to fetch the after-birth, and her best care will be to see that the woman and child be fittingly and decently ordered with necessary conveniences.' He continued, 'I desire that all midwives may gain a good repute, and have a happy success in all their undertakings; and that their knowledge, charity, and patience, with tender compassion, may manifest their worths among their women, and give their women just cause to love, honour, and esteem them.'

But he did not always find things like this. He describes a midwife of Threadneedle Street who 'caused several women perforce to hold the patient by the middle whilst that she with others pulled the child by the limbs one way and the women her body the other way'. Willughby found another midwife tossing her patient in a blanket, 'hoping yet this violent motion would force the child out of her body'. The man-midwife, on the other hand, could employ instruments which might save the day – to his credit and the midwives' chagrin.

The obstetric forceps were introduced into the European practice of midwifery by the Chamberlen family towards the end of the sixteenth century, although it is known that similar instruments were in use in Arab medicine as early as 1,000 AD. Whether the Chamberlens were responsible for an independent invention or somehow learned of the original is unknown, but they were to keep the nature of the instrument a secret for more than a hundred years, during which time they alone employed this means of success when all else had failed. The original Chamberlen forceps only came to light in 1813 when they were discovered beneath a trapdoor in the attic of Woodham Mortimer Hall, near Maldon in Essex, which had been the home of Dr Peter Chamberlen. In this hiding-place was discovered a box containing three sets of midwifery instruments including forceps and a fourth pair of crudely constructed forceps, probably an early model. The box also contained various keepsakes such as a pair of gloves, fans, spectacles, letters – and a packet labelled by Mrs Chamberlen, 'My husband's last tooth'!

Various other means of attempting to extract the child did exist but none was anything like so successful as the forceps. One, known as the fillet, consisted of a single band of linen, silk or leather, which could on occasions be strengthened with whale bone; this was passed as high as possible into the birth canal, either with the finger, or with a special instrument contrived for the purpose, and was looped over some part of the head, such as the chin, or manipulated around the circumference of the head. The ends of the fillet were twisted together to obtain a purchase and the medical attendant pulled as firmly as the material of the fillet would permit. If there was much resistance to the birth of the head such a method was unlikely to succeed. An alternative was the vectis – a single curved fenestrated blade, similar in almost every respect to a single blade of a pair of obstetric forceps. This was inserted alongside the head so that the tip curved inwards over a part of the child's head; attempts were then made to lever the head out or, by applying counter-pressure with the fingers on the opposite side of the skull, to grasp the head and pull it down. Blunt and sharp hooks were also available if the child should be coming bottom first. These could be hooked over a groin and again traction applied.

The forceps were in effect a pair of tongs; the blades crossed over to the opposite side from the handles and each blade could be inserted separately to grasp the fetal head and the handles were fastened together either by binding them with cord or by an interlocking device.

The Chamberlens, who kept a monopoly on them, were a large family and so many were given the same names that they are easily confused with one another. The family were Huguenots who had escaped to England to avoid persecution. Peter Chamberlen the Elder and his brother, named Peter the Younger, were barber-surgeons, an occupation regarded as considerably inferior to doctors who were Fellows of the Royal College of Physicians. The brothers were sometimes in trouble with the Royal College for overstepping their privileges and Peter the Elder was even imprisoned in Newgate in 1612 for his frequent transgression of the Physicians' rules. His release was only obtained through the personal intervention of the Queen, Anne of Denmark, wife of James I, whose confinement he had attended. Peter the Elder had the privilege of serving not only James I's queen, but Charles I's also; he attended Henrietta Maria when she was delivered of a dead child at Greenwich in 1628.

Peter the Elder's royal practice was to be carried on by his nephew, known as Dr Peter Chamberlen, who had been able and astute enough to graduate at the University of Padua and to obtain a degree in medicine at both Oxford and Cambridge before he was twenty years old. He was later to become a Fellow of the Royal College of Physicians. It was Dr Peter Chamberlen who took his uncle's place at the confinement of Henrietta Maria in 1630 when she gave birth to the future Charles II.

Dr Peter's own family was a large one for by his two wives he had fourteen children of whom the eldest, christened Hugh, was to continue the family tradition as royal accoucheur and as custodian of their famous secret. As we shall see, Hugh was to attend James II's wife, Mary Beatrice, and also his two daughters, Anne and Mary.

Not surprisingly the Chamberlens' unknown method of achieving delivery caused much envy and curiosity. Whenever they were called in, which was often when labour had been in progress several days and all else had failed and the poor woman was exhausted or worse, they carried in their secret instrument in an enormous wooden box, elaborately carved and decorated. Two people were always needed to lift it. No one but they was allowed into the birth chamber, which was locked, and the delivery was accomplished in total secrecy with the patient herself being blindfolded so that even she could not tell what had been done.

Of course the Chamberlens were not invariably successful, particularly when faced with the terrible pelvic contraction and deformity so common at that time. Rickets and malnutrition softened and distorted the pelvic bone and so reduced the size of the bony passage of the pelvis, that, in extreme cases, delivery was impossible even for the Chamberlens. Their most notorious failure occurred in 1670 when Hugh Chamberlen took his secret to Paris, in the hope of selling it for an enormous sum to the famous French obstetrician Mauriceau. Mauriceau had at that time a tiny dwarf patient whose pelvis was prodigiously deformed by rickets; clearly if Dr Chamberlen's 'secret' could deliver her it must be worth the money! Chamberlen confidently predicted that fifteen minutes would be sufficient for him to produce the child but, in Mauriceau's words, he 'laboured unceasingly for three hours without pausing except to take breath'; and he failed. The poor patient died the following day. Mauriceau, in accordance with his practice, immediately carried out a caesarean section, in the hope that the child might be saved. Not only did he find a dead child, however, but a ruptured uterus as well, the result of Dr Chamberlen's three-hour attempt at delivery.

This tragic story shows, as well as anything can, the terrible fate of the wretched patient in labour if her pelvis was contracted, or her child lying in the wrong position so that it could not be born naturally. Only some attempt to deliver the woman with forceps, or by crusing the head, or by turning the child and pulling it out by the feet, might save her life – but it would seldom save the child's. Caesarean section had virtually one hundred per cent mortality and the recovery of the mother from the operation was a miracle, so that the procedure was reserved for the patient who was moribund or already dead.

The name 'caesarean section' probably arose from a Roman law, 'Lex Caesarea', which forbade the burial of a pregnant woman until the child was removed from her abdomen. There is no authentic account of it having been performed on a living patient before the seventeenth century, although it is sometimes maintained that a Swiss pig-gelder named Jacob Nufer carried it out on his own wife in the year 1500. But the lady went on to have several more children quite normally, which could scarcely have happened if he had in fact opened her abdomen *and* her womb to extract the child. It seems probable that if the operation were performed at all, it was the removal of a fetus from within the abdomen but outside the uterus – a condition called an advanced extra-uterine pregnancy, an exceedingly rare occurrence, only seen nowadays in underdeveloped countries. Jane Seymour who bore a son, later Edward VI, to Henry VIII on 12 October 1537 was rumoured to have been delivered by caesarean section. But again this seems most unlikely. Contemporary accounts make no reference to it and later ones are cryptic and unconvincing. The probability of the operation being carried out at such an early date is very small – quite apart from the fact that the Queen attended the christening of her infant son four days after his birth, which she would never have been able to do after such a formidable procedure. Jane died twelve days later; it is doubtful if she would have survived so long following a caesarean section. Not until 21 April 1610 is there an authentic account of its performance on a living mother, and she died of infection as did many others for years after. It must be remembered that then there was no understanding of the cause of infection and neither asepsis nor antisepsis had been contemplated. Since the standard remedy for almost anything was blood-letting, it is not surprising that the patient was rarely strong enough to recover from any serious complication during her confinement.

Mauriceau, as we have seen, and a number of other authorities did use caesarean sections post-mortem in an attempt to save children whose mothers had died, but it seldom succeeded even then. Only in desperate circumstances was the procedure contemplated while the mother was still alive. Not until 1793, for example, was a successful operation carried out in England, by James Barlow of Blackburn. Eleven previous attempts had resulted in the deaths of all the mothers and five of the children and it was to be another forty years before there was a second success. As late as 1865 sixty-six out of seventy-seven mothers on whom caesarean section was performed in Britain died; twenty years later in the United States of America, one hundred out of one hundred and sixty died.

Any obstetric procedure, whether a forceps delivery, caesarean section, turning and extracting of the child, caused agony to the patient, of course, since anaesthetics were unknown and pain relief could be obtained only from mandragora, opium, hemp – or alcohol. Even though in the nineteenth century progress was made in relieving the pain of surgical procedures by the newly discovered anaesthetic substances, the suggestion that they should be used for childbirth found bitter and vociferous opponents. 'In sorrow thou shalt bring forth children' had been written in Genesis 3:16 and it was thought by some to be flouting God's will to attempt to change it.

When James Young Simpson first used chloroform to relieve the pains of labour for a doctor's wife on 9 November 1847, a great controversy erupted. Simpson was able to quote the Bible too: 'And the Lord God caused a deep sleep to fall upon Adam and he slept; he took one of his ribs and closed up the flesh instead thereof.' (Genesis 2:21) Nonetheless, despite this apparent vindication of his work, the argument continued until the stamp of approval was put upon anaesthesia for delivery by Queen Victoria, who had chloroform dropped slowly onto a royal handkerchief for the birth of her eighth child, Leopold, in April 1853.

Another important change had occurred during the early part of the eighteenth century when the Chamberlens' monopoly of the obstetric forceps was broken. Other inventors with improved patterns of forceps came along. More men began to involve themselves in the practice of midwifery, although their encroachment was still hotly disputed. Those men who were learned and had undertaken general medical studies and might therefore have advanced the state of knowledge, were still excluded by midwives from normal cases, which they wished to observe and study; they were only permitted to attend abnormal cases which had reached an impasse.

Curiously enough the man-midwife had always enjoyed greater popularity in France and with patients who were higher in the social scale. His acceptance at this social level may have originated at the delivery of Louise de la Vallière in 1663 by a man-midwife laconically referred to as '*l'homme Boucher*'. Louise was among the earlier mistresses of Louis XIV and the employment of a man at her confinement may have set a fashionable trend. At all events, another well-known French man-midwife, Jules Clément, officiated at several of the confinements of Madame de Montespan, Louise's successor as the King's mistress and at that of the Dauphine in 1686, and for the deliveries of the Queen of Spain in 1713, 1716 and 1720. In England, as we have seen, Peter Chamberlen the Elder had attended Anne of Denmark and Henrietta Maria. Hugh Chamberlen was to have been in attendance at the confinement of Mary Beatrice of Modena, James II's second wife, although in the event the birth took place while he was out of London.

Even at court, however, the belief in midwifery as a woman's province was still held. An attempt to call in a man during one of the confinements of Caroline of Ansbach, wife of George II, produced a terrible scene with the midwife in hysterics, refusing to play any further part in the labour. So, although we will see men-midwives at the confinements of the royal ladies in this book more often than they would be found attending more ordinary mortals, their relationship was a delicate one. We find, for example, Dr William Hunter, one of the leading accoucheurs of his day, remaining in the background at the confinement of Queen Charlotte, and leaving the delivery entirely to the midwife, Mrs Draper. If the special skills of the man-midwife were required he would be consulted, but not unless.

By the second half of the eighteenth century though the obstetric forceps had become freely available, many who used them had neither knowledge nor skill to do so safely and efficiently. William Smellie, the greatest of British obstetricians, became a past master of the art – despite surprisingly large hands 'fit only to hold horses'. But others without his ability began to use the instruments too freely, and the suffering women of Georgian England endured agonies and sustained terrible injuries by the unskilled and often unnecessary use of instruments. Mrs Sarah Stone of Piccadilly who in 1737 wrote *A Complete Practice of Midwifery* declared: 'I am certain that when twenty women are delivered with instruments (which has now become a common practice) nineteen of them might be delivered without, if not the twentieth.' In her own practice of three hundred cases a year instruments were needed only four times. But Haggard tells of one obstetrician who used forceps twenty-nine times in sixty-one births, and of another who began 'to cut and slash as soon as everything was not precisely normal', and in this way had a mortality rate of twenty per cent among his patients.

The reaction to such traumatic practices was predictable. An attack on unnecessary instrumental deliveries, written by a Dr Nicholls, a great friend of William Smellie, and entitled 'Petition of the Unborn Babies', so delighted one of the royal midwives, Mrs Kennon, that she presented him with five hundred pounds. But unfortunately the pendulum swung too far and by the end of the eighteenth century a period of ultra-conservatism began. Leading obstetricians of the day put all the weight of their authority against instrumental delivery. Thomas Denman, who will appear again in a later chapter, wrote in 1788 that the forceps were to be used only 'to supply the total want or deficiency of the natural powers of labour'. It became a well-known tenet of Denman's that instruments were never to be used while progress, *however slow*, was being made. Another famous obstetrician, William Hunter, would show students his pair of forceps covered with rust, to prove how rarely he used them.

This violent reaction against forceps delivery was to have a devastating effect upon the course of British history, for it was to lead to the blackest royal obstetric tragedy there has ever been – the deaths in 1817 of Princess Charlotte and of her infant son.

1

The Restoration Stuarts

When Charles I, defeated and deposed, was beheaded in 1649 the fortunes of the Royal House of Stuart were at their lowest ebb. But in 1660 his son, Charles II, had been recalled in triumph and the monarchy had been restored. Two years later when he married Catherine of Braganza there was every expectation that there would soon be an heir who would secure the Stuart succession for many years.

Catherine, then aged twenty-three, was by the standards of the time old for a bride, but she clearly had many possible childbearing years ahead of her and there seemed no reason to doubt her fertility. Charles, nine years older, had already sired a number of bastards and was later to produce more. Antonia Fraser, in her recent biography of the King, gives the total as twelve, one each by Lucy Walter, Elizabeth Killigrew, Catherine Pegge, Moll Davies and Louise de Keroualle, two by Nell Gwynne and five by Barbara Villiers, Countess of Castlemaine. Since Charles's fertility was therefore beyond question, the fault presumably lay with Catherine.

In July 1663 when she was still not pregnant after more than a year of marriage, Catherine visited Tunbridge Wells in the hope that taking the waters there would promote her fertility. Two months later, impatient to conceive, she visited Bath for the same reason. In 1664 Samuel Pepys recorded that she was 'by all reports incapable of bearing children', but in February 1666 he referred to a miscarriage, although there is no reference to this in the King's correspondence or anywhere else. Two years later, though, on 7 May 1668, Charles informed his sister, Minette, in France by letter that the Queen had miscarried that morning. Concerned as he was, the fact that she had proved capable of conceiving gave him hope. On the following day, Samual Pepys recorded that the miscarriage had been of a perfect child about ten weeks old; but since a fetus of ten weeks does not yet have a human form, we can only conclude that Pepys's evidence for its perfection was questionable.

A year later Charles wrote again to his sister, who had heard a rumour that Catherine had missed two periods; Charles confirmed this, but mentioned that the Queen was experiencing the occasional passage of a small show of blood, which some of the experienced women at the court construed as a sign of a successful pregnancy. In fact though, the outlook cannot have been promising. There is a significant passage in the King's letter to his sister: 'She missed those [her periods] almost if not altogether, twice about this time she ought to have had them and she had a kind of colic the day before yesterday which pressed downwards and made her apprehend she would miscarry.' The colic was in all probability due to contractions of her womb which, in association with intermittent bleeding, made the likelihood of miscarriage high. Indeed, two weeks later, on 7 June, Charles was obliged to write to his sister telling her of a second miscarriage. Since the Queen had missed two periods and miscarried some two weeks later, she again appears to have been about ten weeks pregnant when the mishap occurred. Dr Willis, the eminent physician, told Dr Lloyd, who told Bishop Burnet that the Queen had miscarried so late that the sex of the child could have been identified. Sex cannot be identified at ten weeks and this hearsay evidence seems to have been inaccurate.

Catherine never became pregnant again. She was still only in her twenties and there is no evident explanation for her failure to produce an heir, but as time passed it seemed more and more likely that Charles would be succeeded by his brother James, Duke of York, a prospect that was viewed by Protestants in the government and in the country with deep misgivings, for James and his wife, Anne Hyde, were suspected by many to be secret supporters of the Catholic faith, if not indeed Catholics themselves. In fact by 1669 both were seeking communion with the Church of Rome and before long they made little attempt to hide their conversion. To many in England Catholicism spelt 'Popery'. There were memories of the burning of Protestants by Bloody Mary and of the Guy Fawkes plot to blow up the Houses of Parliament. The Catholic rulers of France were regarded as oppressors, determined to impose religious tyranny throughout Europe. The fear of the growing strength of the Catholic Church was so great that it led, in 1673, to the Test Act, which excluded from public office anyone who refused to take communion according to the rites of the Church of England. James, faced with such a dilemma, stuck to his religious beliefs, and resigned all his public offices. Any lingering doubts about his own religious persuasion and the strength of his attachment to it were dispelled. On Charles's death the country would be faced with its first Catholic monarch since Mary Tudor; and the question of James's own successor became one of increasing political significance.

James's wife, Anne, had died in 1671, leaving him with two small daughters, Mary and Anne. James had met Anne, daughter of the Earl of Clarendon, while they were both in exile in France during the Interregnum and she had become pregnant by him. After the Restoration the couple were secretly married in London, two witnesses only being present. Then James, alarmed by the hostile reaction provoked by the news of his marriage, tried to withdraw, protesting that others too had slept with Anne and that in any case without the King's consent the marriage was illegal. Charles, however, gave his permission without demur and indeed insisted that James must honour his marriage contract. In the eleven years of marriage that followed, the Duchess of York gave her husband six children but her childbearing history was a sad one. The first baby, which she was carrying at her wedding, was a son who died when he was six months old. In 1662 a daughter, Mary, was born and the following year a son, James, created Duke of Cambridge. A second daughter, Anne, came into the world in 1665, the year of the Great Plague. Few at the time recorded her birth, since it seemed unlikely to be of national importance, though her father noted it briefly but precisely in his diary – thirty-nine minutes past eleven on the night of 6 February. The next year brought a third son, but 1667 brought tragedy to the young family. The four-year-old Duke of Cambridge and his baby brother both died while another boy born during the year lived only a few hours. So when Anne herself died in 1671, out of her four sons and two daughters only the daughters remained.

Despite their parents' adherence to Catholicism, the two girls were brought up as Protestants and were soon showing every sign of being staunch supporters of the Church of England. Any attempt made by their father to convert them produced no impression on them. So long as they remained his heirs there seemed a possibility that the country would be prepared to tolerate a Catholic king. But in 1673, two years after the death of Anne Hyde, James decided to remarry and chose as his bride a Catholic princess, Mary of Modena. Should she produce a son then he would replace his half-sisters in the line of succession – and there seemed no doubt whatsoever that such a son would be brought up a Catholic. Before receiving James's proposal Mary of Modena had been planning to enter a convent and showed great reluctance to abandon this idea. By her own account she objected to the marriage so strongly that she screamed for two days and nights and had to be restrained by force during the worse of her tantrums. Even the Pope intervened. He wrote to her mother asking that Mary overcome her reluctance to be married, since the marriage would further the cause of Catholicism more than her entry into a religious life. She was urged to reflect upon the benefits which her marriage would bring to England, so that she would 'open to yourself a field of merit wider than that of the virgin cloister'.

Not surprisingly, in view of her family's influence with the Holy See, in England Mary personified all the evils of Popery, and it was even rumoured that she was the natural daughter of the Pope. Papal effigies were burnt in public and Parliament tried, unsuccessfully, to persuade the King to prevent the marriage. On Saturday, 30 September 1673 James and Mary were married by proxy in Italy, the Earl of Peterborough representing the Duke. Mary was then only fourteen years old but already a striking individual. Lord Peterborough wrote that 'she was tall and admirably shaped, her complexion was of the last degree of fairness, her hair black as jet, so were her eyebrows and her eyes, but the latter so full of light and sweetness as they did dazzle and charm too. There seemed given unto them by nature sovereign power to kill and power to save; and in the whole turn of her face which was of a most graceful oval, there were all the features, all the beauty and all that would be great and charming in any creature.'

With such a young and beautiful wife the Duke of York seemed about to confront the country with the prospect of a new Catholic line of monarchs. Moreover neither he nor Mary was prepared to modify their religious practices which so inflamed public opinion. In 1678 the so-called Popish Plot erupted, a strange tissue of lies and rumours feeding on public prejudice to produce a politically explosive situation. Two rogues, Titus Oates and Israel Tonge, maintained that they had uncovered a plot in which the Pope was accused of plotting to murder Charles in order to put James on the throne as a Catholic sovereign. The intensity of public feeling which was stirred up by this totally fabricated plot led to riots and vicious anti-Catholic demonstrations. Thousands of Catholics were accused of involvement and were thrown into prison. Some, including James's own secretary Edward Coleman were executed and the Duke of York's own unpopularity was so marked that he was sent abroad until things became calmer.

In February 1685 Charles 11 died and James became King. After twelve years of marriage Mary had not borne him a son so perhaps after all James would be succeeded by his Protestant daughter Mary. The storm of the Popish Plot had blown itself out and at first the country seemed prepared to tolerate him even though he appeared to be going out of his way to antagonize public opinion by celebrating Mass openly and – despite the Test Act – by appointing Catholics to public offices. Then, in 1688, Mary of Modena gave birth to a son.

Although she was still not yet thirty, it was a very surprising turn of events. By the time she became Queen, Mary had been pregnant eight times but had no living child. She first became pregnant some three months after her marriage but miscarried in March 1674 following an indisposition in February. However she soon conceived again and in January 1675 gave birth to a daughter. Evidently her labour and delivery went smoothly. On 8 January she played ombre with the Duchess of Monmouth until midnight, then supped and slept well. On the morning of the 9th she heard two Masses and dined before her pains began. The King and Queen were informed that she was in labour and they arrived in time for the birth of the child, a girl, who was christened Catherine Laura in honour of the Queen. But the infant lived only until 3 October when she died in convulsions. Poor Mary who was by then pregnant again miscarried the following day. Three pregnancies had come to nothing.

Then it seemed that her fortunes had changed. On 28 August 1676 she gave birth to a second daughter, Isabella, who was born so rapidly that the King and Queen did not arrive in time for the birth. Isabella survived and a little over a year later came the event that Mary and James had hoped for: Mary became pregnant soon after a visit to Bath and a son was born to her on November 1677 at 'just a quarter before ten at night', as the Duke recorded in his diary. The boy was christened Charles and created Duke of Cambridge. But he lived only five weeks; after a brief illness of two days he died of smallpox shortly before noon on 12 December. There seemed no end to the couple's misfortunes when in March 1681 their only surviving child, Isabella, who had been repeatedly ill during her short life, died, aged four and a half, during the absence of her parents in Scotland. This tragic event was followed by the birth of another daughter, Charlotte Mary, in August 1682 who died in convulsions only two months later; this in turn was followed by a miscarriage in October 1683 and by another in May 1684. Eight pregnancies had led to no living child.

The Duchess of York was far from well after her last miscarriage. A few weeks afterwards she went to Windsor to convalesce. A little later in the summer she accompanied her step-daughter, Anne, to Tunbridge Wells to take the waters, but she did not think they suited her. Her health was giving cause for concern and there now seemed very little likelihood of her having a son to inherit the throne. For the next three years there were no more pregnancies; then in 1687, soon after she became Queen, Mary decided to visit Bath, in the belief that it had been the waters there that had helped in the conception of her first son, ten years earlier. Most of her doctors believed that the visit was unwise since it would prove too much strain on her constitution, but one of her physicians, Dr Waldegrave, whom Mary trusted, supported the project and it went ahead, even though the court was in mourning for Mary's mother who had died earlier that summer. After visiting the Duke of Somerset at Marlborough Mary proceeded to Bath while James went on a progress to Portsmouth, Southampton and Salisbury, before joining her there on 16 August. He remained with her until the 21st when he set off again, this time on a progress through Gloucester, Ludlow and Shrewsbury, and prayed for a son at the Well of St

Winifred in Flintshire. He returned to Mary in Bath on 6 September and remained with her until the 15th when he returned to London.

All this time each morning Mary had been assiduously bathing in the Cross Bath, so called because a white marble cross had been erected to commemorate the birth of her son Charles, the Duke of Cambridge, who had been born nine months after her previous visit. She got little privacy there, for there was no shortage of spectators eager to watch their Queen bathe. To do this Mary and her ladies-in-waiting who accompanied her, wore a voluminous stiff yellow canvas covering with large sleeves which ballooned out with the water so that the shape of the body could not be seen. When the Queen entered the water an Italian string orchestra burst into activity and the galleries thronged with people!

Despite the faith which many women then placed in 'the waters' as a means of promoting fertility, there is no evidence to suggest that they had any physical effect, although they may have been of psychological benefit. We know that emotional factors do influence conception. This is probably why, for example, pregnancy can occur in women who have failed to conceive for many years, soon after they adopt a child. So, if Mary's visit to Bath did have any effect this may well have been simply due to her belief that the waters had helped her to conceive her first son. At all events the bath certainly appeared to have been a dramatic success for, although the precise date of her conception is uncertain, the Queen clearly did become pregnant very soon after her visit.

Her son was eventually born on 10 June 1688 but for some time the first week of July was thought to be the expected date. The infant at birth was not considered to show signs of prematurity, so a birth date of 10 June would correspond to a conception date in mid-September, which fits well with the King's presence in Bath until the 15th. Had the birth taken place in early July, this would have corresponded to a conception date about the second week of October when Mary and James were together again in London and Windsor. But though either date remains a possibility later events support the earlier one. Carola Oman, Mary's biographer, says that shortly after returning to London in the first part of October, the Queen began to feel ill. Agnes Strickland, her earlier biographer, wrote of whispers around the court by the end of November that the Queen might be pregnant, while James in a letter to his daughter, Mary of Orange, on 29 November, informed her of the pregnancy of which the Queen had told him some time earlier. The matter was formally made public by royal proclamation on 23 December, and a day of general thanksgiving was ordered.

For a pregnancy conceived about early to mid-October, the public announcement on 23 December is remarkably soon for those days, when no precise means of confirmation of an early pregnancy existed. Moreover the Queen would hardly have been feeling indisposed in the first part of October if conception had been then, but such indisposition is to be expected at precisely that time had she become pregnant in September. It seems justifiable therefore to conclude she conceived before the King left Bath on 15 September.

The news of the Queen's pregnancy was received by Anne and her sister Mary with rage, which quickly led to incredulity. A series of letters full of malice and vindictiveness passed between the sisters. They were highly sceptical of the existence of the pregnancy, and in this they were not alone. Rumour was rife in many quarters that the Queen was not pregnant at all, or, if she was, the doubters affirmed, the King was not the father. Her confessor Father Petrie or the Papal Nuncio Count D'Adda were suggested as the real father, and, not surprisingly, puns on their names were commonplace. In Holland Dutch caricatures were drawn showing the Queen pinning on a cushion beneath her dress in front, whilst other sources credited her with dropsy.

Anne had made a number of attempts to be present when Mary was dressing or undressing. The Queen, however, probably realizing Anne's motives, always changed alone and on one occasion threw a glove at her step-daughter to get her to leave the room. Anne aired her suspicions in a letter to her sister Mary in March three months before the child was born. 'I cannot help feeling [the Queen's] great belly is a little suspicious', she wrote, 'it is true indeed she is very big but she looks better than she ever did which is not usual for people when they are far gone for the most part look very ill.' This is, in some ways, a strange letter. It is far from true that women in late pregnancy look very ill, and Anne must have known this very well. Many look the picture of health, and it would not have been surprising if Mary, carrying a pregnancy successfully for

the first time for almost six years, had been one of them. Moreover
if Anne believed the child was not due until early July, as she afterwards stated, the phrase 'when they are far gone' is a strange one.
But Anne felt that she had such cause for suspicion that 'when she
is brought to bed no one will be convinced it is her child except
it prove a daughter. For my part I declare I shall not except I see
the child and she parted.'

Anne was not to see 'the child and she parted' for when the delivery took place she was in Bath. Why, since her suspicions were
so strong, she had made the journey as late in the Queen's pregnancy
as 12 May, is difficult to explain. David Green, her biographer,
suggests her decision was a sudden one, and says that in her
entreaties to the King for permission, she 'pleaded pregnancy'. She
was not, however, pregnant then, having miscarried in April, so presumably the real reason was to expedite her full recovery. 'James',
Green writes, 'who had been begging her to stay gave in to her
and her doctors and agreed to her going.' But her absence was
remarked upon by many who thought it odd that she did not pay
the Queen the courtesy of waiting until she was delivered before
going.

Another possibility that has been suggested is that Anne's husband's asthma was troublesome and he always found Bath eased
his breathing; but he could have gone alone. Agnes Strickland,
the Victorian authoress of *Lives of the Queens of England*, suggests
that Anne's absence was deliberate. 'Can anyone believe', wrote
Miss Strickland, 'that if Anne did suspect a cheat she would have
shown so little regard for her own interests as to have invented a
pretext for going to Bath, instead of remaining on the spot to expose
it? But the Queen had given her indisputable proofs that she was
about to become a mother, and Anne purposely went out of her
way that she might not be a witness of the birth of a brother whose
rights she intended to dispute.' So one biographer saw it, and it
is more convincingly explained in those terms than in any others,
as her behaviour after the confinement bears out.

The Queen decided that she would not be delivered at Windsor
but at St James's, a decision perhaps prompted by the doubts about
her pregnancy. St James's Palace was at the centre of things, readily
accessible to the members of the Privy Council, who should be

present at the birth. A confinement so far away as Windsor, especially if it were to occur quickly, as in the event it did, might take place before the necessary witnesses arrived, and without official authentication the deepest suspicion would attach to it. As things turned out, the quarters selected in the Palace for the confinement were ready only in the nick of time. Work was in progress on the rooms adjoining the Queen's apartments, and was only finished during the evening of Saturday 9 June. The Queen, then at Whitehall, had sent word several times that day to enquire about the progress, but was so determined to go to St James's, come what may, that she insisted that she would sleep there that night even if she did so on the floor. When word finally came that the rooms were ready it was after dinner, and Mary was playing cards. She finished the game, and was then carried in her sedan chair through the park with her Chamberlain, Lord Godolphin, beside her, and her ladies-in-waiting ahead. She and the King spent the night together, and in the morning between seven and eight o'clock he returned to his own rooms. Within fifteen minutes Mary sent word to him asking him to summon witnesses. Her labour had begun.

The events of the labour of Mary of Modena have been subjected to the closest scrutiny in view of the immense importance of the birth of her son. Despite suspicions prior to the event, and accusations after it, of the smuggling in of a spurious child in a warming pan, there can now be no real doubt that she gave birth to James Francis Edward Stuart, unhappily and unfairly known to posterity as the Old Pretender.

Many readers will doubt whether a new-born child could possibly be smuggled in a warming pan into a room containing a number of people with any real hope of escaping detection. The warming pans with which people are now familiar are eighteenth-century ones and those of the seventeenth century were larger; a fine example can be seen in the Victoria and Albert Museum. Even in the smaller eighteenth-century pattern, I was able to place a $5\frac{1}{2}$-lb child comfortably without closing the lid but this might have been achieved if the baby had been folded up more tightly. It is probable that a child between six and seven pounds could have been completely enclosed in a seventeenth-century warming pan although he would presumably have required to be drugged to prevent him crying.

Soon after her pains began, the Queen was attended by the midwife, Mrs Judith Wilkes, and her nurse, Pelegrine Turini.

The next person to arrive was Mrs Dawson, a Protestant and a Woman of the Bedchamber. Sunday, 10 June 1688 was Trinity Sunday and Mrs Dawson had to be summoned from church as indeed had a number of others who arrived later. She found the Queen sitting beside her bed on a stool, looking disconsolate. Her Majesty asked for the couch in the ante-room to be made up, but Mrs Dawson said it had not yet been aired, and pressed the Queen to get back into the bed in which she and the King had spent the night. At this point a warming pan did indeed enter the scene, perhaps rather unnecessarily, to warm the bed from which Mary had so recently arisen. Although the presence of this warming pan is beyond dispute, at the time of its appearance at 8.15 a.m., an hour and three-quarters before the birth, it could not possibly have contained a spurious child whose presence could have been kept secret from the many witnesses who were shortly to enter the room.

Anne, Countess of Sunderland, another Woman of the Bedchamber came next; she had also been at her devotions. The Lord Chancellor and other members of the Privy Council followed at varying intervals, and took up their positions at the foot of the bed, where the curtains were closed, although they were open at the bed sides. The Lord Chancellor approached the bedside, after his arrival, to inform the King and Queen of his presence, but then retreated to the foot. Catherine, the Queen Dowager, came in at 9.15 and stood by the clock.

A little before ten o'clock the Queen cried out to Mrs Wilkes, 'I die, Oh you kill me, you kill me.' She then gave three large pushes, and with the third the child was born. Mary Beatrice, relieved but apprehensive, cried out, 'I don't hear the child cry', and at that very moment he did. Madame de Labadie, one of the Queen's bed women, then took the baby from Mrs Wilkes and was about to carry him into an adjoining room, when she was stopped by the King, who called upon the Privy Council to witness that the child had been born to the Queen.

The sex of the infant was not immediately announced. A system

of signals had been prearranged, however. Mrs Wilkes was to pull
her dress if the child was a boy, thereby informing the watching
Lady Sunderland, who, in turn, touched her forehead, as a sign to
the King that he had a son. He could not contain himself, however,
and eagerly asked Mme de Labadie 'what is it?.' 'What your
Majesty desires', was the reply whereupon the Earl of Faversham,
who had overheard the exchange, forced a passage through the
crowd for Mme de Labadie and her charge, calling out 'room for
the prince'. The possibility that Mary did not bear a male child is
negligible. More than sixty people were in the room at the time
including Catherine, the Queen Dowager, and the Privy Council.
Three of the ladies in close attendance by the bedside of the labouring Queen were Protestants, one of whom was Baroness Bellasys,
herself a faithful companion.

The King was of course in the seventh heaven with happiness.
He knighted the Queen's physician Dr Waldegrave on the spot and
gave the midwife Mrs Wilkes five hundred guineas 'for your breakfast'. The royal accoucheur, Dr Hugh Chamberlen, who should
have been present to deal with any difficulty which might arise, was
unhappily for him out of town, having been summoned to Chatham
to another case. He too, it seems, must have expected the Queen's
confinement somewhat later, or else he would hardly have absented
himself, even briefly, so near to the possible date. Chamberlen's role
as accoucheur was, in any event, essentially that of a man-midwife
available to be called in by the female midwife if delivery could not
be accomplished naturally, and no doubt he would be more accus-
tomed to answering a summons, whenever it came, rather than holding himself in readiness at any particular time. It has already been
stressed, however, that estimates of the duration of pregnancy at
that time were imprecise, and no tests to confirm the accuracy of
the date estimated from the last menstrual period were available.
Mary Beatrice had indeed told the King that she had two dates,
and that in her previous confinements the doctors had calculated
a month too long.

There was no proper understanding in those days of when in the
menstrual cycle a woman actually became pregnant. Not until 1830
was a convenient and reasonably accurate method of calculating the
expected date of confinement devised. This was called Naegele's

rule after the obstetrician who devised it; it consisted in adding 280 days to the date of the first day of the last menstrual period which was done in practice by adding a week to that date and counting backwards 3 months—i.e., last menstrual period 3rd September 1687, expected date of confinement 10 June 1688. We now know that confusion can occur when the expected date of confinement is calculated in this way, in, for example, patients whose menstrual period comes less often than every twenty-eight days or is irregular. Furthermore, some women do not miss their first period when they become pregnant but instead have a much reduced show of blood, and it is uncertain whether the calculation should be made from this date or that of the previous normal period. Something of this sort probably occurred in the case of Mary Beatrice who, as she said, had two dates – one probably calculated from the last normal period and one from a shortened period which followed it about a month later by which time it seems likely she had conceived.

On 12 June James wrote to the Prince of Orange informing him of the birth of the child, and a few days later to Mary, his daughter, giving her further details. Mary at once bombarded her sister Anne with a list of eighteen questions, all evidence of the envy and hatred the sisters felt for their stepmother. 'Had anyone felt the child move?' 'Did any woman other than her confidants see the Queen's face when she was in labour?' 'Who was present in the room?' 'When did they arrive?' 'Where did they stand?' 'Who held the Queen?' 'Had Anne ever known the Queen so suddenly and mysteriously delivered in such privacy?' and so on.

The answers Anne was obliged to give can scarcely have given her sister any comfort:

Question 1: 'I never heard anyone say they felt the child stir; but I am told Lady Sunderland and Madam Mazarin say they felt it at the beginning. Mrs Dawson tells me she had seen it stir but never felt it.'

Question 10: 'There was no screen.'

Question 11: 'The feet curtains of the bed were drawn and the two sides were open. When she was in great pain, the King called in haste for my Lord Chamberlain, who came up to the bedside to show he was there; upon which the rest of the Privy Council did the same thing. Then the Queen desired the King to hide her face with his head and periwig, which he did for she said she could not be brought to bed and have so many men look upon her; for all the Council stood close to the bed feet and the Lord Chancellor upon the step.'

Question 12: 'As soon as the child was born the midwife cut the navel string because the afterburthen did not follow quickly.'

Question 13: 'When the Queen Dowager first came into the room she went up to the bedside and after that stood all the while by the clock. There was in the room' – and here Anne named forty-two individuals who were present to whom she added 'two of the Queen Dowager's Portuguese's' and 'pages of the back stairs and priests'.* The midwife and various other women she did not mention.

Question 15: 'Her labour was never so long.'

Anne's source of information for these answers was Mrs Dawson, whom she questioned 'in such a manner that I might know everything, and in case she should betray me that the King and Queen might not be angry with me'. Towards the end of the letter Anne added rather ungrammatically, 'all she says seems very clear but one does not know what to think; for methinks it is wonderful if it is no cheat that they never took no pains to convince me of it.'

This may have been Anne's view but why need she require such convincing? The Queen had been pregnant eight times previously, and despite a lapse of more than three years without another pregnancy, it cannot have been thought surprising that at the age of thirty she should conceive again. Moreover, Anne's doubts may have been ill-concealed and her surreptitious prying may have so irritated the Queen that she was determined to deny her step-daughter the satisfaction of knowing for certain that she was pregnant. It is scarcely credible that the masquerade of a pretended

---

* Anne named as present in the room: Lord Chancellor: Lord President: Lord Privy Seal: the two Lord Chamberlains: Lord Middleton: Lord Craven: Lord Huntingdon: Lord Powis: Lord Dover: Lord Peterborough: Lord Melfort: Lord Dartmouth: Sir John Ernley: Lord Preston: Sir Nicholas Butler: Duke of Beaufort: Lord Berkeley: Lord Moray: Lord Castlemaine (constituting the members of the Privy Council). Lord Faversham: Lord Arran: Sir Stephen Fox: Mr Griffin, Lady Peterborough: Lady Bellasys: Lady Arran: Lady Tyrconnel: Lady Roscommon: Lady Sophia Buckley: Lady Fingall: Madame Mazarin: Madame Bouillon: Lady Powis: Lady Strickland: Lady Ceary: Mrs Crane: two of the Queen Dowager's Portugueses: Mrs Bromley: Mrs Dawson: Mrs Waldegrave: Lady Wentworth and Mrs Turine.

Agnes Strickland quotes Lord Melfort (who was named by Anne as being present) as saying that there were in all sixty-seven persons present.

pregnancy could have been sustained throughout nine months and then throughout labour, in the presence of more than sixty people.

If Anne had been as determined to discover the truth as she after-wards alleged to her sister, she had a very simple remedy to the problem: stay with the Queen, uncover the deception and denounce it. But she was not prepared to take this ultimate step, which would have proved her in the wrong, and she departed to Bath. Neither was she prepared to make any open challenge to the truth of the confinement, nor to listen to any evidence concerning it. Later when James, in view of the persistence of rumours of his son's birth, set about gathering evidence from 'more than 40 persons, most of them of the first quality' who were prepared to testify that James Francis Edward was his mother's son, he convened a Council and invited Anne. She said she was pregnant and declined to come; when the evidence was sent to her she refused to read it 'for I have so much duty to the King that his word must be more to me than those depositions'. She did not really doubt, but she did not want to believe, and was not prepared to put herself in the position of having to accept the truth.

The depositions before the Privy Council contained evidence from Lady Bellasys which Agnes Strickland describes as 'most im-portant and conclusive and such as must have substantiated it in any court of justice'. Lady Isabella Wentworth, another Protestant in the Queen's household, also certified to the genuineness of the birth on oath to the Privy Council and long afterwards to Bishop Burnet – the arch-sceptic about the confinement – and others in forthright terms: 'She was as sure the Prince of Wales was the Queen's son as that any of her own children were hers.' She affirmed the truth as strongly as she knew how in saying, 'Out of zeal for the truth and honour of my mistress I spoke in such terms as modesty would scarce let me speak at another time.'

In the event the birth of a son acknowledged by the King and Queen as theirs was enough to tip the scales and to lead to an invita-tion being sent to William of Orange to depose James. On 5 November 1688 William landed with a small force at Torbay. James mustered his own troops at Salisbury, but his position was undermined by desertions. His son-in-law Prince George of Den-mark and John Churchill, who had gone to Salisbury, deserted to

William and there were risings against the King elsewhere in the country, which clearly showed him that his position was hopeless. He returned at once to London, but Anne escaped to Nottingham as soon as she learnt of his return. James and Mary Beatrice fled to France with their infant son, and William and his wife Mary were later declared joint sovereigns. Instead of ensuring the succession, the birth of James Francis Edward Stuart had destroyed it.

2

The End of a Dynasty:
Mary and Anne

The Declaration of William and Mary as joint sovereigns in 1689 was accompanied by an Act to ensure that the throne should never again pass to a Catholic. Should Mary and William have any children, then they would inherit the throne. If not, Mary's sister, Anne, would become Queen and any children she might have would follow her. Catholics were explicitly barred from the succession. The fertility of the two sisters now became vitally important for the future of the House of Stuart lay in their hands, or, more correctly, in their wombs. But not only did no heir survive to inherit, but the obstetric history of Anne was more poignant and tragic than that of any British queen or queen consort and can have few equals anywhere.

Mary and Anne were, as we have seen, the only surviving children of Anne Hyde, James II's first wife, but despite their parents' leanings to Rome had been educated in strict Protestant principles. Their governess was Lady Frances Villiers, a staunch Anglican, and their chaplain and tutor was a devoted Protestant minister, Edward Lake. Their rigid upbringing in the Anglican faith was, if anything, further strengthened later when a bitter anti-Catholic, Henry Compton, became their preceptor. Their lives were led in a devout atmosphere of regular church going and frequent prayers, and they acquired religious convictions which were never to waver and which were to give Anne in particular an inner strength she was, one day, to need.

In 1677 Mary married William of Orange and left England. She was then fifteen, he twenty-seven. She is said to have cried for a day and a half when informed that the marriage had been arranged, which is perhaps not surprising when we consider the curious differences between them. William was a solemn, silent man, thin, short and unprepossessing; Mary was fashionable, loquacious, stately and four inches taller than her husband! They were first cousins, he being the only child of William II of Orange and his wife, also named Mary, who was the daughter of Charles I of England.

William's birth had been notable in a number of ways. His father died of smallpox in October 1630 when his wife was in the last month of her pregnancy. She was not told immediately since it was feared that the news might precipitate premature labour and possibly other complications too. Labour, when it did ensure on 14 November, was conducted in a bedroom draped in deep mourning whilst all the women who attended the Queen wore black. Fortunately labour was kind to her; the pains came on at 2.30 in the afternoon and she was safely delivered six hours later.

Her daughter-in-law's attempt to produce an heir for William III of Orange over forty years later was brief, abortive and curious. Early in 1678 Mary became pregnant, but miscarried in April during the third month. She had been especially active, travelling to Rotterdam and to Breda to meet William, and then back again to The Hague; the bumpy coach journeys involved had been blamed for what happened, although there is no certainty that these were really the cause.

Later the same year Mary thought herself pregnant again. Writing to her friend Anne Bentinck in July, she spoke of being some six to seven weeks pregnant, but of not yet wanting it generally known. By the end of August, however, it was common knowledge at court that a pregnancy had been confirmed by the doctors. Towards the end of the summer she was indisposed, and there were, naturally enough, fears that she might miscarry. Then she improved, and all seemed to be going well. In October her stepmother, Mary Duchess of York, and her sister Anne visited her, remaining until early November when it was believed Mary was more than half-way through her pregnancy. Preparations for the confinement went ahead, and, by Christmas, William was choosing the godparents.

But strangely as nine months was reached and passed, nothing happened. The Duchess of York, this time with James' visited her stepdaughter again in March on their way to Brussels. The visit this time coincided with the sad and mysterious announcement that there was to be no baby, since there was no pregnancy – perhaps there never had been one, despite the doctors' 'confirmation' in August.

What the explanation was, we can now only surmise. Possibly Mary's indisposition in the late summer had been a miscarriage which was unrecognized, and her periods had not returned afterwards, as sometimes happens. Perhaps she had never been pregnant, but had missed her periods for some other reason. Anxiety to become pregnant can, though rarely, cause this, and Mary, with William going so often away to war, may have hoped to be pregnant too desperately. A similar false alarm was to affect Caroline of Ansbach later in our story when her husband George, later George II, also went away to fight.

It seems strange, however, that so experienced a woman as her stepmother did not notice something amiss in October. This suggests that there might have been some apparent enlargement of the Princess of Orange's abdomen, even though this was not due to a pregnancy. Perhaps, after all, Mary's problem was emotional – pseudocyesis.

A pseudocyesis is sometimes called a phantom pregnancy. Menstrual periods cease; the patient experiences symptoms of nausea and sickness suggestive of pregnancy; the abdomen appears to be enlarging. Careful examination, however, shows that it is not the womb which is enlarged but the whole abdomen which appears more distended and protruberant than usual, though it certainly outwardly resembles pregnancy. Exactly how and why such distension occurs is not always apparent. The intestines are partly blown up by the patient swallowing air and the whole abdomen is thrust forward as it is in pregnancy. Such patients may be so sure that they can feel fetal movements that they disbelieve assurances that there is no pregnancy and that what they are feeling does not exist. The disorder always has an emotional explanation relating to anxiety to be pregnant.

Mary never became pregnant again, although for some years she continued to hope for a child. It is sometimes said that she had several miscarriages – Stephen Baxter, William's biographer, speaks of 'a series of miscarriages' – but there is no evidence to support this and for such a series of disasters we must turn to Mary's sister, Anne.

Anne, two years younger than Mary, was not yet of marriageable age at the time of her sister's wedding. Then towards the end of 1680, Prince George of Hanover visited the court with, it seemed, some intention of viewing Anne as a possible bride. The couple disliked each other, however, and other more official difficulties arose; George was recalled to Hanover, where he remained an object of dislike to Anne for the rest of her life. For more than two years there were no further matrimonial negotiations, until, in the early summer of 1683, when Anne was eighteen, a marriage was arranged between her and another Prince George, the younger brother of the King of Denmark.

George, despite being the progenitor of Anne's numerous pregnancies, does not otherwise greatly influence our story. Indeed, he scarcely ever influenced events, even during his lifetime. He was an unintelligent, uninteresting man with few abilities. His repeated asthmatic attacks and colourless character prompted John, Lord Mulgrave, to remark that he was forced to breath hard, lest he be taken for dead and removed for burial! Charles II was no more complimentary, alleging he had tried George drunk and had tried him sober, drunk or sober there was nothing in him. But he was handsome and affable, and Anne became greatly attached to him, devoting much time to him and giving him great personal care and attention during many illnesses and indispositions from which he suffered. And in one respect, at least, he could not be said to have been ineffectual for he produced for Anne seventeen pregnancies in the twenty-five years of their marriage. What royal consort, it may be asked, could have done more?

Anne's pregnancies, however, produced disappointment after disappointment, failure after failure. So numerous were her conceptions, yet so uncertain many of the facts relating to them, that it is not easy to obtain an accurate account.

A belief existed from the time of Anne's reign that she gave birth to seventeen children, a notion probably arising from Bishop Burnet. Writing about Anne's son, the Duke of Gloucester, for whose education Burnet was given responsibility, he stated, 'He was the

only remaining child of seventeen that the Princess had born, some
to the full time, the rest before it.'

M. R. Hopkinson, writing in 1934, was unable to confirm this
and pointed out that a broadsheet, which was issued at the time
of the Queen's death, and an anonymous publication in 1738,
entitled *The Life and Reign of Queen Anne*, gave the number of her
children as six, and listed them as follows:

1 A daughter who was stillborn on 12 May 1684
2 Mary, born 2 June 1685
3 Anne Sophia, born 12 May 1686
4 William, Duke of Gloucester, born 24 July 1689
5 Mary, born October 1690
6 George, no date of birth given

Of these six children, the Duke of Gloucester died aged eleven
in 1700; the first Mary died in 1690; Anne Sophia died in February
1687; the second Mary and George lived only a very short time,
perhaps no more than an hour or so.

The Calendar of State Papers at the Records Office, which Hopkinson consulted, contained references to only two of these births
and to 'two of the four or five miscarriages which took place'. No
information was available from the royal archives at Windsor, since
no such records were kept before the reign of George II. A search
of the Court Announcements in the *London Gazette* disclosed that
the statements officially issued from Whitehall corresponded with
those given by *The Life and Reign of Queen Anne* and the broadsheet,
but there were two minor differences; the first Mary's death was
given as February 1686 instead of 1690 and the date of the birth
and death of George was recorded as 1692. This careful search by
Hopkinson therefore disclosed six babies and 'two of the four or
five miscarriages' – perhaps ten or eleven pregnancies in all.

David Green, writing in 1974, has provided a helpful appendix
on the problems of Queen Anne's health in general and her childbearing history in particular. This history is recorded by Green as
follows:

1684 12 May a stillborn daughter
1685 2 June Mary or Marie (died 8 February 1687)
1686 2 June Anne Sophia (died 2 February 1687)

1687 Between 20 January and 4 February a miscarriage
1687 October a miscarriage (male)
1688 16 April a miscarriage
1689 24 July William Duke of Gloucester (died 30 July 1700)
1690 14 October Mary (two months premature, lived two hours)
1692 17 April George (born at Syon, lived a few minutes)
1693 23 March a miscarriage (female)
1694 21 January a miscarriage
1696 18 February a miscarriage (female)
1696 20 September a double miscarriage ('a son of 7 months' growth,
       the other of 2 or 3 months')
1697 25 March a miscarriage
1697 December a miscarriage
1698 15 September a miscarriage (male)
1700 25 January a miscarriage (male)

Green's account therefore differs from Hopkinson's in several respects. He records a total of seventeen pregnancies instead of ten or eleven; Mary and Anne Sophia are recorded as dying in the same week in February 1687 whilst the latter's date of birth is given as 2 June instead of 12 May. The total number of children born still remains the same, the extra pregnancies all ending in miscarriages. David Green in an effort to find the cause of this remarkable history questioned several leading doctors, but after considering the information he provided, none of them could explain it convincingly.

This is not perhaps surprising since Green's summary of Anne's eventful obstetric career tells us only the barest facts; no assessment of the likely explanation of them can be arrived at without further details. Perusal of contemporary references to Anne's confinements brief though these are, throws light on the problem in one very important respect.

We learn from these original sources that Anne's first pregnancy ended on 12 May 1684 in the birth of a stillborn daughter. The child's death was attributed to Anne's fall from a horse but we do not have enough information to judge whether this was really the cause or not. The second pregnancy was initially successful. On 2 June 1685 Anne was safely delivered of a daughter, christened Mary. Tragically she lived only until February 1687 when she died of an acute infection, the nature of which we cannot now determine.

Francis Sandford, the herald and genealogist, reported that she was buried privately on 10 February in the vault of Mary Queen of Scots in Westminster Abbey.

Another daughter had been born alive from the third pregnancy on 12 May 1686. According to the Register of St George's Chapel, Windsor Castle, this confinement took place in the Prince of Wales's Lodgings in the chamber over the staircase which goes down into the Terrace Walk. But this child, Anne Sophia, succumbed to the same infection which led to the death of her elder sister and was buried on 4 February in the royal vault in King Henry VII's Chapel in Westminster Abbey.

Pregnancy number four ended in a miscarriage on 21 January 1687. As we will see presently the phrase 'miscarriage' was then used in a more general sense that it is now and whether this was an early miscarriage or whether Anne carried the child to a later stage of gestation we cannot say. She, herself, blamed the 'miscarriage' on the exertions involved in taking part in a new dance lately introduced from France called the rigadoon. 'I have no reason to like it now', she wrote sadly, 'for I believe it was the dance that made me miscarry for there is a great deal of jumping in it.'

Anne conceived pregnancy number five very quickly and was to be confined on 22 October that same year, 1687. But the child is reported to have been dead about one month in the uterus before it was born.

Narcissus Luttrell, the annalist and bibliographer who painstakingly chronicled the events of his time, reported the sixth pregnancy as ending in a miscarriage on 16 April 1688. Again no further details are available.

There may have been another pregnancy later in the same year but without confirmation we cannot accept this as certain. Luttrell wrote that after a visit to Bath 'the Princess proves with child' and she kept within doors to prevent a miscarriage. We do not know what happened to this pregnancy, if indeed it was one, and not some kind of false alarm. A not dissimilar episode was to occur in 1695 which was ultimately to prove not to have been a pregnancy at all.

Leaving aside this possible second pregnancy in 1688, therefore, Anne's next conception was her seventh and it was to be her most successful. A son, William, Duke of Gloucester, was born at Hampton Court on 24 July 1689 and was to live eleven years before his death on 30 July 1700.

The year 1690 saw Anne delivered of a daughter from her eighth pregnancy. Sandford reported that the child was born at St James's on 14 October, but lived only two hours, dying soon after baptism. Luttrell recorded that 'she came two months before her time'.

The ninth pregnancy led to another child who died within a short time of his birth. Sandford referred to a son, christened George, being born at Syon House on 17 April 1692 but dying within an hour after he was baptized. His body was buried on the following day at Westminster Abbey. Luttrell, wrote that 'Dr Chamberlen had the honour to lay the Princess on Sunday last of a son which immediately died; he had a hundred guineas for his pains.'

No more children were to be born alive to the Princess after this. According to Sandford the tenth pregnancy ended in the birth of a stillborn daughter at Berkley House, St James's Street, on 23 March 1693. Luttrell recorded the event as a 'miscarriage of a dead daughter on Thursday last'.

Pregnancy number eleven resulted in the birth of a dead child on 21 January 1694; the sex was not recorded.

In April 1695 there were again rumours of a pregnancy as there had been in 1688 but they were not substantiated and in June the 'Princess of Denmark declared herself not with child'.

The twelfth pregnancy ended on 17 February 1696 when in Luttrell's words 'the Princess miscarried a daughter'.

Later on 20 September the same year Luttrell again described the miscarriage of a son from Anne's thirteenth pregnancy. The Danish Ambassador said that she was six months pregnant which was just possible if she had conceived immediately after her delivery in February.

On 25 March 1697 the Princess miscarried again in her fourteenth pregnancy. It was recognized that there were twin embryos but their sex could not be determined.

Number fifteen was again a miscarriage early in December the same year. The Calendar of State Papers Domestic referred to a visit which King William made to the Princess at St James's on 10 December, she having miscarried some days before.

There are a few more details available of Anne's sixteenth pregnancy. This time the Calendar of State Papers Domestic reported in April that 'The Princess does not stir out being about twenty weeks gone with child and she hopes by care to avoid those misfortunes that she is too subject to.' By July she was planning to go to Windsor but in Luttrell's words 'her physicians have held a consultation upon the same and were divided; many being against it for fear she should miscarry, being big with child.' Whether the physicians ultimately agreed or not we do not know, but Anne went to Windsor just the same. On Thursday morning 15 September 1698 she gave birth to a dead son. James Vernon, the Secretary of State, reported that a surgeon, Bassier, opened the body of the child and found no obvious defect or deformity but supposed it to have been dead eight to ten days. The child was buried in a vault in the choir of St George's Chapel in Windsor near the body of Charles I.

Anne's final pregnancy, her seventeenth, ended as had so many others in the birth of a dead son. Luttrell recorded the event as occurring 'within six weeks of her time'. The child which was reported by Vernon to have been dead for a month within her womb was eventually born on 24 January 1700. Later in the same year her only surviving child, William Henry, Duke of Gloucester, was to die from scarlet fever a few days after his eleventh birthday. Seventeen attempts to produce an heir had led to nothing.

These, then, are as many of the facts concerning Anne's pregnancies as we can discover. They are only a sketchy record and they tell us nothing of Anne's state of mind as disappointment followed disappointment. How profound must her emotional distress have been!

Consider, for example, the disastrous blows that she suffered in the single year 1687. In January she had two daughters and was pregnant again. Before the month was out she had miscarried; by early February both her daughters were dead and buried and by October she had borne a dead son. She was still only twenty-two years old. When eventually in 1689 she gave birth to a son who survived his birth he was to be nearly overwhelmed when six weeks old by an illness which, as we will see presently, in all probability caused him permanent handicap; despite his struggle against his disabilities he remained for his mother 'my poor boy'. Even he was snatched away from her in the same year as her last pregnancy came to its almost inevitable end in yet another stillbirth.

There can have been few women, even in those fateful days, whose childbearing brought them such a deluge of disasters. Without her faith Anne could scarcely have borne so much grief. But she had been brought up to accept God's will and as a deeply religious woman she gained sufficient inner strength to survive. Even her husband, to whom she was deeply attached, died in 1708 and she was left to reign a lonely Queen for her last six years on the throne.

To return to our examination of Anne's reproductive failure, we find that the dates of the pregnancies given here and compiled from contemporary records correspond in most respects with Green's list given earlier, but there are several small differences, and one of considerable importance. Green recorded the miscarriage of twins as pregnancy number thirteen, occurring in 1696; here it is recorded as number fourteen in 1697. Moreover in Green's account the twins are reported as 'a son of seven months and the other of two to three months' whilst here they are recorded as too early to determine sex. It is possible for twins of different maturity to be born. One twin dies at an early stage in the pregnancy but is retained in the uterus until the other is born much later. The retained dead twin is then small and shrivelled and is compressed by the second fetus and becomes known as a 'fetus papyraceous'. I have been able to trace no record of such an episode but merely that of the early twin miscarriage mentioned.

But the really significant distinction between the accounts is the different interpretation which we now put on the word 'miscarriage'. A miscarriage nowadays has a specific meaning and refers to a pregnancy which comes to an end before the child is viable, that is to say before twenty-eight weeks of pregnancy. Most miscarriages occur around eight to twelve weeks, and this has generally been understood when Anne's history has previously been considered by medical commentators. However it is clear that this was not the case in some pregnancies to which the label 'miscarriage' was given since the child reached viability but then died within the uterus, to be delivered several weeks later.

The picture gained from David Green's notes on Queen Anne's health – six children and eleven miscarriages – does not accord with contemporary accounts. In seven of these eleven 'miscarriages' it is clear that Anne carried the fetus to viability although it was born dead sometime later. In three instances death had preceded labour by a week or more. This happened in pregnancy number five when the fetus was dead at least a month before birth; pregnancy number sixteen when the fetus was dead eight to ten days before the birth; and in pregnancy number seventeen when the fetus again died a month before birth.

It is not unreasonable to assume that the same probably happened in pregnancies numbers ten, eleven, twelve and thirteen. What remains uncertain, despite the facts now disclosed, is whether the remaining pregnancies recorded as miscarriages – numbers four, six, fourteen and fifteen – were miscarriages in the modern sense, or whether they also might have been deliveries of dead babies in later pregnancy. Since in the twin miscarriage, number fourteen, the sex of the children could not be determined, it is evident that this at least was an early miscarriage. About the others we just do not know.

In medical terms the difference between an early miscarriage and the death of a fetus in utero in late pregnancy is a very important one. The conditions which give rise to the one do not cause the other and vice versa. It is evident now that we should be seeking to determine not why Anne miscarried so often, but why her babies died in utero in late pregnancy, or died at, or very soon after, birth. Before we can do this, however, we must look at her remaining confinements, especially those which resulted in children which survived for a time, to see if they provide helpful information.

Little is known about Anne's first confinement beyond the fact that the child was stillborn, and that a fall from a horse is thought to have been responsible. Such a fall may indeed have injured the fetus, although it is more likely that it was coincidental. Trauma of this kind may result in fetal death, but not usually. The risk to the first child is always greater than that to the next three or four children, since the birth passages have not previously been dilated and this risk, in 1684, was far greater than it is now. There are several possible reasons why Anne's first child might have been stillborn, but in the absence of more detailed information, we cannot say what the particular cause was.

Her second and third children are very significant to our story. Mary was born on 2 June 1685 and Anne Sophia in May or June 1686. We here record 12 May as does Hopkinson whilst Green gives 2 June. Both children died in February 1687, when Mary was twenty months of age and Anne Sophia nine months. Agnes Strickland and Hopkinson reported these deaths as occurring on the same day, 6 February, their mother's birthday. This is almost certainly not the case, however, and the dates given by Green are probably the correct ones, Anne Sophia's death being on 2 February and Mary's on 8 February. They died as a result of acute infection, probably the same one which affected their father and believed to be smallpox. George had certainly been very ill and was being devotedly nursed by his wife, when their infant daughters were taken ill as well and quickly succumbed.

Mary had never been a robust child. Agnes Strickland described her as 'weakly and languishing' and Hopkinson as 'always ailing and delicate'. But the younger child had apparently been in excellent health. Their bodies were examined after death, as Lady Rachel Russell reported in a letter to her friend Dr Fitzgerald, on Ash Wednesday, 9 February. She referred to Prince George as 'ill of fever', then commenting on the deaths of the little girls she remarked 'both children were opened; the eldest was all consumed, but the youngest was very sound and likely to live'. It is not easy to decide what the phrase 'all consumed' might mean and it is too imprecise to speculate upon.

The deaths of these two children were clearly due to their contracting a severe infection and were unrelated to the process of their birth.

We must now move on to Anne's ninth pregnancy when 'It pleased God to bless the Princess with the birth of a Prince at Hampton Court at five in the morning of 24 June 1689.' The baby was christened William Henry, and the title of Duke of Gloucester was at once bestowed upon him. We learn of the events of his life from the delightful record of Jenkin Lewis, a servant in the Household of the Prince and Princess of Denmark, who was with the Duke a great deal, and clearly developed a considerable affection for him.

At birth he was reported to be a 'very weakly child; and most people believed he would not live long'. We do not know anything more precise than this about his weight at birth, but the phrase used suggests a small child lacking vigour, and therefore clearly at risk of succumbing to the huge dangers children then ran during their early lives.

Lewis's record, however, makes it clear that for a time he did well. There was a brief period of concern about difficulty in feeding which was judged to be due to the nipple of the wet nurse, Mrs Shermon, 'proving too big'. Mrs Wanley, who had suckled one of Anne's earlier babies was therefore substituted and for six weeks the boy did well and began to gain weight. 'All people now began to conceive hopes of the Duke's living when Lo! he was taken with convulsion fits which followed so quick one after another that physicians from London despaired of his life.'

The physicians from London, uncertain what to do, ordered a change of milk as have other physicians many thousands of times since. Mothers of young babies flocked to Hampton Court hoping to be selected as wet nurse and many were tried without success. Some were not above sharp practice: one 'said her milk was younger than it proved to be' but her subterfuge was detected by Lady Charlotte Beverwort 'by examining the Parish books'.

Eventually Prince George, passing through the Presence Room where several candidates were waiting, detected a Mrs Pack, the wife of a Quaker from Kingston Wick who seemed 'a strong healthy woman'. She was ordered to go to bed with the baby who sucked well and 'mended that night'.

It is improbable that the Duke's fits were in any way concerned with the milk which he had been taking satisfactorily for six weeks, and much more likely that he had developed a serious disorder, such as an acute infection, which often causes convulsions in young children. Mrs Pack (or Peck as Lewis later calls her) was, in all probability, the lucky person whose arrival simply coincided with his recovery. She made the best of her notoriety, despite being an unpleasant, uncouth individual who was 'fitter to go to a pigsty than to a Prince's bed'. In Lewis's words 'by artifice, [she] availed herself of whatever she chose by way of advancement which women of good quality would have gladly obtained.' Orders were given that she should not be contradicted by anyone, and for a while she made great profit from her privileged position. As we shall see later when wet nurses are considered in more detail in Chapter 6, it was not uncommon for them to achieve such a position of importance.

This illness, whatever it was, evidently led to what Lewis mysteriously calls 'an issue from his pole'. This fluid discharge from somewhere on the Duke's head had evidently 'been kept running ever since his sickness at Hampton Court'. It is not possible to be certain what this was. He may have developed a sinus from the infection which precipitated his convulsions; perhaps an infection of the middle ear caused both his fits and the subsequent discharge of pus through a ruptured ear drum. But it is evident, from what Jenkin Lewis wrote, that it was the illness at six weeks which led to it, and it was not a consequence of his birth.

The subsequent development of the young Prince was in some respects quite normal. He has often been represented as a tiny, weak, chronically ailing child, but it is doubtful how correct this picture is. Lewis reported only two or three attacks of 'ague', which appeared to have responded to treatment without difficulty. The Duke eventually began to talk and walk at more or less the proper time, although his locomotion was never normal. Despite being a very active boy in most respects, he could not go up or down stairs without help, nor could he get up when he was on the floor. It is possible that not all these difficulties were entirely physical, since it was the opinion of some who knew him that they were 'occasioned by the overcare of the ladies about him'. On one occasion Lewis reported that 'an unaccountable fancy seized him of not going at all without two persons to hold him'. His father clearly believed that the boy was shamming, and beat him with a birch rod for the first time in his life, whereupon the Duke said 'he would go if one would hold him'. 'He was whipt again and went ever after well', reported Lewis laconically.

The Duke of Gloucester did, nonetheless, definitely have certain physical disabilities. His faithful servant measured him when he was about five years old and recorded his height as 3 foot 4 inches. About the same age 'the Duke's head was then grown very long; insomuch that his hat was big enough for most men'. Ninety-five per cent or so of modern children of five years of age would be taller than this. We know, of course, that seventeenth-century children were somewhat smaller than children are now, and Lewis does not tell us the Duke's precise age at the time he was measured. Whilst it is clear that he was well below average height, his smallness has probably been somewhat exaggerated in other accounts. It is often recorded, for example, that he went for outings in his special coach drawn by horses which were 'no larger than a good mastiff' which the Duchess of Ormond had given to him, the implication being that he was a very tiny individual for whom such miniature ponies were necessary. What is seldom mentioned, however, is that he was some two years old at the time and such an equipage would be quite appropriate for a child of that age, however big or small he might have been.

The size of the Duke's head was obviously larger than that of most children, which in combination with his somewhat small stature would have made it appear even bigger still. The word Lewis used to describe his head is curious; it had, he said, 'grown very *long*' but he does also say that he wore a hat which would fit most men. Again judging from modern measurements only one or two per cent of five-year-olds would have a head equal in size to that of an average man, and these would be children whose body size was appropriately large. Judging from this evidence, it is highly probable that the Duke had some degree of hydrocephalus, a view which post-mortem examination of his brain was later to confirm.

His physical disabilities do not seem to have been associated with any intellectual incapacity. Both Lewis and Bishop Burnet record numerous instances of his ability to assimilate knowledge, and he clearly had an acute, inquiring mind. He showed interest in many things, but guns, soldiers and war were his favourite subjects. He even formed a number of local boys into a military detachment and drilled and manoeuvred them.

On the Duke's eleventh birthday there were festivities in which he joined with enthusiasm. 'The boy reviewed his junior regiment', Agnes Strickland wrote, and 'exulted in the discharge of cannon and crackers and presided over a large banquet.' He went to bed somewhat indisposed, and it was thought he was over-excited and had eaten more than was good for him. But on the following morning it was evident that this illness was more serious; he complained of sickness, headache and a sore throat, and later became delirious. The next day he was no better and a rash appeared. His physicians thought he might have caught smallpox, and he was bled and blistered without benefit. Dr Radcliffe, the foremost physician of his age, was prevailed upon to attend him. Radcliffe declared the malady to be scarlet fever, and when he discovered that the boy had been bled, he exclaimed, 'you have destroyed him; and you may finish him for I will not prescribe.' The child languished for four days until his death on 30 July when he was eleven years and five days old.

The findings at his post-mortem examination (printed in full in the appendix) are typical of those associated with a severe infection. One important finding, however, indicates clearly that the Duke of Gloucester had a degree of hydrocephalus.

It is recorded that when the head was opened 'out of the first and second ventricles of the cerebrum ... was taken about four ounces and a half of a limpid tumour'. The ventricles spoken of are two of the four spaces in the brain through which cerebro-spinal fluid flows to the outer surface of the brain and spinal cord where it bathes these vital structures. Four and a half fluid ounces is 130 ml which was found in these two ventricles alone. The total volume of cerebro-spinal fluid in an adult is 100–150 ml and for a child aged eleven perhaps 60–100 ml. Since that amount occupies the whole of the brain and spinal cord area, the volume normally present in the first and second ventricals (or lateral ventricles as they are now called) would be much less than the total figure. In fact these ventricles when seen during autopsy are usually flattened spaces which are relatively inconspicuous with little fluid within them. Clearly, four and a half fluid ounces is an excessive amount.

He cannot, however, have suffered from gross hydrocephalus. In such a condition the head is huge, and the child is a distressing sight, with an enormous swollen head which can scarcely be supported. Hydrocephalus may arise during development in utero or may be acquired after birth. Had the Duke suffered from it before birth, his head would probably have been far too large to permit him to be born normally. Lesser degrees of congenital hydrocephalus do occur but it is much more likely that he acquired the disorder after birth as a result of his illness at six weeks.

One of the commonest causes of such acquired hydrocephalus is an acute infection such as meningitis, which interferes with the normal process of absorption of cerebro-spinal fluid, which thus accumulates in excessive amounts in the brain. As we have seen, such an acute infection is also the likeliest cause of the convulsions which affected him at that time. It is most probable therefore that a severe infection – such as meningitis or a middle ear infection (*otitis media*) as already postulated – caused his convulsions and led to his hydrocephalus. Had the Duke contracted meningitis it is not very likely that he would have survived and a middle ear infection is more likely. Such hydrocephalus is of course an acquired and not a genetic condition. Although the Duke suffered from a minor degree of it, therefore, there is no reason to suppose that any of Anne's other children did so as well.

The death of the Duke of Gloucester was, moreover, unrelated to his hydrocephalus and was directly due to an acute infection – scarlet fever according to Dr Radcliffe. Death, therefore, as in the case of his younger sisters who died before he was born, was unrelated to the process of his birth.

The other two children who were born alive, from Anne's eighth and ninth pregnancies, died within the space of an hour or two. The daughter born in the eighth pregnancy was two months premature, and therefore survival was unlikely, but whether the son born in the ninth pregnancy was also premature or not we do not know.

What explanation therefore can be offered for Anne's reproductive failure?

Several opinions have been expressed in the past, probably without the facts at our disposal being available; these opinions cannot now be substantiated.

R. Scott Stephenson, a medical journalist and editor, suggested the Duke of Gloucester's hydrocephalus and Princess Anne's long series of 'miscarriages' were due to syphilis. There is no evidence to support this, and much to refute it. There is nothing else, for example, to suggest that George, Prince of Denmark was syphilitic. Moreover, the pattern of childbearing in a syphilitic mother is not like Anne's. Typically, an early pregnancy or two may miscarry or the child may be born dead; then, an infant may be born alive but with obvious evidence of infection; later children may be alive and apparently normal, although they will later be shown to have congenital syphilis.

James Kemble, a surgeon with a keen interest in medical history, in *Idols and Invalids* attributes the disasters to Anne's having a contracted or deformed pelvis. This we now realize cannot be the explanation, since the infants were, on several occasions, known to have died in utero some weeks before birth. This could not result from a contracted pelvis which would only cause problems during labour. Another previous suggestion, which is now equally untenable, is chronic pelvic infection, since this causes infertility, not repeated unsuccessful pregnancies.

When the Princess Anne's obstetric history is considered carefully, a number of significant facts are evident. Firstly, it is clear that no single explanation will account for it all. Her second and third children died from an infection which was in no way related to the process of birth, so whatever caused the deaths of her other babies before or about the time of birth, it was not the infection which caused the deaths of these two children. The Duke of Gloucester died from scarlet fever, again unrelated to his birth; his hydrocephalus too was probably acquired as a result of another infection and there is no reason to suppose any of Anne's other fetuses suffered from it.

But we know also that on three occasions, and in all probability more, the fetus was dead in utero some time before it was born. These deaths therefore were not concerned with the process of *delivery*, but with the process of *development* inside the womb. Furthermore, scrutiny of all Anne's pregnancies shows a tendency for the trouble, whatever it was, to get worse as time went by. In the initial phase two of her early children were born alive and were well for a time. Then in the second phase, of four infants who reached viability, one survived, two died almost immediately and one succumbed some weeks before it was born. In the third phase no child survived birth from the last eight pregnancies.

Three conditions could account for this pattern: Rhesus disease; diabetes; and what is called intra-uterine growth retardation due to placental insufficiency.

Rhesus incompatibility is certainly a possible explanation. In this disorder the mother's blood lacks the Rhesus factor – she is known as Rhesus negative – and the father's blood has the factor – he is known as Rhesus positive. If the child is Rhesus positive the mother responds to the presence of the child's Rhesus factor by forming antibodies. These antibodies then react on the baby's blood, destroying the corpuscles and the child becomes increasingly anaemic. The antibodies do not normally develop in the first pregnancy but usually in a subsequent one, perhaps the second or third. Initially the antibody strength is low but it tends to rise with subsequent pregnancies. If a Rhesus negative mother develops antibodies in, say, her third pregnancy, her next pregnancy may show a fetus moderately affected, the following one a more severely affected fetus, and eventually a very severely affected child indeed. The more severely affected the child, the more likely it is to die in utero before term and, as pregnancy follows pregnancy, as in Anne's case, these deaths may occur earlier and earlier.

If we accept the death of Anne's first child as due to another cause, as it could easily have been, the chain of events in her later pregnancies could fit the pattern of Rhesus incompatibility. The fifth to the ninth pregnancies could be regarded as showing moderately to severely affected fetuses only one of which, the Duke of Gloucester, survived. After his birth, however, no other child was born alive, the process becoming so severe that the fetus perished as early as the sixth or seventh month. The aspect which is not typical is the death in utero of Anne's fifth child, and the later survival of the Duke of Gloucester. Usually the condition becomes progressively worse; if Rhesus incompatibility caused the death of the fifth child, it is unlikely that a child of the seventh pregnancy would have survived. There are occasional variations in the degree of affection, however, and such a sequence of events is possible.

More likely than Rhesus incompatibility, perhaps, is insufficiency of the placenta causing intra-uterine growth regardation. The placenta is a rich vascular organ, which allows the fetus to take oxygen and nutrient substances from its mother, and to pass carbon dioxide and waste products back to her. If the placenta is poorly formed, or if some of its blood vessels become thrombosed and unable to permit this essential exchange, growth of the fetus may be limited, and if the oxygen supply is very poor, it may die in the uterus before the end of pregnancy. Fetuses so affected therefore may die in utero before birth, or be born very small with a serious risk of dying in the first few days or weeks of life.

This is precisely the pattern of the Princess Anne's pregnancies after the early ones, and could easily be the explanation for her reproductive failure. Such intra-uterine growth retardation is usually associated with a raised blood pressure in the mother, although this is not invariably the case. We have no knowledge of Anne's blood pressure, but her health pattern in her later life is at least compatible with high blood pressure.

Anne certainly did not enjoy good health. As a child she suffered from sore eyes. When she was twelve years old she had smallpox. Towards the end of her childbearing years, in 1698, when she was thirty-three, she was reported to be afflicted with gout which affected her principal joints and was later said to be present in her stomach and brain. Whether in fact she had gout we cannot say. It is not a common disease in women, and seldom, if ever, has the widespread effects which were alleged in the Queen.

As she got older Anne became so fat that she could scarcely walk. This was certainly due to over-eating, and perhaps over-drinking too, but it may have been aggravated by dropsy. Her physician, Sir David Hamilton, disputed the dropsy, declaring her 'constitution as without any tendency to it' and the examination of her body after death (a fuller post-mortem report is included in the appendix) did not confirm excessive fluid to be present.

In her final illness the Queen was seized with pain in her head, trembling of her hands, loss of speech, convulsions and unconsciousness. The description her physician used to refer to her disorders, however, does not have a precise meaning, and we can only speculate about what it might have meant. Sir David Hamilton wrote that she suffered from 'the common effects of a sharpness in her blood discharging outward in the common forms of ails to preserve her constitution till within those few years a succession of disquiets happened which weakened her nerves and prepared them for receiving a translation of this sharpness threatening first to discharge on the foot and knee in the form of gout, but her spirits being weakly at the time it would not perform it and translated upwards upon the nerves and brain'. Such a description has no meaning to us now, and regrettably we do not know enough of the facts to form a firm conclusion on the Queen's disorder, or whether or not it might have been a contributory factor in the death of her babies.

One other explanation for her stillbirths and neonatal deaths is that the Princess was a diabetic. The effect of established diabetes on pregnancy is, in some cases, to cause death of a child in utero during late pregnancy or soon after birth. If the children are born alive they are often large in size – ten, twelve, or fourteen pounds being not uncommon in a patient whose diabetes is uncontrolled. There is nothing to suggest that any of Anne's babies was unduly large – indeed William, Duke of Gloucester was probably smaller than average. Although diabetes is a possibility, therefore, it is less likely than Rhesus incompatibility and much less likely than intra-uterine growth retardation, which on the evidence we now have seems the most probable explanation.

Lastly, whenever a mother loses a series of pregnancies as Anne did, the possibility of a genetic cause must be given some thought. If she had had a series of early miscarriages, as the more superficial consideration of her history suggested, a genetic fault could have been the explanation; but her true history as recorded here fits no recognized pattern of repeated genetic abnormality. Moreover, neither a perusal of her own family tree nor that of the Danish Royal Family, Prince George's relatives, suggest the likelihood of any such familial tendency.

The death of the Duke of Gloucester, in the year 1700, was the death knell of the House of Stuart. In that same year Anne lost her last child. Although she was only thirty-five she did not become pregnant again, and even had she done so a successful outcome would have been a vain hope.

In 1701 the Act of Settlement was passed. If Anne were to die without issue, as seemed all too likely, the Crown would pass to the heirs of Elizabeth, daughter of James I of England and briefly Queen of Bohemia. The Hanoverians were waiting in the wings to become Kings of England. To learn something of their reproductive history before their dynasty became established we must now move backwards in time and go with Elizabeth to Germany.

3

The Hanoverian Succession

Elizabeth, daughter of James VI of Scotland, who later became James I of England, was to bear a large family, but was to manifest in her first pregnancy a most unusual abnormality – flat refusal to accept that she was pregnant.

She had been born to James and his wife, Anne of Denmark, in Scotland in August 1596. When she was sixteen Elizabeth married Frederick V, Elector Palatine, on Sunday, 14 February 1613. It is clear that she became pregnant quickly, probably shortly before the couple left England on 26 April that year, bound for Heidelberg Castle. The British Resident in Brussels wrote to his colleague, Sir Ralph Winwood, in The Hague on 25 June, to say that on the previous Sunday gentlemen from the Electorate had passed through Brussels bound for England to tell her father that Elizabeth had arrived safely and to recount that 'Her Majesty's physicians do report that in all appearances she should be with child.'

Elizabeth, however, shut out all notion of pregnancy from her mind, and refused to discuss it. She hunted, made expeditions to the country and continued to entertain visitors, and many expressed doubts about the effect this activity might have on her pregnancy and subsequent labour.

There was concern in London that, since all her medical attendants were German, some attempt should be made to provide a companion and a midwife from England. On 20 November the Privy Council discussed which 'noble English matron should go out to attend her', and selected Lady Cecil, who at that time was conveniently in the Netherlands. The King wished a midwife to go too, and on 8 December Lord Suffolk wrote to Sir Thomas Lake to say: 'I can hear of none more fitting for this employment than Mrs Mercer who hath in this city an excellent good report both for skill, carriage and religion.' In a writ dated 10 December 1613, when

Elizabeth was already in the last month of pregnancy, Margaret Mercer was ordered to proceed to Heidelberg to attend the delivery of 'His Majesty's dearest daughter Princess Electress Palatine'.

Elizabeth was not to be attended by her English midwife nor companion for neither Mrs Mercer nor Lady Cecil arrived in time – which perhaps explains why Mrs Mercer had to wait so long before being paid for her services. It was not until January 1616, more than two years later, that an order was given authorizing that she be paid £84 4s. 'in full payment and discharge of the charge of her said journey and six other persons attending and accompanying her from London to Heidelberg and back again appearing by her bill of particulars subscribed and allowed by us according to the tenour of the said privy seal'. Margaret Mercer, although one of the first royal midwives in Britain of whom we have any real knowledge, was not one of the highest paid. As we have seen, Alice Dennis, her predecessor by more than ten years, had received £100 for officiating at the confinements of Anne of Denmark, James's Queen, in 1605 and 1606. Towards the end of the century Mrs Wilkes was to receive 500 guineas from James II for the birth of James Francis Edward, 'The Old Pretender'.

Nor was Elizabeth the only royal person to be deprived of the services of her midwife. J. H. Aveling, a most distinguished gynaecologist of the ninteenth century, in his book *English Midwives* reports that when Henrietta Maria, wife of Charles I, was delivered at Greenwich of a son in 1628, she 'had neither physician nor other professional aid near her; and when her terrified attendants brought the good old midwife who usually officiated at Greenwich, that functionary, overcome by the idea of the exalted rank of her patient, fainted with fear the moment she approached the Queen, and had to be carried out of the royal chamber.'

But to return to Elizabeth in 1614, the Electress Palatine was still refusing to admit her pregnant state right up to the month before her confinement. When an envoy from France, Monsieur de Sainte Catherine, brought felicitations to her on 29 December, he was amazed to learn that 'although Madame la Princesse, must be according to calculations very near her accouchement she will not have a word said about her pregnancy'. The envoy was in a dilemma since he could hardly bring official felicitations without refering to it.

When he was admitted to her presence, on 1 January 1614, he took the plunge and remarked that he hoped she would soon be a happy mother. Elizabeth seemed satisfied with his sentiments and complacently replied, 'Since they consider me *enceinte* that helps me to believe I am so.' *Enceinte* she undoubtedly was, for labour started that very evening. She was delivered of a son by Dr Christian Rumph at 1.00 a.m. on 2 January. Her father was so delighted he settled £2,000 a year on her, whilst, at the next meeting of Parliament, the boy, Frederick Henry, was naturalized English.

Elizabeth's refusal to accept either the evidence of her own body, or the assurance of her physicians that she was pregnant is difficult to understand. This reaction is not unknown, but it is a profound psychological response usually associated with fear, or with an unwanted pregnancy, or with a regretted illicit act of intercourse. For it to occur in the context of a normal married life as hers did, and to be so prominent as to persist to the last day of the pregnancy, is rare, and in this instance unexplained.

Elizabeth was ultimately obliged to acknowledge the reality of the pregnant state many times. There was an interval of three years between the births of her first and second children, but thereafter she conceived regularly, and bore in all thirteen children. By the year of the passage of the Act of Settlement in 1701 transferring the succession to Elizabeth's descendants, only two of these survived – Louise, the sixth child, and Sophia, the twelfth. Louise had disappeared to France in 1657 where she was received into the Catholic Church, later taking the veil, and eventually becoming Abbess of Maubuisson, an elegant convent not far from Paris. Since she had renounced all worldly rights, Sophia became the heir and very nearly succeeded Anne as Queen of Britain. She died, however, at the age of eighty-four, less than two months before Anne, and so it was her eldest son, George Lewis, who became King in 1714.

George Lewis was born to Sophia on 28 May 1660 – the same month and year that Charles II was restored as King in Britain. George was an uninteresting person, dull of intellect, shy and withdrawn, and suspicious of what was new or unfamiliar. When he was twenty he came to Britain, as we saw earlier, and there seemed a possibility of a marriage between him and Princess Anne. However, as we have seen, nothing came of this plan and in 1682 George married his cousin, Sophia Dorothea of Celle, the daughter of a morganatic marriage between the Duke of Celle and a French woman. The relationship between George Lewis and his wife was unimportant obstetrically; maritally it was a *cause célèbre*. Sophia Dorothea's history was tragic and her crime perhaps no more than indiscretion; her punishment was cruel and prolonged.

It seems probable that she and her husband did not have any affection for each other, even at the outset, and as time went by their mutual dislike increased. Nonetheless, despite their feelings, an heir had to be produced. Sophia Dorothea gave birth to a son, also christened George, within a year of marriage, but not for a further five years did she have a second child, when a daughter was born.

George, during this time, had at least one mistress and probably more. The social position of the mistress was then very precise. As Joyce Marlow has so engagingly written, 'going to bed on the odd occasion with the ruler was not sufficient to turn a woman into an official mistress. The relationship had to be further defined until it was recognized that Madam X was the King or Elector's mistress and she then received the deference due to her status. If there were several ladies who acquired the status, the one who emerged on top, metaphorically speaking, was known as the *maîtresse en titre* or chief mistress.'

Sophia Dorothea learned of these mistresses, but did not submit meekly to the situation, as many royal wives did. She first objected violently and demanded to be sent home; later, when the opportunity presented, she was prepared to carry on her own intrigue, from which such disastrous consequences stemmed.

Her lover was Count Philip Von Königsmark, appointed at the court as Colonel of Dragoons. He was a handsome man and an experienced womanizer, and he captivated the Princess. Initially perhaps he paid her compliments, flattered and danced attention on her from force of habit. But his advances met with instant success, and the couple soon became the gossip of the court and even of the duchy. Sophia Dorothea was anything but discreet, and whatever their true relationship they seemed outwardly to be lovers. The truth was never really established. Whether the relationship was precisely what it seemed was not in the end important. Sophia Dorothea was open in her attachment to the Colonel at court, and he was boastful of his relationship with her. The Elector and his son, George Augustus, were both being held up to ridicule, and something had to be done. Their solution was sudden, drastic and savage.

Count Philip Von Königsmark was seen to enter the apartments of the Princess on 1 July 1694 and was never seen again. It has been widely believed since that he was murdered, and there seems no other reasonable explanation. But how the deed was done, and by whom, and what happened to his body remains unknown. Rumour suggested that, immediately the murder was accomplished, he was dismembered and buried beneath the floorboards. Stories of his bones being discovered later, during reconstruction in the palace, continued to circulate. Even those who might indirectly have been implicated in the supposed killing are in doubt. The Princess was not thought to have been in the apartment when Königsmark arrived. George Lewis was probably not even in Hanover when the deed was done, although some stories suggested that he was even present in the room. One rumour said that the couple were to elope that very night, another that they were to part for ever, realizing that their affair could not continue.

What really happened to Konigsmark remains unknown. What happened to Sophia Dorothea is tragic. A few months after Königsmark's disappearance she was tried by a Consistorial Court of Hanover and Celle, and her marriage to George was dissolved. She was forbidden to remarry, forbidden ever to see her two children again, and at the age of twenty-eight was imprisoned in the Castle of Ahlden where she remained until her death thirty-one years later. George was implacable, and at no time seemed willing to commute the sentence.

George never remarried but, as before, there was no shortage of mistresses. His two principle ones, who were to remain with him all his life, were his *maîtresses en titre* Mlle von der Schulenberg and Mme Kielmansegge. Neither was a person of special physical attraction, nor indeed of particular accomplishment. Kielmansegge was to accompany George to England when he came to assume the throne and was created Countess of Darlington. Schulenberg was to follow later and to become Countess of Kendal.

George I did not like his son – indeed this bitter relationship between father and son was to be a characteristic feature of the Hanoverian dynasty. The boy was resentful of his father's severe treatment of his mother, and their antipathy was seldom mellowed throughout their relationship.

George, the son, married Caroline of Ansbach in August 1705, nine years before his father became King of Great Britain. The marriage was to produce a large family of eight children, and to make ample provision for the continuation of the Hanoverian succession. It is of special interest to us, however, in several ways – Caroline's early pregnancies illustrate the difficulties, which existed in those days, of knowing when a baby was expected to be born; a violent controversy broke out during the birth of her fifth child – a stillborn son – concerning the rights of midwives or doctors to conduct the confinement; whilst the birth of her sixth child was to foment the ill-feeling which characterized the relationship between the father and son throughout this whole era.

George and Caroline had been married for a little over six months when he expressed a wish to go to war. His father refused him permission till Caroline produced an heir, and George was obliged to stop at home and control his martial feelings as best he could. In May 1706 Caroline believed that she was pregnant. As time went by and she began to show clear signs of her abdomen enlarging, it seemed certain that this was so. As the end of the year approached, however, and she showed no signs of going into labour, people began to have their doubts. Ernest Augustus, Sophia's youngest son, had ceased to believe that Caroline was pregnant, and attributed her condition to 'wind, I expect'. Finally when the court had, in the words of her biographer, R. L. Arkell, 'for some time past almost despaired of the princess electoral's being brought to bed', she was delivered of her first-born son on 31 January 1707.

The most likely explanation for this apparent prolongation of pregnancy, is that Caroline's menstrual cycle was irregular, and the intervals between periods somewhat prolonged. In these circumstances with, shall we say, two months between one menstrual period and the next, a woman may believe herself pregnant before the conception actually takes place. In those days no one knew when, during a menstrual cycle, the conception actually occurred, although it was known that to miss periods was a sign of pregnancy. If Caroline sometimes had periods every month, and sometimes as far apart as two or even three months, she might easily believe she had conceived when more than four weeks elapsed from her last period without another one appearing. We now know that ovulation takes place in regular relationship to the next menstrual period – fourteen days before it to be precise. Caroline could easily go for eight or ten weeks from the last menstrual period, believe herself to be pregnant when she was not, but then become pregnant when she ovulated. She would then imagine herself to be further on in pregnancy than she was. Hence she thought herself already pregnant in May when it was probably about the time that the conception actually occurred.

Uncertain of what was happening, anxious no doubt that something might be going wrong with her pregnancy, and harrassed by constant enquiry, she kept out of the way of all except her immediate family. Sophia's biographer, Maria Kroll, described Caroline as 'keeping to her bed behind barricaded door and shuttered windows'. No one was allowed to visit her. Indeed she overdid the secrecy. In Arkell's words, 'a wretched furtiveness concerned the baby's arrival as if he had entered his mother's room in a warming pan'. The Electress Sophia thought that her son Max, George's younger brother, 'might be of a mind to dispute the genuineness of the baby'.

In fact the genuineness does not seem to have been questioned, although the confinement eventually took place behind locked doors without any one from Hanover present and with only a small number of people from Ansbach. Sophia was outraged at not being allowed into the room before the child was born; she saw him for the first time several days later at his christening, which was held privately in the birth chamber. Mr Hall, the British envoy, heard the news of the birth some time later, and then only from one of Caroline's ladies-in-waiting, and he did not see the child until the last week of February. George apologized to him for the small respect paid to him as Queen Anne's representative.

So in this hole-in-the-corner fashion was Frederick Lewis, Prince of Wales – 'poor Fred' to posterity – born. His life was to be characterized by bitter antipathy with his parents and by little else.

In the spring of 1708, with one son thriving, and his wife believing herself pregnant again, George was allowed to go to war. On his return in the autumn, however, he found no baby, and no expectation of one. Again Caroline's missed periods had not been caused by pregnancy but by some other factor which we cannot now determine.

It is not uncommon for women to miss periods in this way for several months or even, in rarer cases, for several years. There are many possible explanations, but the commonest is that, in certain women, the delicate balance of hormones, which controls the process of menstruation, is disturbed by quite simple events, which might not affect another individual. Emotional stress is often the precipitating cause; weight loss is also frequently involved. We cannot now say why the Princess Caroline should have suffered from missed periods – secondary amenorrhoea, as it is called – in this way, but it seems clear that she did, at least from time to time. Anxiety about her husband's departure to war could have been quite enough to produce it.

It had no lasting effect, however. George's return in the autumn of 1708, must have been followed within a few months by a return of her menstrual rhythm, since she became pregnant again early in 1709, and was delivered of her second child, Anne, on 2 November. Amelia was born in 1711, and Caroline in 1713. Then in Caroline's fifth pregnancy, problems were to arise which might have had far more serious consequences.

By this time George I was King. The two Georges with Caroline and her three youngest children had come to England in 1714, the oldest boy Frederick having been left behind in Hanover. Caroline planned to have her expected confinement at Hampton Court and, because the surroundings were unfamiliar, she had brought her midwife from Hanover with her. During the pregnancy the English ladies about the court expressed concern that she was too active. Caroline was fond of taking long walks, and could not be dissuaded from continuing to do so. Lady Cowper remarked in mid-August that 'the Princess has been mightily out of order. She was in great danger of miscarrying ... she has taken some things Sir David Hamilton gave her and I hope she is out of danger this time though I wish she would take a little more care of herself.'

On Sunday, 4 November Caroline's labour began and the Privy Council was called. They and the Prince did not go to bed all night waiting for news, but none came. The Princess was to be looked after by the German midwife 'whose countenance prognosticated ill', wrote Lady Cowper. Sir David Hamilton was in attendance as physician: he had formerly been physician to Queen Anne and was, at the time of Caroline's labour, not only a Fellow of the College of Physicians and a Fellow of the Royal Society but also one of the country's leading exponents of midwifery.

The court ladies were full of anxiety and distrustful of the Princess's midwife, whom none of them knew. In Lady Cowper's words they 'pressed to have the Princess laid by Sir David' but the Prince, when approached, was loathe to agree unless it was absolutely necessary, and when the suggestion was put to Caroline herself, she refused to consider it. The labour dragged on desultorily all through the Monday and Tuesday. Caroline was disturbed by noise from the courtyard and other rooms in the palace. At one point on the Tuesday she had a violent shivering attack which took a long time to subside.

The members of the cabinet, anxious yet helpless, sent the Princess's old friend, the Countess of Buckenburgh, to the Prince with their petition that Sir David should take over. Despite the eminence of the Royal Physician this precipitated an ethical crisis, offended George, and provoked a storm of protest from the midwife. Feeling that her professional competence was being slighted, she objected violently, and refused to continue unless she was protected from the court ladies, who, she alleged, threatened to hang her if things went wrong. Prince George was incensed, and when the Duchesses of Bolton and St Albans entered the room, in all innocence, he harangued the astonished pair, insisting that he would fling anyone who attempted to interfere out of the window. The old German midwife still proved obstinate, and everyone set about coaxing her to return to her duties. Lord Townshend the Secretary of State 'met the midwife in the outward room and ran and shook and squeezed her by the hand and made kind faces at her; for she understood no language but German'. Eventually she capitulated and returned to supervise the remainder of the labour.

It continued to be slow and not until Friday, when Caroline was exhausted and almost beyond endurance, did she bear a dead son. 'Prudery', wrote Arkell, 'had cost her a babe and nearly her life.'

This distressing and dangerous confinement did not, however, delay Caroline's next pregnancy. The following year she gave birth to another boy. He was named George after his father and grandfather, but so far from improving the already strained relationships between the King and his heir, the christening of the child caused a violent flare-up in their antipathy.

George I and his son and family were at that time living in St James's Palace. The Prince of Wales invited his father to be godfather to the boy, and wished his uncle, who was Bishop of Osnabruck, to be the second godparent. The King, however, although normally little influenced by British customs, seemed determined to be difficult and insisted that by tradition the Lord Chamberlain, the Duke of Newcastle, should be godparent. The Prince of Wales heartily disliked the Duke of Newcastle, but could do nothing but agree.

After the christening, however, the Prince could contain himself no longer. Making his way in a menacing fashion towards Newcastle, he shook his fist and uttered a threat, which was so misunderstood by the Duke, that he was filled with alarm. The Prince called the Duke a rascal, and then said, 'I will find you out', by which, he later explained, he meant, 'Sooner or later I will get my own back upon you.' What Newcastle thought had been said was, 'I shall *fight* you out', and imagined he had been challenged to a duel. He at once told the King, who was so angry that he ordered a cabinet meeting, and sent his ministers to question Newcastle. The Prince of Wales denied that he had said what Newcastle alleged and called him a liar. The King was further incensed. He first ordered the Prince and Princess to be put under house arrest, and finally, having been dissuaded by his ministers from actually arresting them, banished them from the palace. They were not allowed to take their children with them, and they could see them only once a week. Thirty years later when George and Caroline were King and Queen, they were to banish their eldest son in a similar manner.

Caroline bore three more children, a son William Augustus, born in 1721, a daughter Mary in 1723, and her childbearing finally came to an end with the birth of Louisa the following year, when Caroline was forty-one years old. Three years later she and her husband became King and Queen in 1727 on the death of George I.

4

Frederick, Prince of Wales, and Augusta

Frederick, Prince of Wales, eldest son of George II and Queen Caroline, showed little in his character or behaviour to commend him to posterity. He has remained:

> 'Poor Fred, who was alive and is dead
> There's no more to be said.'

We nowadays recall scarcely anything to his credit. His relations with his parents were appalling even by the standards of the Hanoverian royal family and on one occasion led him to such a prodigious act of folly that his wife, Augusta, might easily have lost her life bearing their first child.

It is clear that both George II and Queen Caroline disliked their eldest son from an early age. When he reacted to their antipathy and goaded them by behaviour he knew would be offensive to them, their dislike became hatred, and their opposition implacable.

The origin of their hostility is uncertain, but it must have begun when he was very young. Left behind, as we have seen, when his parents came to Britain as Prince and Princess of Wales in 1714, the seven-year-old Frederick Louis spent a lonely childhood in the enormous house of Herrenhausen with an old great-uncle, Ernest Augustus, as his guardian. Perhaps, it is not altogether surprising that, growing up as he did in the company of adults, he became a precocious child. When George I returned to Herrenhausen, two years later, he was to find the nine-year-old Prince holding courts and levées at the palace, whilst his governor was writing to Caroline complaining of the boy's addiction to cards and drink!

When George II succeeded his father in 1727, he continued to resist his ministers' advice that the rightful place for his eldest son, now Prince of Wales, was in Britain. Not only does it seem that the King was bent on preventing Frederick's presence in the country, but that he had previously sought means of excluding him from the succession. Lord Chancellor King's diary records: 'The Prince of Wales [George II] and his wife were for excluding Prince Frederick from the throne of England, but that after the King and Prince he should be an elector of Hanover and Prince William (his brother) King of Great Britain; but the King said it was unjust to do it without Prince Frederick's consent.' It seems probable that only the opposition of George I foiled this scheme. Sir Robert Walpole indeed advised George I that his grandson would never reach the country at all unless the King – brought him over himself.

Frederick finally did arrive in England on 7 December 1728 when almost twenty-two years old. He had forced his father's hand by appearing determined to marry Wilhemina, Princess Royal of Prussia. Since a Prussian alliance was not at all in keeping with the policy of George II and his government, the King, unwillingly no doubt, demanded his son's presence in London.

Neither he nor the Queen made any attempt to make Frederick welcome. He was refused an adequate allowance, although Parliament, subject to the King's agreement, had voted him £100,000 a year; but the King withheld his consent. Frederick was also denied an establishment of his own, and was obliged to make do with apartments in St James's Palace. After a period of conformity with his parents wishes, with no improvement in his own position, Frederick's patience became exhausted, and he began courting the Opposition and flouting royal authority whenever he had the opportunity. Relations became strained to breaking point, and the Queen would openly refer to her son in the most unflattering and degrading terms.

It was Caroline's expressed view that Frederick was impotent, despite a good deal of evidence to the contrary. Much of our information on Caroline's opinion of her son's sexual incapacity comes from her favourite, Lord Hervey, who was also closely associated with Frederick. Hervey's famous *Memoirs* concern not only the affairs of the government at home and abroad, but also the extraordinary relationship between the King, the Queen and the heir apparent.

Lord Hervey was the second son of a rich Suffolk gentleman who had been created Lord Bristol by George I. The Countess, Hervey's mother, was for a quarter of a century Woman of the Bedchamber to Caroline, both as Princess of Wales and as Queen, and was in a fortunate position to further the career of her son. Hervey was described by Sir Charles Hanbury Williams as excessively handsome, but 'so effeminate as to bring even his sex into question'. Hervey's friend, Pulteney, with whom he had a violent quarrel, ending in a duel, described Hervey as 'a delicate hermaphrodite' and 'a pretty little master miss' and made other offensive references to his effeminacy.

If his sex was in question from his appearance, however, it can hardly have been so from his behaviour. Not only did Lady Hervey, who was a Maid of Honour to Caroline, then Princess of Wales, bear him eight children, but he also maintained as a mistress another Maid of Honour, Miss Anne Vane. It was Miss Vane who was to be one of the reasons for Hervey's break with the Prince of Wales.

Frederick and Hervey had been on excellent terms during the first three years of the Prince's time in England. Towards the end of 1731, however, Hervey, on returning to London from a visit to the country, was chagrined to find his place as the Prince's confidant and adviser had been taken by George Bubb Doddington, whilst Miss Vane had been set up by Frederick in an establishment in Soho Square. In June the following year she gave birth to a son who was named Fitz Frederick after his putative royal father. In the *Gentleman's Magazine* there appeared the following notice: 'On the 17th June 1733 the son of a Lady much talked of at St James's was christened by the name of FitzFrederick of Cornwall; the Honourable Henry Vane and Lord Baltimore were Godfathers and Lady B. Mansel Godmother. He was born on the 4th instant.'

Hervey, out of favour, railed against Miss Vane, believing her to have poisoned the Prince's mind against him. This insulting behaviour to his mistress did in fact incense Frederick, who rejected Hervey completely, and spurned any attempt at reconciliation. Unpopularity with the Prince of Wales was, however, synonymous with acceptance by the King and Queen. Hervey was soon a favourite, especially with the Queen, becoming 'constant companion and distinguished favourite' – which further angered her son. It is not to be wondered at, therefore, that in Hervey's *Memoirs* Frederick Louis, Prince of Wales, appears in an unfavourable light.

The *Memoirs* record conversations between Queen Caroline and Hervey about the Prince of Wales's supposed impotence, which make remarkable and distressing reading. According to Hervey, the Queen had heard many conflicting stories of Frederick's sexual prowess – or lack of it. Sometimes he was supposed to have referred to himself as Hercules or 'as if he were the late King of Poland' (Augustus the Strong of Poland was alleged to have fathered 354 bastards); 'at other times with a despondency of having children, and in so pathetic a tone that he is ready to cry and seems to think it impossible'.

There were whispered references to a mysterious operation performed by a *valet de chambre*, one Vreid, who was also a surgeon and man-midwife. What this procedure may have been can only be surmised. His mother, not unnaturally, found the conversation both incomprehensible and repellent and begged him 'to talk of something else'. Hervey, asked by the Queen for his opinion, said, 'Your Majesty must know that the chief intelligence I have had in this subject must be from Miss Vane who I do not tell Your Majesty always adhered to truth. She used to describe the Prince in these matters ignorant to a degree inconceivable' (scarcely as it turned out an appropriate word) 'but not impotent, and my firm belief is that he is as capable of having children as any man in England.'

So we turn to the Princess of Wales herself. Augusta, the seventeen-year-old Princess of Saxe-Gotha, had been seen by George II during the summer of 1735, and approved as a suitable bride for his son. Frederick had been demanding a wife for some little time. He was after all twenty-seven years old, and nothing could be more reasonable than his wish for marriage and a family. The King had proposed the Princess of Denmark, but she was described by Lord Egmont as 'ugly, crooked and not very young'. Frederick declined with vehemence, only to be offered instead the daughter of the Duke of Wurtemburg-Stutgard who was more attractive but only thirteen years old. Augusta of Saxe-Gotha seemed an altogether better bet, and how could the Prince tell who, if anyone, might be proposed if he declined again? He was not prepared to take his father's recommendation entirely on trust, however, but sent a gentleman to Saxe-

Gotha to report to him in person. Perhaps to Frederick's surprise, and certainly to his relief, the account he received of the Princess was highly satisfactory, permitting him to acquiesce to his father's wishes with equanimity.

His agreement to marry Augusta spelt the dismissal of poor little Anne Vane. Upon Frederick's betrothal, Lord Baltimore was sent to see Anne, bearing a message that she should go abroad for two or three years. Her compliance would mean the continuance of her allowance the Prince was making to her. If she refused, payments would cease.

Frederick also wished her to leave their child behind in his care, so that proper provision could be made for his education. Anne appeared indignant at the proposal, but to what extent she was truly distressed is uncertain. She had resumed her liaison with Hervey, and with his help wrote a reproachful answer to the Prince. There was much wrangling, with Hervey and others using the affair to further their own ends. Lord Egmont records that the Prince actually visited Anne himself formally to end their relationship 'making a visit purposely to Wimbledon to tell her that since His Majesty deigns to bring him over a wife, decency required that he should quit correspondence with herself before her arrival, but that he would allow her £1,500 per annum pension till she could find a husband and on her marriage give her £20,000'.

The affair had a tragic end. Anne retired to Bath on doctor's orders, and wrote from there to Hervey in optimistic vein believing her life would be happier than at any time. Within two months her son died in convulsions; twelve days later Anne too was dead.

The boy was buried in Westminster Abbey, no doubt by the direct order of the Prince of Wales, who was deeply affected. Hervey records that the Queen and Princess Caroline 'thought the Prince more afflicted for the loss of this child than they had ever seen him on any occasion or thought him capable of being.' The brief entry in the register at Westminster Abbey merely reads, 'FitzFrederick, natural child of the Prince of Wales by Anne Vane, daughter of Gilbert Lord Bernard, aged 4.'

Augusta landed at Greenwich on Sunday morning, 25 April 1736. She proceeded to Greenwich Palace, whence Frederick made his way that same afternoon. He was attentive, seeing much of her during the ensuing days. On Tuesday, 27 April, Augusta was conveyed to Lambeth in one of the King's coaches, and from there to Whitehall by the royal barge, and from Whitehall to St James's in the King's chair. It is recorded that, upon first being presented to the King and Queen, Augusta prostrated herself on the floor, first before the monarch, then his wife, who were most favourably impressed by the gesture.

Her arrival in many ways foreshadowed that of Charlotte of Mecklenburg-Strelitz twenty-five years later to marry Augusta's eldest son. Neither spoke English; neither had come with any retinue of friends or servants. Indeed Augusta had one retainer, and had been escorted from The Hague by Lady Irwin, one of her new ladies-in-waiting, whom she did not know. Both Augusta and Charlotte were to be married within hours of their arrival at St James's Palace, although Augusta had at least enjoyed two days of her husband-to-be's company before the ceremony.

Hervey records that she was composed, and did not appear at all embarrassed by her arrival at the palace. He may have been impressed by her demeanour but not by her appearance, for his description is anything but flattering. 'The Princess', he says, 'was rather tall, and had health and youth enough in her face joined to a very modest and good natured look to make her countenance not disagreeable, but her person, from being very ill-made, a good deal awry, her arms long and her motions awkward, had in spite of all the finery of jewels and brocade an ordinary air, which no trappings could cover or exalt.' But Frederick seemed pleased with her, which was all that mattered.

They were married at 9.00 p.m. on 27 April with little formality in the Chapel at the Palace. The Court was not assembled, and there were no processions to or from the ceremony. Supper followed at which in Hervey's words 'nothing remarkable happened but the Prince eating several glasses of jelly'. After supper the Queen retired with the Princess to the latter's apartment, where Augusta was undressed and put to bed beside her bridegroom. 'Everyone', reported Hervey, 'passed through their bedchamber to see them, where there was nothing remarkable but the Prince's nightcap, which was some inches higher than any grenadier's cap in the whole army.' Augusta is said to have retained her composure admirably throughout the ordeal and Frederick, sustained no doubt by his several glasses of jelly, did likewise.

Their marriage was, of course, followed by much speculation on the possibility of a royal birth in the near future. Frederick did much to further the notion that his wife was pregnant, giving frequent and obvious instructions to his coachman to drive carefully whenever the Princess was with him. 'Several hints of like nature were often thrown out', says Hervey, but the Queen refused to believe the Princess of Wales was pregnant and persisted in her belief that Frederick was impotent.

At one point she asked Lord Hervey if he could discover from Lady Dudley, who, she said, had 'lain with half the town', whether the Prince was 'like other men or not'. Lord Hervey was disinclined to involve himself with Lady Dudley to the extent which would be necessary to find this out. The Queen, however, was insistent about her son's urge to have children, which she said 'was to such an extent that there was nothing he was not capable of to give the point of the Princess being with child'.

Caroline quizzed Hervey as to whether it would be possible for a man to lie with the Princess without her knowing that it was not her husband beside her. 'Supposing the Prince has never consummated his marriage with her, I believe it could,' Hervey replied, 'but if he never has, it would be impossible.' 'Do you think', continued the Queen, 'that you could contrive, if he and you were both willing, without her knowledge to go to bed with her instead of him?' 'Nothing so easy', replied My Lord. 'My God is it possible', wondered the Queen. 'Why, for a month before and after the time of putting the design in execution, I would advise the Prince to go to bed several hours after his wife, and to pretend to get up for a flux several times in the night, to perfume himself always with some predominant smell, and by the help of these tricks it would be very easy, not using himself to talk to her in bed, to put the change of any man near his own size upon her as he pleased.'

A more unsavoury conversation with a mother about her son it would be difficult to imagine – nor indeed why a man would wish to commit it to his memoirs for the benefit of posterity. But it shows beyond any doubt the depths of Caroline's suspicion of Frederick

and of his capacity to beget a child. When later she was told that
the Princess was pregnant, at first she did not believe it, and when
it proved true she was highly suspicious that the Prince was not
the father.

Early in July 1737, however, Frederick wrote to his mother, indicating that Dr Hollings and the midwife, Mrs Cannons, had no
doubt about the fact that Augusta was with child, and asking his
mother to inform the King. The Queen's suspicions, already strong,
were re-doubled when she met the Princess shortly afterwards. Her
enquiry about the date of the forthcoming confinement met with
the unhelpful reply that the Princess did not know. This of course
may well have been true, but together with Augustua's continued
evasion of further questions on the subject, this answer merely
served to underline the Queen's suspicions. She was convinced that
a plot existed to fob off the newborn child of another woman as
the infant who might one day inherit the throne. Although others
observed that physically the Princess showed all the signs of pregnancy, Caroline was still unwilling to accept this: 'for my part I
do not see she is big; you all say you see it and therefore I suppose
it is so and that I am blind.'

To fan the flames of doubt further, the Prince was determined
that this child should be born at St James's Palace. The Queen was
equally adamant that it should not and demanded that instead the
confinement should take place at Hampton Court where she and
the King were living. Advised by Sir Robert Walpole, they had
resolved to send a message to Frederick informing him of this decision. It was Hervey's view, however – which he lost no time in
passing on to Queen Caroline – that even if this message were dispatched, the Prince would thwart their wishes.

Lord Hervey said the Prince would pretend it was by chance; for as
Dr Hollings and Mrs Cannons would be made to say that exercise was
good for the Princess in her condition, she would be carried once or twice
a week to Kew or London and whichever of these two places the Prince
intended he should lie in at, he would make her when she was within
a month of her time affect to be taken ill; and nobody could disprove
her having the pains she would complain of, the King and Queen could
not take in prudence upon them to say she should be removed: and there
of course her Royal Highness would bring forth.

'Well, if that be so', replied the Queen, 'I cannot help it, but at her labour I positively will be, let her lie in where she will; for she cannot be brought to bed as quick as one can blow one's nose, and I will be sure it is her child.'

With her anxieties about her son's trickery increasing daily, the Queen urged Walpole to have the King's message forwarded to him without delay. Walpole's reply was that the Princess did not expect the child until the beginning of October, which gave them time enough, since it was still only July. From whom he had been given that information concerning the expected date of the Princess's confinement we do not know, but his procrastination, in the event, gave Frederick the opportunity he needed to embark on his desperate enterprise. The poor Princess of Wales, who should have been the centre of attraction, was a pawn in the game, and a dangerous game it proved.

The drama began at Hampton Court on Sunday evening, 31 July. After dinner the King retired below stairs to play at commerce; the Queen was engaged at quadrille and the Princess Caroline and Hervey played cribbage. None was aware of the events taking place elsewhere in the palace.

During the evening the Princess's labour began. Frederick instantly ordered a coach to transport her to London. The pains became stronger and more frequent; before she could be removed from the palace her waters broke. Frederick pressed into service Monsieur Dunoyer, the dancing master, and Mr Bloodworth, one of the equerries, and with one on each arm and the Prince himself whipping them on from the rear, poor labouring Augusta was dragged downstairs, urged along passages, and, finally, thrust into the coach which set off with full speed. The Princess's lady-in-waiting, Lady Hamilton, remonstrated strongly against this very unwise move, but Frederick would not be prevented. With what Hervey calls 'the encouragement of a toothdrawer or the consolatory tenderness of an executioner' he assured his wife that 'it would all be over in a minute'. It very nearly was.

In the coach with Frederick and Augusta on their hair-raising drive to London were the Princess's lady-in-waiting, Lady Hamilton, and two of her dressers, Mrs Clavering and Mrs

Paine. On the box was Vreid, the Prince's *valet de chambre*, who, as we have already seen, was a surgeon and man-midwife. Behind the coach came Mr Bloodworth and several more determined to get Augusta to a place of safety at all costs.

There are few details of the journey available to us, from sources sufficiently reliable, to judge the extent of the poor Princess's suffering. Her distress must have been acute, and despite the encouragement and support of her husband and her ladies, the jolting and pitching of the coach must have been hard to bear. The Prince later admitted to his mother that so strong were the pains, that they thought they would be obliged to take her into one of the houses they passed along the road, to be delivered there. And – according to the Prince – it was not only the mother-to-be who was in pain; he himself 'with holding her and her pillows in the coach, had got such pains in his own back he could hardly stir'!

Eventually, about ten o'clock, the party arrived at St James's Palace. According to Hervey, with his customary zeal to record the unsavoury, 'notwithstanding all the handkerchieves that had been thrust up Her Royal Highness's petticoats in the coach, her clothes were in such a condition with the filthy inundations which attend these circumstances, that when the coach stopped at St James's the Prince ordered all the lights to be put out, that people might not have the nasty ocular evidence which would otherwise have been exhibited to them of his folly and her distress.' But she had arrived, and not a moment too soon. Forty-five minutes later she was safely delivered of a daughter who, in Hervey's words, was 'a little rat of a girl, about the bigness of a good large toothpick case'.

To what extent anyone at the Palace might have been expecting an event such as this is not easy to decide. Before leaving Hampton Court Frederick had sent a message to the Lord President of the Council, Lord Wilmington, bidding him to attend St James's, to witness the confinement. To have done this, and not at the same time have sent a second message to the Palace itself to ensure that suitable preparations would be made for the Princess's comfort and safety on arrival, seems inconceivable.

According to Hervey, however, nothing was ready. The midwife 'came in a few minutes'. 'Napkins, warming pan and all other necessary implements for this operation were sought by different emissaries in different houses in the neighbourhood; and no sheets being to be come at, Her Royal Highness was put to bed between two table cloths.'

How unlikely all this sounds! If, as seems highly probable, the Prince had been full of schemes to outwit his parents, and to contrive that his wife be confined away from Hampton Court, St James's Palace was surely one of the places in which he would have ensured that preparations were made. Even if, despite his intentions ultimately to employ a stratagem to this end, he was caught unawares by the sudden onset of premature labour, is it reasonable to suppose that St James's could not supply such simple articles as a pair of sheets and a warming pan? No doubt there was excitement and much apprehension for the safety of the Princess of Wales, arriving late in the second stage of labour; certainly there would be attendants rushing hither and thither to give the necessary help in the nick of time, but one can hardly imagine that they would need to beg assistance from 'different houses in the neighbourhood'. What Hervey wrote seems to be intended to emphasize the Prince's undoubted folly, in subjecting his wife and the heir to the throne to such danger, to spite his parents.

Only two officers of state were present when the child was born – Lord President Wilmington and Lord Godolphin, the Lord Privy Seal, who lived close to the Palace and who was sent for immediately the Prince reached London. Messages were also sent to the Lord Chancellor, who was out of London, and the Archbishop of Canterbury, who eventually arrived – a quarter of an hour too late.

But Lord Godolphin later assured Sir Robert Walpole that he and Lord Wilmington had been in the Princess's bedroom for at least fifteen minutes before the child was born. They had been on the same side of the bed as the midwife, the Prince close to the bed on the opposite side. When Augusta complained of one very strong pain, the Prince asked 'is the child born?'. 'Don't you hear it cry?' replied Mrs Cannons, and at once lifted the baby from beneath the sheet (or table cloth if we are to believe Hervey) and gave her into the Lord President's arms, not into the Prince's. Frederick not unnaturally inquired if it was a boy or a girl; the astonishing reply from the midwife was that the Princess should not be surprised with either the joy or mortification of knowing which it was! How long the Princess and he were obliged to wait for such an elementary piece of information is not recorded.

So the Princess was safely delivered, and as the excitement subsided at St James's it broke out soon afterwards at Hampton Court. The King, the Queen, the Princesses and Lord Hervey had retired to bed at eleven. Incredible though it seems, they were blissfully unaware of the drama which had been going on around them. It is hard to imagine how a labouring Princess, borne along by a strong man on each arm and her husband behind, with her waters broken and amniotic fluid dripping onto the floor, could have been spirited away without anyone realizing it.

It was not until 1.30 a.m. on 1 August that a courier arrived from London with the news that the Princess was in labour. He was received by Mrs Tichburne, the Woman of the Bedchamber, who immediately went to wake the King and Queen to tell them. The Queen, demanding to know why she was being woken at such an hour, enquired if the house was on fire. She might almost have wished it so, rather than hear the news which followed. The Prince, Mrs Tichburne said, had sent to inform their Majesties of the Princess being in labour. 'My God, my nightgown. I will go to her this moment', cried Caroline. 'Your nightgown, madam, and your coaches too', responded her informant. 'The Princess is at St James's.' The Queen was incredulous, 'Are you mad or are you asleep my good Tichburne?' she demanded. Mrs Tichburne, of course, insisted on the truth, which invoked violent passion in the King, who, in German (but translated later for all by Lord Hervey) upbraided the Queen: 'You see now with all your wisdom', he cried, 'how they have outwitted you. This is all your fault. There is a false child will be put upon you and how will you answer it to all your children?'

The Queen wisely made no reply, but dressing as rapidly as possible, set out for London. She took with her the two eldest Princesses, two of their ladies, Lord Hervey, the Duke of Grafton and finally Lord Essex, who was to be sent back to the King with news from St James's Palace. By 2.30 they were assembled and set out; by four o'clock they were in London.

Upon entering the Prince and Princess's apartments the Queen was met by her son in nightgown and cap, who told her what had transpired and that her granddaughter was born. He was received coldly, with frosty enquiries as to why no messenger had been sent sooner to Hampton Court to acquaint her with the news. Frederick replied that he had written the message as soon as he could, and since he had written only three lines had wasted no time. The Queen then went into her daughter-in-law, offered her congratulations and felicitations and kissed her. Then addressing her in French she said, 'apparently madam you have suffered terribly'. 'Not at all', responded the Princess in the same language. 'It is nothing.'

The Queen withdrew and joined Lord Hervey in his quarters, where, after dispatching a note to the King by Lord Essex, she announced to him and to Lord Grafton and her daughters, her acceptance of the child as that of her son and his wife. 'Well, upon my honour', she cried, 'I no more doubt this poor little bit of a thing is the Princess's child than I doubted either of these two being mine, though I owe to you I had my doubts upon the road that there would be some juggle; and if instead of this poor little ugly she-mouse there had been a brave large fat and jolly boy I should not have been cured of my suspicions.' Walpole's account of Lord Godolphin's story of the delivery was later to put an end to any lingering doubt she or the King might have had.

Medical comment on the rash act of the Prince of Wales is almost superfluous. One does not have to possess specialized knowledge to be aware of the huge risk to which he subjected his wife and his unborn child. The distance from Hampton Court to St James's Palace is twelve miles, little enough in modern times, but in an eighteenth-century horse-drawn coach along roads little better than cart tracks, how different the matter would have been. Had they encountered any obstacle whatever, they could have been many hours on the journey. Early the following morning, when the Queen and her entourage travelled the same road, it took one and a half hours for them to reach London, and such was their agitation that we can safely assume they lost no time.

Whilst Augusta was being transported in strong labour, any one of a score of events might seriously have delayed her. Admittedly the Prince had taken the only precaution open to him, if he was to make the journey at all, and had taken along his valet-cum-surgeon-cum, man-midwife, Vreid. But we have no means of knowing how competent he was and the most skilful obstetrician in England at that time would have been able to do little if the delivery had taken place *en route*, and had been followed by a serious haemorrhage.

Such post-partum haemorrhages are still a hazard to this day, in an era when blood transfusion can swiftly be administered and powerful drugs are available to stimulate the uterus to contract to stop the bleeding. Bleeding from the womb following delivery is controlled by one mechanism only – by strong contractions of inter-weaving muscle fibres, between which pass the arteries to the pla-centa or after-birth. Once the placenta separates from the inside of the womb, these arteries are torn, their ends open, and the blood pours out. If the muscle of the uterus contracts firmly the arteries are gripped tightly and kinked and compressed, and the bleeding is stopped; if the muscle does not contract properly the blood-flow through the arteries continues, and this blood loss is a serious risk to the mother's life. Nowadays we have drugs available to cause muscular contraction of the uterus, drugs which can be injected into a vein for rapid action, and the uterus will respond with a powerful contraction within minutes. But no such drug existed in the eighteenth century, and it is safe to say that a post-partum haemor-rhage occurring on the Princess's journey to London might well have caused her death, as it was to cause the death of her great-grand-daughter eighty years later. Vreid might have been present in the coach, but any serious complication of this kind would have left him helpless.

The Princess, moreover, was not the only patient at risk. A child, unexpectedly born in such circumstances, with little or no means available to establish respiration or to maintain body heat, or to deal effectively with such a simple task of cutting and tying the umbilical cord, may well have lost its life. Added to these and the other general risks which would have affected any child so born, it seems probable that an additional complication here was prematurity.

Premature babies are especially prone to lose body heat rapidly, and may suffer serious harm or die as a result; their breathing is difficult and serious oxygen lack can occur also. A coach travelling to London along eighteenth-century roads late at night, even though the date was 31 July, is scarcely an ideal place to give such a mite proper conditions for survival. We cannot be certain, of course, that the child was premature. Augusta had said that she did not know when her confinement was due. Walpole had told the Queen the birth was expected in October. If he was right, the Princess's confinement might have taken place five or six weeks before the pregnancy reached its full time of forty weeks. We have no accurate – or even approximate – idea of the infant's weight at birth. It is not easy to envisage how big a 'good large toothpick case' of the eighteenth century might have been. This unflattering description, together with the Queen's references to the baby as 'this poor little bit of a thing' and 'this poor little ugly she-mouse' strongly suggest a tiny baby, and gives weight to a diagnosis of prematurity.

Frederick's behaviour also supports the conclusion that labour was premature. That he was determined to outwit his father and mother somehow there seems no doubt. One way or another, he intended to get the Princess away from Hampton Court near to her time, and to have the child born elsewhere, but in the event one is forced to conclude that he was not ready. Whatever scheme he had in mind, it was not yet unfolded. Hence his desperate remedy of a headlong dash to London, risking the loss of his wife, or child, or both, on the way.

The Prince later wrote to the King, giving as an explanation of his conduct that labour began prematurely, leading to his precipitous departure. He assured his father that the Princess had suffered with the colic for several days. Dr Hollings and Dr Broxome, along with Mrs Cannons, the midwife, had been consulted several times, and on each occasion had assured the Prince that his wife was not yet near her time. This, Frederick said, was the opinion of the two doctors as recently as midday on that fateful Sunday.

So, according to his account, when labour began so unexpectedly at Hampton Court he had one thought – to get Augusta to St James's and to her medical attendants as swiftly as posssible. Indeed he went further and insisted that it was the Princess who urgently desired him to take her – a view she later confirmed. It is possible it was so, but it seems unlikely. His wife, one imagines, was giving her husband the support he very much needed.

Perhaps the kindest view to take is that Frederick really had no conception of the terrible risk he was running. History has severely criticized him for it and it is difficult to offer anything more convincing than this in his support. We will leave the last word with the Queen that 'it was a miracle that the Princess and the child had not both been killed'.

The aftermath of the Princess's confinement was characterized by continued deterioration in the relationship between the King, the Queen and the Prince. Soon after the birth itself, Frederick, possibly elated by having outwitted his mother, and by the safe delivery of his wife, had been more forthcoming with the Queen than he had for some years. But when Caroline and her daughters visited Augusta again a few days later, Frederick was offhand and offensive. He received his mother only at the door of the Princess's room, instead of at the entrance to the Palace. He spoke not a single word to her nor his sisters during the visit, although he chatted to other members of her suite. On her departure, after a far more brief visit than she had anticipated, in view of his rudeness, he escorted her still in silence to her coach, where he knelt and kissed her hand. The Queen, incensed by his behaviour, and imagining his public gesture to be only for the benefit of the crowd of spectators, informed the King, who flew into a rage and resolved to expel his son from the Palace as soon as the Princess's condition permitted.

On 29 August the child was baptized Augusta at a ceremony which took place in the Palace at 8 p.m. The King and Queen had agreed to act as godparents – however unwilling they were they could scarcely do anything else – and the Dowager Duchess of Saxe-Gotha was the other godmother. All were represented by proxy. It is recorded that the infant was placed in an elaborate cradle which was approached by steps and covered with a canopy of State; after the ceremony she was placed on her nurse's knee on a sumptuous cushion embroidered with silver. The Princess, who was still regarded as convalescent, in accordance with the practice at the time, was sitting up in her State bed, the pillows of which were covered with the finest lace and elaborately ornamented. The font and flagon normally used for royal christenings, and kept at the Tower, were brought especially to the Palace for the occasion.

But the King and Queen were not disposed to give Frederick any more rein. The Prince sent letters of thanks to them the following day, hoping for reinstatement in his father's favour, but the King was unmoved, and returned a bitter letter complaining of Frederick's extravagant and undutiful behaviour, 'in a matter of such great consequence as the birth of an heir to the crown'. Frederick was ordered to leave St James's Palace. On 10 September a letter was delivered to him, and on the 12th the Prince and Princess and the infant Augusta departed. The sentiments of the King and Queen were bitter. 'Thank God', said the King, 'tomorrow night the puppy will be out of my house.' 'I hope in God I shall never see him again', was the Queen's only comment. She never did.

In November, two months later, she was taken ill from strangulation of a large hernia from which she had suffered for years. Hervey describes her last illness in distressing detail, but his account is not appropriate here. To the last she refused to see her son. When her illness was announced, Frederick had sent Lord North to St James's Palace to say that he was deeply distressed by the news of her suffering, hoping that he might be allowed to see her. But the King, anticipating some such action, had informed Hervey, 'If the puppy should, in one of his impertinent affected airs of duty and affection, dare to come to St James's, I order you to go to the scoundrel and tell him I wonder at his impudence in daring to come here ... bid him go about his business'; which, in more euphemistic terms, Hervey did. The Queen, to the end, begged the King not to allow her son to see her, and throughout her fatal illness sent him no message of any kind.

Augusta bore Frederick eight further children – George, afterwards King George III, was born, also premature, in 1738 and there was doubt if he would live; Edward Augustus, Duke of York, was born in 1739, Elizabeth in 1741, William Henry, Duke of Gloucester, in 1743, Henry Frederick, Duke of Cumberland, in 1745, Louisa Anne in 1749, Frederick William in 1750 and Caroline Matilda in 1751. The infant Augusta, superseded as heir to the throne by her brother George, was later to marry Charles William Frederick, Duke of Brunswick, and through the unhappy marriage of their daughter Caroline to the Prince of Wales (later George IV), was to be grandmother to Charlotte, whose tragic confinement was to occur eighty years later.

Frederick never became King. He died of pneumonia on Wednesday, 20 March 1750. Ten years later, in 1760 his elder son, George, was to succeed to the throne as George III.

5

A Royal Success Story:
George III and Queen Charlotte

When George III ascended the throne, on the death of his grand-father, George II, on 5 October 1760, he was twenty-two years old. He was also the first unmarried sovereign since Charles II, and it was clearly in the national interest that he should marry and produce an heir. The nation was not to be disappointed. George's marriage to Charlotte of Mecklenberg-Strelitz was to be the biggest repro-ductive success story of any royal couple in the history of this country – at least numerically – and scarcely to be surpassed by any royal house in Europe. Sadly though, the behaviour of many of their offspring was extravagant, unprincipled, irresponsible – even ludicrous at times – and was to cause their parents much distress.

However, in 1760 not only was it a matter of national importance for the King to marry and produce an heir, it was something he was very anxious to do. In the year before he came to the throne he had fallen in love with Lady Sarah Lennox, one of the most beautiful women of her day, and had hoped for a time to make her his Queen, but eventually accepted that marriage to a commoner who was one of his own subjects would be unwise. And so his search for a German princess began.

The manner in which Sophia Charlotte of Mecklenberg-Strelitz was selected to be the wife of George III has been a matter of specu-lation and misrepresentation ever since. The fact that a search was being made at all was kept so secret that, when the choice was even-tually announced, rumour and Court gossip and tittle-tattle were the only sources of information about the negotiations. We learn from the historian Romney Sedgwick that in a letter to Lord Bute, whose influence over him was enormous, George expressed the wish that, 'we could next Summer, by some means or other, get some account of the various princesses in Germany that binds me to nothing, and would save a great deal of trouble whenever I consent to enter into these bonds'.

'Some account' of these various ladies was available in the New Berlin Almanac of Princesses, which was consulted by the Prince and his mother, and which helped to the extent of disclosing the existence of three new princesses, not previously considered. Nothing more aetive was done, however, until George became King.

He then sent for the Hanoverian representative in London, Baron Munchausen, and invited him to confer with Lord Bute to determine which German princesses might be appropriate consorts. It seems likely that very few people knew of these negotiations, perhaps no one beyond the small select committee of the King, Bute and Munchausen. The Dowager Princess of Wales, who had been involved in the earlier perusal of the Berlin Almanac of runners was evidently not involved now.

The King's requirements did not stipulate a beautiful woman, but he did ask for one of good understanding, an amiable disposition, and with no inclination to meddle in politics. Munchausen made two initial suggestions – the Princess of Saxe-Gotha and the young Princess of Brunswick, both of which met with a poor reception. Reports of the Princess of Saxe-Gotha indicated that she was interested in philosophy, which 'was repugnant to him from every point of view; he wanted a wife who had no idea of such studies'. The Princess of Brunswick was from a house which had no attraction for the King, who remarked there were many other princesses available.

Accordingly Baron Munchausen's elder brother in Hanover was consulted, and other names were put forward and a short list compiled. It consisted of:

The Princess of Brandenburg
The Princess of Brandenburg-Schwedt
The Princess of Saxe-Gotha
The Princess of Brunswick
The Princess of Anhalt-Dessau
The Princess of Darmstadt

With the utmost discretion, enquiries were made about all of them. The Princess of Anhalt-Dessau's grandfather had married the daughter of an apothecary, a misalliance not considered at all proper; her name was crossed off. The Princess of Brandenburg's mother, who was also a daughter of this misalliance, had been put in prison for having had an affair with a courier; her name was crossed off. The Princess of Saxe-Gotha, the philosopher, had other disadvantages, for, in addition to being much marked by smallpox, she was believed to have a deformity of figure, which raised doubts about her ability to bear children, who might in any case inherit the abnormality; she was crossed off. The Princess of Brunswick, although thought to be very beautiful, was not only from a house ill-favoured by the King, but was only fourteen years of age and was rejected as too young, though almost certainly this was an excuse.

Only two candidates were thus left for more serious consideration – the Princesses of Brandenburg-Schwedt and Darmstadt, and since the list had become so short, the name of an outsider was added – Sophia Charlotte of Mecklenburg-Strelitz.

The Princess of Brandenburg-Schwedt did not fulfil one of the King's requirements, since she was reported to be obstinate and bad-tempered, although admittedly good-looking; she was crossed off. Only two now remained of whom Princess Charlotte, little known and coming from a small Court, seemed an unlikely winner. This was especially so when a favourable report on the Princess of Darmstadt reached the King. His inclination was 'for settling this as soon as possible – the worst thing for my liking is her size' (she was said to be a big girl). But it turned out that this was not the worst thing. Munchausen the elder reported that she was 'stubborn and ill-tempered to the greatest degree, in short much the same character as the Princess of Schwedit'. To this alarming information was added the disturbing news that her father was under the influence of mystics and in communication with spirits. This was too much for the King, and she too was eliminated. Only Charlotte of Mecklenburg-Strelitz remained.

What was known about Charlotte was satisfactory so far as it went, but it did not go very far. The elder Munchausen at first knew nothing about her at all. He later learnt that she was of good character, but, since she came from a small Court, she could not have been brought up with the idea that she would ever aspire to be Queen of a powerful country such as Britain. He despatched an emissary to

Strelitz therefore, whose report permitted a further letter to the King, giving the Princess an amiable character and disposition, so that 'a little of England's air will soon give her the deportment necessary for a British Queen'.

As the only remaining candidate from the original short list, it became imperative to send someone from Britain to obtain more facts, to get another opinion, and to establish the reaction of the Court at Strelitz if the King were to demand her hand.

The choice of emissary fell upon Colonel David Graeme, who went to Mecklenburg-Strelitz in June 1761 bearing a letter from the Princess Dowager of Wales to the Duchess of Strelitz. This letter is said to have asked several specific questions, to have indicated that the King was in no way committed yet, although a desire was felt to render communications between the two families more intimate. The reply, satisfactory in all respects, was dispatched to England at once, and was followed a few days later by a further letter from the Duchess, suggesting that Charlotte would be able to set out by the beginning of August; perhaps, should it be required, even earlier.

The Colonel also forwarded his own detailed report. Her complexion was 'delicate and fine', her hair 'pale brown, more than cendré', but 'advancing a little too much across the face at the upper part of the temples'. Her nose was 'good and not flat'. The 'back part of the cheek especially well turned' but the 'mouth rather large'. She was 'above the middle size and promises to be taller still'. Her general appearance was 'not quite that of a woman fully formed' although 'her bosom is full enough for her age'. Graeme summed up the princess as 'not a beauty, but what is little inferior, she is amiable and her face agreeable than otherwise'.

The King was more than satisfied. The choice was made, and it was announced to the Privy Council on 8 July 1761.

The Court was astonished. Horace Walpole's surprise is evident; 'the handkerchief had been tossed a vast way; it is to a Charlotte, Princess of Mecklenburg. Lord Harcourt is to be at her father's court – if he can find it – on the 1 August, and the coronation of both their majesties is fixed for the 22 September.'

Gossip was rife. Since few facts were known, these were elaborated and embroidered, and others were invented. The King's mother, the Dowager Princess of Wales, was blamed by almost everyone for insisting that the King marry a German princess – almost any German princess. Walpole insisted that it was she who had despatched 'one Colonel Graeme ... in the most private manner ... to visit various little Protestant courts, and make reports on the various unmarried princesses'.

A more romantic version of Charlotte's selection credits her with having written to Frederick the Great of Prussia, whose war with the Empress of Austria was devastating Charlotte's country; the letter was sent to George III, who caused enquiries to be made about one who could write such a letter, 'not inferior, except in its brevity, to the finest compositions of the most celebrated orators in ancient and modern times'. Delightful though this story might be, it is untrue as we have seen. The real process of selection was far more mundane.

Charlotte, like others before and since, was to make her journey to Britain to marry the King in most trying conditions. As an immediate prelude to marriage it was formidable by any standards. The Earl of Harcourt, who had been appointed Master of the Horse in the household of the future Queen, journeyed to Mecklenburg-Strelitz to escort her to England. He travelled with two ladies-in-waiting, the Duchesses of Hamilton and Ancaster, in a handsome squadron of ships, under the command of Admiral of the Fleet, Lord Anson. Lord Harcourt arrived in Mecklenburg-Strelitz on 14 August, the marriage contract was signed on the 15th, and Charlotte was left just one day, 16 August, to say goodbye to a country she would never see again.

Lord Harcourt's impression of the young princess was as favourable as Colonel Graeme's. 'Our Queen that is to be', be wrote to a friend, 'has seen very little of the world, but her good sense, vivacity and cheerfulness I daresay will recommend her to the King and make her a darling of the British nation. She is no regular beauty, but she is a very pretty size, has a charming complexion, very pretty eyes and finely made; in short she is a fine girl.'

'Fine girl' or not, she must have had to make a remarkable adjustment to her life and her outlook to adapt to the proposal from George III. Charlotte was the younger daughter of the brother of the former Duke, and had an elder sister Christina, who was twenty-six and still unmarried. Indeed, it had seemed so unlikely that Charlotte would find an acceptable suitor that preparations had been made for her to be attached to a convent, if not to enter it in the formal sense. She later told Fanny Burney, her Assistant Keeper of the Robes, that her name had been enrolled and her cross and badge bestowed upon her when the proposal of marriage was made.

On 17 August the Princess left Mecklenburg-Strelitz with her brother, the reigning Duke, and many relatives and friends in a long cortège of coaches. They travelled for five days to the town of Stade on the lower reaches of the river Elbe, which was reached on Saturday, 22 August.

The Queen-to-be boarded the royal yacht, renamed *Royal Charlotte* and lavishly refurbished, on Monday, 24 August, and the fleet sailed. Almost at that moment, however, the wind changed, adding to the problems of what was already a difficult passage down the Elbe; then, as they approached the open sea, the wind shifted again, and Lord Anson put back into Cukshaven roads. Here they remained to ride out the gale – an unpleasant interlude for someone who had never before been to sea – until dawn on Friday 28th when, despite the strong winds which continued to blow, the convoy weighed and headed for England. It was to be a nightmare journey. Gales continued and thunder, lightning, rain and hail had to be contended with, until finally Lord Anson, finding himself off Harwich, put in there on the evening of 6 September.

This long and very rough crossing must have been trying to a degree for all, but especially for the seventeen-year-old Princess, with the ordeal ahead of marriage to a King she had never seen. It is recorded, however, that Charlotte was not sick, and made great sport of the Earl who was. It is said that she played hymns and 'God Save the King' on the harpsicord – which must have been a not inconsiderable feat in a North Sea gale!

The party's arrival brought to an end a period of anxiety and speculation in the capital. Many people, impatient no doubt to see their future Queen, had been expecting her for days or weeks. 'As to our future Queen', Lord Hardwicke wrote to his son on 22 August, 'they are in daily expectation of her. She was to embark at Stade yesterday. Her future progress will depend on the wind, which, as it is in London, is at present contrary.'

Contrary it undoubtedly was, and as time passed rumour piled on rumour. There was a report that the ships had been sighted off the coast of Sussex on Saturday, 5 September, but if the yacht had been seen out at sea, or if she were on land, any certain information was lacking.

Charlotte's arrival at the wrong place took everyone by surprise. The King had earlier given Lord Anson detailed instructions, 'a full sheet – all writ with his own hand'. The Duke of Devonshire, as Lord Chamberlain, was to go as far as Gravesend, and was to kiss the Princess's hand when he first saw her. The Lord Chamberlain apart, however, no one but the King himself was to kiss her hand until she was Queen. George intended to meet his bride at Greenwich, but to go there only with his usual attendants, and without any extraordinary parade.

But the King's instructions, even though 'writ with his own hand', were unavailing in the face of such violent North Sea storms. Hasty rearrangements were necessary, so not until the afternoon of 7 September did Charlotte disembark. She was then driven to Colchester where, no doubt to her surprise, she was presented with a box of candied eryngo root, for which the town was famous, and regaled with an account of the events of historic interest in Colchester's past. Not the least of these was that the town had stood for Queen Mary and Popery against Lady Jane Grey and Protestantism, an event scarcely likely to commend Colchester to a future Queen, whose purpose was to make secure the Protestant succession! Charlotte might, moreover, have taken exception to the indelicacy of the gift had she known that eryngo – the candied root of the sea holly (*Eryngium Maritinum*) was used as an aphrodisiac!

Eventually, about quarter past seven, 'twixt the gloaming and the murk', she arrived at the house of Lord Abercorn at Whitham, where she was to spend the night. There was to be no immediate relaxation, however. Dr Doran describes how she was made to dine in public, sitting at table with all the doors and windows open, so that all comers might watch her at dinner.

The last stage of Charlotte's journey began early in the morning of 8 September. At Romford the royal party changed carriages to those which had been sent from St James's, and after a short rest they set off again for London.

One wonders what her thoughts must have been as she approached the capital, by what can hardly have been its most picturesque route. According to Dr Doran,

> She entered the capital by the suburb of Mile End which for dirt and misery can hardly be equalled by anything at Strelitz. Having passed through Whitechapel, which must have given her no very high idea of the civilization of the British people, she passed on westward, and proceeding by the longest route, continued along Oxford Street to Hyde Park, and finally reached the garden gate of St James's at 3 in the afternoon.

The Duchess of Devonshire, who had ridden out beyond Islington to see the arrival, reported that 'the Princess was (as was very natural) a good deal agitated when she came into the parks and was almost ready to faint'. Dr Doran suggests that she had shown astonishing spirit on the long journey from Mecklenburg-Strelitz, and only when she came in sight of the Palace did her courage seem to fail her. And well it might. Not only was she about to see for the first time the man she was to marry – but the man she was to marry at nine o'clock that evening!

In the six hours that remained before the ceremony much was to be done. Rest and refreshment were the most important. In addition Charlotte had to be coached in the responses to the marriage service (since she spoke no English), and the wedding dress which had been made from measurements supplied by Mecklenburg-Strelitz, had to be altered. Horace Walpole's later account of the ceremony – exaggerated as always – suggests that these alterations cannot have been entirely successful. Writing to Sir Thomas Mann, he says, 'The Queen was in white and silver; an endless mantle of violet coloured velvet, lined with ermine and attempted to be fastened on her shoulder by a bunch of large pearls, dragged itself and almost the rest of her clothes half way down her waist.'

The ceremony that evening took place in the Chapel Royal, and was conducted by the Archbishop of Canterbury, Dr Secker. It was preceded by a procession accompanying the King and his bride, which took time to assemble and to reach the Chapel. Charlotte's train was borne by ten unmarried daughters of Dukes and Earls. So much time was taken up by these processions to and from the Chapel Royal, and by the service itself, that it was not until 11.00 p.m. that supper – which could hardly at that hour be called the wedding breakfast – was served. The meal finished at 2.00 a.m. because the Duke of Cumberland complained of feeling sleepy!

Then, or shortly afterwards, we may assume, the royal marriage was consummated. Charlotte had been travelling for five days by coach, fifteen days by sea and two more days by coach; she had been up since an early hour the previous morning, and had endured an emotional time meeting her future husband and his family, none of whom she had ever seen before. It can scarcely be regarded as an ideal beginning to married life, to find oneself in bed with a husband one has seen for the first time less than twelve hours earlier, with sexual intercourse firmly in his mind. Despite this inauspicious start, however, the King and Queen were to be the happiest of married couples for many years.

These were, of course, different times with different values, and Charlotte had not come to be happy but to bear an heir and ensure the royal succession. In this she was overwhelmingly successful.

Few Queens have so speedily and so successfully fulfilled their obligations to provide an heir to the throne. The wedding had been on 8 September and the consummation, it is presumed, in the early hours of the 9th. It is recorded by her obstetrician, Dr William Hunter, that the date of Queen Charlotte's last menstrual period was 26 October, from which it was calculated that the expected date of her confinement would be 3 August 1762. She had lost no time in becoming pregnant.

The medical and nursing attendants on Queen Charlotte, during her first pregnancy and labour, were the Royal Surgeon, Mr Caesar Hawkins, the royal accoucheur or man-midwife, Dr William Hunter, and the royal midwife, Mrs Draper. Mr Caesar Hawkins was on the staff of St George's Hospital, London, and was reputedly extremely skilful at blood-letting, at which procedure alone he was said to make £1,000 a year – a considerable sum in 1762. Dr William Hunter was a most distinguished man, a Scot born in Lanarkshire who had received his medical training in Glasgow before seeking his fortune in London: he achieved undying fame with his book on the *Anatomy of the Human Gravid Uterus*. But it was Mrs Draper, the midwife, herself a grandmother, who was to play the most important part in the proceedings.

Hunter has left a detailed diary of the events of Queen Charlotte's first three confinements. He saw her first on 3 May 1762, when the Queen was about thirty-one weeks pregnant. He was informed by Mr Hawkins that prior to that time she 'had had very good health and had been very regular in menses. At eighteen weeks of the pregnancy she was taken ill at Chappell with giddiness, palpitations, difficulty in breathing and with a pain round the hypochondria [below the ribs]; for which he [Mr Hawkins] bled her six ounces [in characteristic fashion] and upon keeping quiet, all symptoms went off.'

From time to time during her pregnancy the Queen suffered a troublesome cough. On 3 May Hunter records, 'At different times she had a cough, but without any pain and without any considerable heat. This cough was enough to shake her body disagreeably, and as she had been giddy the day before and had bled from the nose, we thought it safest to take away five ounces of blood.'

Hunter complied with Hawkins's suggestion on that occasion, perhaps diplomatically, since this was the first time that he had been consulted; but later, with considerable wisdom, he advised against bleeding which was not undertaken again. Hunter wrote to Hawkins in the following terms;

I am clear in my opinion that it is judicious practice to take away some blood in the last month of pregnancy, when the patient is heated or has symptoms of fullness – that, as labour is not a disease, it does not require that the constitution should be reduced by way of preparation, and therefore when the patient is cool and has no marks of having too much blood, the taking it away cannot do good and may do harm.

The Queen clearly remained well for most of her pregnancy and 'took air every evening'. No further record appears in Hunter's diary until 12 August when labour began.

Charlotte's pains came on very early in the morning, probably around 2.30 a.m. The King got up to inform the dry nurse, who awakened the Dowager Princess of Wales, the King's mother. She, satisfied that labour had begun, sent for Mr Hawkins and Dr Hunter. Hunter's arrival at St James's Palace, at 5.30 a.m., coincided with that of several officers of State, and it is of interest that as a man-midwife, whose involvement would be required only if some problem arose, he remained in the anteroom with Mr Hawkins.

Before long he was informed by the midwife of the state of play. 'A little after six Mrs Draper came to us and told us that all was in a very natural way, but that the appearances indicated that it would be slow.' Alas, how many midwives and obstetricians over the years have been wildly inaccurate in their efforts to forecast the probable length of labour. Hunter's next sentence in the diary is remarkably restrained in the circumstances: 'At half after seven, when I little expected it from what Mrs Draper had told us, the Prince was born.'

Charlotte had not only produced an heir after less than one year of marriage, but had produced a male heir – and in only five hours.

Her lying-in period is described by Hunter in the greatest detail, and it is plain that as a qualified physician he then came into his own. His attention to detail was considerable, and his supervision of Charlotte's puerperium excellent. His account of the first two days of the lying-in period will be given in full, since it gives an admirable insight into the practice of the time:

Soon after this [the birth of the Prince] we examined him all over, and found him perfect, with every mark of health, and of a large size. Then we examined the placenta which was sound and very compleat, and Mrs Draper told us that the Queen had had a very good time, and was very well.

A little after 9, when her Majesty was shifted, we saw what was taken from the bed, and found it just moderate or what is most common: then I saw the Queen (who had taken a little N. meg and Sugar after delivery) and found her without any complaint and with a good pulse. We ordered for Her Majesty:

R – Spt. Cit. Sol. Ɵi
   Pulv. Contr. C. Ɵiss
   Aq. Alex. Simp. ℥iss
  – N. M. ℨiss
   Syr. Croc. ℨss M ft Haustus

6ta quaque hora sum
and for the Prince
    R – Ol. Amygd. d. ʒii
      Syr. Ros. ʒvi
      Rhubarb gr. iii. M.
    Cap. Cochl parvum omni hora.

These are delightful examples of the types of prescription used by doctors many years ago. They are written in the Latin shorthand then employed and their translation is:

For the Queen: Spirits of Lemon 1 scruple
                Compounded powder of Contrayerva 1½ scruples
                Alexiterial Water 1½ fluid ounces
                Nutmeg 1½ fluid drams
                Syrup of Saffron ½ fluid dram
                Mix to make draught
                to be taken every six hours

The spirits of lemon were regarded as excellent for nausea since they were believed to harden the fibres of the stomach. The compounded powder was made from the root of the exotic species Dorstenia, a native of tropical America and it was used for skin disorders since it was thought to improve discharge through cutaneous pores. Alexiterial water was made by the addition of spearmint leaves, angelica leaves and sea wormwood tops to water; it was sometimes used as a vehicle for alexipharmic medicines (antidotes to poisons). Nutmeg had astringent qualities which led to its use for diarrhoea and dysentery. Syrup of saffron was believed to cleanse the womb and promote menstrual discharges.

For the Prince: Sweet Almonds oil, 2 drams
                Syrup of Damask Roses, 6 drams
                Rhubarb, 3 grains
                A. Small spoonful every hour

Sweet almonds were believed to relieve colic in children; many nurses gave a little as soon as the child was born. The damask rose syrup was a mild purgative as was the rhubarb.

Hunter's account continues:

At 12 o'clock we saw the Q. again and found her perfectly well, and her pulse more quiet than when we left her in the morning. She had taken some broth and one draught, and had had a refreshing sleep. She desired to live some days upon broth, caudle and tea, rather than to eat chicken.

The Prince had taken the 2nd large Tea Spoonful of the purging mixture, was quiet and looked extremely well.

At 6 in the evening the Q. had slept an hour and was remarkably well. She had eaten with appetite – had made water plentifully and with ease – the cloths were of a full colour and in plenty. She now took her 2nd Haustus and was ordered a Spoonful of Wine in each half pint of caudle.

At this time the Prince had his first stool and made water but had not sucked.

At 10 at night we were informed that the Q. was well, and therefore did not go in. We gave orders that, if any considerable rigor should come on within 36 hours from delivery, to give immediately a small glass of Brandy and to send for me.

The Prince was quite well, had had another stool, and had sucked several times.

Friday, 13 August 1762. At ½ after 10 we visited the Prince. He looked well, had sucked and slept comfortably through the night, and had 3 or 4 stools. Order: to let the Beast (sic) be his principal support, but to feed him twice a day, as had been the custom in the Princess of Wales' family. The Princess desired a little milk to be put into the Pap.

The Queen had rested well, particularly had one continued sleep from midnight to four o'clock; her pulse remarkably quick, yet not slow. She was cheerful and said she had no complaint; cleansed well and still of a deep or full colour, and made water easily; had not desire to eat chicken: thought the draught made her thirsty, therefore I wrote thus:

R – Spt. Cit. Sol. ℈i.
Pulv. Contr. Co. ℈ss.
Aq. Ros. ℥iss.
– N. M. ℨi.
Syr. Ros. ℨss.
ft haust 6to quaque h. Sum.

Her Majesty asked if she might see the Prince. We allowed it with proper caution and gave Direction to Mrs Scott.

At 7 in the evening. The Prince perfectly well.

The Q. had taken plenty of Berry or caudle (which she liked better than broth), and bread and Butter with Tea, had slept $\frac{1}{2}$ hour twice – was in cheerful spirits and fine perspiration. The clothes still of deep colour, order to continue.'

The prescriptions he wrote were harmless – but probably valueless too.

As the lying-in continued Charlotte made excellent progress and continued to gain strength. Hunter was curiously insistent that she take chicken, which however, on Friday, 13 August she 'had no desire to eat', on Sunday 15th 'she did not choose to eat' and on Wednesday 18th 'she could not eat'. But Hunter persisted. On Friday 20 August at 12 noon he recorded 'was to eat chicken' and at 8.00 p.m. 'the Queen ate with appetite almost a whole chicken and was up three hours.'

And so the uncomplicated course of her lying-in period continued. She got up for the first time on the sixth day, and spent a little more time out of bed each day thereafter. The Prince too gave little cause for concern until Sunday, 22 August, when he 'had a kind of fainting fit on the Queen's bed, occasioned we supposed by having been laid with his head low just after suckling. He took a little Peppermint water, and was instantly well again.' Later he had a rash which was considered 'a symptom of teeth, and hardly did anything. He was quite well.' Her Majesty did not feed her son, etiquette not permitting royal mothers to do so. The wet nurse was Mrs Margaret Scott, who had just been delivered of her twelfth child, appropriately name Charlotte.

There was of course great excitement in the capital. It was customary for the heir to be presented to the ladies of the nobility and gentry from Britain and of nearby countries. Receptions were held daily, and the crowds of women, anxious to get a glimpse of the royal child, were admitted to the room in groups of about forty at a time. Dr Hunter recorded that 'near the cradle sat Mrs Nurse, a small velvet cushion on her knee, for the Prince to rest upon when out of the cradle. The part of the apartment where she was, latticed off in the chinese manner, to prevent curious persons from approaching too close. So he came to no harm.'

It was the custom to serve cake and caudle (a warm concoction of wine and eggs, said to be very nourishing to children and invalids) to all who attended, and when the ladies came in such numbers a great deal was consumed. Five hundred pounds of cake were eaten and eight gallons of caudle drunk each day. The daily cost of the cake was computed to be £40 whilst the cost of the wine was in Hunter's words 'more than could readily be counted'.

The Queen's confinement set the pattern for the whole of her astonishing obstetric achievement. She took pregnancy and delivery in her stride, and let it influence her everyday life to only a minor extent. Her second pregnancy followed so closely after the first that in Hunter's words 'the reckoning was nearly the same as of the first child'; and her Majesty remained so well that 'there was no occasion for my being consulted'. Charlotte decided to have her baby in her own home – Buckingham House – where all her remaining children were to be born, because of its better ventilation. The previous August confinement had clearly proved more taxing in this regard than Hunter had realized. It was fortunate that she made the change, since the month of August 1763 was remarkably hot, and her apartments at St James's might have become insufferable.

So rapidly was her second child born that Hunter did not arrive until some time after the delivery. He was sent for at 11.00 a.m. on 16 August, and on arrival was told, first by Mr Hawkins and then by the King, that 'the Queen had complained lightly for about two hours and was delivered with three pains of a fine boy, so that there was no time to call the proper people together'.

Dr Hunter was not unnaturally somewhat put out. 'Then accompanied by Mr Hawkins', the royal accoucheur wrote,

I saw Mrs Draper who told us that she was called from St James's, where she had been in waiting for some days, at 9 o'clock in the morning – that she, upon her arrival, found the waters broken, and that the Queen was wet even to her stockings; upon which she immediately got the bed properly made and put her Majesty into it – that the pains continued so trifling that she did not imagine the Queen was near delivery, till three strong pains came suddenly and close together and finished it. This she *said*.

Again his account of the puerperium – somewhat shorter this time – shows the same care and attention for detail as the first. The Queen was troubled by nothing beyond the heat. 'August 19th. She had been almost melted by the heat of the night, which indeed had been excessive. We ordered the door of an adjacent room to stand open, and a window in that room to be put up, and to take no draughts as she perspired so profusely.' However that evening again she 'complained of being melted with the heat of the weather. There had been much lightning all day, with a storm of Wind, Rain and Thunder'; and by a fitting juxtaposition of sentences Hunter continued, 'As she had had no passage a spoonful of rhubarb water and a little Peppermint was prescribed.'

The diary then records a miscarriage at Richmond after the birth of the second son, 'of which I only received accounts from Mr Hawkins'.

9 August the following year, 1765, however, brought a third son for Charlotte, but no better fortune for Dr Hunter. 'I was called at 4 o'clock in the morning, and was told that her Majesty had dined at Richmond the day before, and came home at 9 o'clock, and felt as if tired, and went to bed rather uneasy; and at 1 o'clock found that it would be her labour. It had advanced in the most kindly way, and she was delivered between two and three in the morning.' The confinement and lying-in period which followed were almost a repetition of the second, even to the Queen's complaining of the heat, so that doors and windows were again left open. Dr Hunter's account is even more brief, and on its conclusion we have no further written word from him of the details of subsequent pregnancies. This is surprising, since the Queen's third confinement was to be Mrs Draper's swansong, and the royal midwife is not heard of again.

Dr Hunter, on the other hand, was to come into his own, and was to play an increasingly large part in Charlotte's remaining confinements. Mrs Johnson took Mrs Draper's place as midwife, but she was much more under Dr Hunter's control. Lady Mary Coke, in her enchanting diary, records of the Queen's fourth child in 1766, 'Mrs Chetwynd told me the Queen was to be brought to bed by Dr Hunter, instead of the old woman, but that it was kept as great a secret as if the fate of the country depended on the change.'* This time a daughter, Charlotte Augusta Matilda; the Princess Royal,

---

* This is a prophetic remark, when one considers that little more than fifty years later, when the Princess Charlotte and her son died during childbirth, the fate of the country may indeed have depended upon the change.

was born on 29 September – 'the Michaelmas Goose' in Charlotte's own words.

1767 brought a winter confinement for the first time; a fourth boy, Edward, later Duke of Kent, was born on 2 November and was, so Lady Effingham told Lady Mary Coke, the largest child the Queen had ever had. During the next pregnancy, which followed almost immediately afterwards, we find Charlotte appearing at a birthday ball when she was thirty-three weeks pregnant, and dancing four times with the King of Denmark.

Her exertions were without ill effect, however, for a year and six days after the birth of Edward, on 8 November 1768, came the second daughter, Augusta. Her birth led to Dr Hunter offending the King, however unwittingly. Hunter, fearing that the birth of another son might disappoint the King, said to him, 'I think Sir whoever sees those lovely Princes above stairs must be glad to have another.' 'Dr Hunter', exclaimed George, 'I did not think I could have been angry with you, but I am; and I say whoever sees that lovely girl, Princess Royal, above stairs, must wish to have a fellow for her', and he stamped off to the Queen's bedside and narrated the whole episode to her. Augusta, their second daughter, was born in one and a quarter hours.

The year 1769 was the first year since her marriage that the Queen did not have a child or a miscarriage. But her respite was brief. Elizabeth was born in 1770, Ernest Augustus in 1771, Augustus Frederick in 1773, Adolphus Frederick in 1774, Mary 1776, Sophia 1777, Octavius 1780, Alfred 1778 and Amelia 1783.

There were few incidents of note. With Ernest Augustus, the eighth child, we find the Queen at a tiring drawing-room in the morning, attending the King's birthday ball at night and being delivered at 4.45 a.m. the following morning. So quick was her eleventh confinement that, in her own words, 'I was taken ill and delivered within fifteen minutes'. Almost the only evidence of abnormality was a period of depression after the birth of Augustus, later Duke of Sussex, although this seemed to stem from her concern about family problems rather than from a puerperal depression.

Child-bearing finally came to an end in 1783 when Charlotte was thirty-nine years old. Amelia was born that year on 7 August, and for the first time for eighteen years Dr Hunter was not with her, although Mrs Johnson had lasted the course. Hunter had died on 30 March, during the fourth month of her pregnancy, and his place as royal accoucheur was taken by Dr James Ford, a consulting man-midwife to the Westminster General Infirmary. It was not a happy end to childbearing. The King and Queen had been deeply affected by the deaths of their two younger sons. Alfred had died at the age of two the previous year, and the three-year-old Octavius in May of 1783 – sad events from which the King never fully recovered. We do not know the nature of their diseases. Alfred, the first to die, had never been a strong child and had suffered a long final illness throughout 1782 until his death on 20 August, but Octavius, de-scribed by Charlotte's biographer, Olwen Hedley, as 'a strong and beautiful child, the pet of all and the King's pride', was over-whelmed by an acute illness and, in Queen Charlotte's words, 'in less than eight and forty hours was my Son, Octavius, in perfect Health, Sick and struck with Death immediately.' Miss Hedley makes the sad comment on the infant mortality of the time that, by losing a child, Charlotte had at last become 'a proper mother'.

Amelia's birth brought the total of Charlotte's children to fifteen, born over a period of twenty-one years. By any standards this is a truly remarkable achievement. In British history there is none to match it. Edward III and his wife Philippa had twelve children, seven sons and five daughters, of whom three died in infancy or childhood; Queen Victoria and the Prince Consort Albert had nine, and Frederick Prince of Wales and Augusta also had nine; George II and Caroline had eight, one of whom was stillborn. In Europe there were some distinguished performances which match that of George III and Charlotte, but do not surpass it. The Empress Maria Theresa bore sixteen children, but eight of these died before the age of sixteen years; her son, whilst Duke of Tuscany, also fathered sixteen children, but all were born before he reigned as Emperor of Austria.

Within Charlotte's own family there was tremendous fertility. She was the eighth of ten children, six of whom survived infancy. Her grandfather had three wives, the first bearing six children, the second none and the third one – Charlotte's father. But pride of place in the Duchy goes to Charlotte's great-grandfather, who had two wives and nineteen children, the first wife bearing eight and the second eleven. It is perhaps not so surprising that her own obstetrical career was of Olympian standards.

The survival into adult life of thirteen out of Queen Charlotte's fifteen children is not only remarkable, in an age when many died in infancy, but even more surprising in that all were fed by wet nurses. The members of the aristocracy had employed wet nurses since ancient times and sometimes 'the wet nurses held an important position in the household and exerted much influence; Mrs Pack who, it will be recalled, successfully fed Queen Anne's son, the Duke of Gloucester, was precisely in such a privileged position, despite her uncouth nature.

But the use of a wet nurse was not without its risks. The widespread farming-out of newborn babies to wet nurses, many of whom either neglected their duties or employed a woeful lack of hygiene, resulted in infants wasting away or dying of infection. The practice of giving the child animal milk or pap (a kind of gruel made by soaking meal or bread in water) or panada (cereal cooked in broth) was even worse and resulted in an appalling mortality from infection. Dr Wickes, in an entertaining account of the history of infant feeding, quotes several eighteenth-century authors loud in their condemnation of these practices. Pap, which as we have seen was added to the feeds given to the Prince of Wales at the request of the Dowager Princess of Wales, was described as 'the most dangerous of all foods'. If, as one author described, large amounts were often given to the infant after having been previously chewed by the wet nurse, who then put the child to the breast 'to better dilute the pap', this is not surprising!

It was during the latter part of the eighteenth century that the employment of wet nurses was at its height and Queen Charlotte was no exception to the customary practice. To feed your own child was not only unfashionable, but was believed to ruin one's health, to say nothing of one's figure, and of course it seriously interfered with the social round. But a number of impassioned appeals were made in an attempt to persuade the aristocracy of the errors of their ways.

The Dowager Countess of Lincoln, who had fed none of her eighteen children and had had the misfortune to see only one, the fourth Earl of Lincoln, reach adult life, was so put to shame by his wife

who breast-fed and reared their first child successfully, that she
wrote a book devoted to *The Duties of Nursing Due by Mothers
to Their Own Children*. One of Queen Charlotte's most syco-
phantic biographers, W. M. Craig, waxed eloquent in his plea for
more mothers to feed their own children:

> I must be allowed to take this opportunity of addressing my fair and
> amiable Countrywoman of the sacred obligation they are under to sustain
> and strengthen the children they bring into the world with the all suf-
> ficient nutriment of their own bosoms. Sometimes it is true this may not
> be practicable; constitutional or other impediments may tend to make
> it so; but where there is not such impediment, the responsibility of
> neglect becomes most serious and weighty. Is there anyone so devoted
> to the vain and fleeting pleasures of dissipation as to neglect the gratifying
> duty of paying back to society, in the only way that it allowed her, the
> tender cares she received from her affectionate mother? Is there anyone
> so enchanted by the public admiration of her beauty as to prefer it to
> the thankful smiles of a lovely infant that clings close to her breast? I
> am persuaded there are but very few such in this land of domestic virtues.

But the Queen, Craig was careful to point out, was an unwilling
victim of this practice for

> She had all the lively and fond affections of a young and amiable Mother;
> and regretted most deeply the customs, the duties, of royalty which pre-
> vented her supplying to her infant the nutriment to which it had a claim
> by birthright and for which she was amply qualified. To perform this
> important duty by proxy had long been a prevalent custom on the Conti-
> nent; but Her Majesty . . . had caught the tenderness of maternal feeling
> on her landing in this Country; and it burst forth as soon as an object
> calculated to excite it was put into her arms. She grieved that she could
> not be to her son all that a mother should be; but she submitted and
> endeavoured to make amends by a most scrupulous attention to other
> points in watching over the young prince.

Whether Craig was anywhere near the truth in his assertion that
Queen Charlotte, against her own inclinations, was obliged to
employ a wet nurse we do not know, but most of the fashionable
ladies of the seventeenth and eighteenth century were hard to convince of the importance of breast-feeding. The royal family, in fact,
adhered to the practice of using wet nurses until the latter part of
the nineteenth century. The choosing of a good wet nurse therefore

became a very important matter upon which it is presumed Queen Charlotte eventually became an expert.

From the earliest times there was no lack of advice about the qualities the wet nurse and her milk should possess. Wickes refers to the advice of Paulus Aegineta in the seventh century AD that a wet nurse should be between twenty-five and thirty-five years of age, with well-developed breasts and chest, and be recently delivered of a male child. She must avoid salty and spicy foods, venery and debauchery and should take regular exercise, especially using the shoulders and arms as in grinding or working a loom. Ancient Brahmin medicine of the second century BC advised against using a wet nurse who was feverish, dyspeptic, hungry or pregnant. Jacques Guillemeau, a late sixteenth-century French obstetrician, writing in his book *Nursing of Children*, recommended a paragon who should be 'of healthy lineage, good behaviour, sober, even-tempered, happy, chaste, wise, discreet, careful, observant, understanding, conscientious and always willing to give the breast'. Mauriceau, the famous French obstetrician of the eighteenth century, advised against the use of red heads since their milk had a 'sour stinking and bad scent'.

Examination of the milk itself was most important. Good milk was sweet, odourless and white; red milk was not well concocted; blue milk meant melancholy, yellow milk choler, watery milk was sure to be followed by undernourishment and thick milk by indigestion, curdling, obstruction and stones. To ensure that the milk was in every way satisfactory, its appearance must be noted and the 'Nail Test' applied.

The Nail Test appears to have been used almost unchanged for more than a thousand years. A drop of milk was put upon the finger or thumb nail and the nail rocked from side to side, then turned into a vertical position to allow the milk to run downwards. The milk was too thin if it flowed freely over the nail with ordinary movement and too thick if it 'hange faste upon your naile when ye turne it downeward'. Milk which lay between these two extremes was good.

An entertaining poem originally written in Latin in the sixteenth century by S. de Saint-Marthe and subsequently translated into English by H. W. Tytler at the end of the eighteenth century is quoted by Wickes. In it all the virtues of a satisfactory wet nurse and her milk are enumerated.

> Chuse one of middle age, nor old nor young,
> Nor plump nor slim her make, but firm and strong,
> Upon her cheek, let health refulgent glow
> In vivid colours, that good-humour shew;
> Long be her arms, and broad her ample chest;
> Her neck be finely turn'd, and full her breast:
> Let the twin hills be white as mountain snow;
> Their swelling veins with circling juices flow;
> Each in a well projected nipple end,
> And milk, in copious streams, from these descend;
> This the delighted babe will instant chuse,
> And he best knows what quantity to use.
> Remember too, the whitest milk you meet,
> Of grateful flavour, pleasing taste, and sweet,
> Is always best: and if it strongly scent
> The air, some latent ill the vessels vent.
> Avoid what, on your nail, too ropy proves,
> Adheres too fast, or thence too swiftly moves.

Nowhere was the wet nurse more in demand with the aristocracy than in France, where the trade was so highly organized that in the early eighteenth century there were four employment agencies in Paris which kept lists of available wet nurses. Many abuses of the system led to a new law being passed which prevented a wet nurse taking another child until her own was more than nine months old; fees were fixed by law, the nurse had regular medical inspection and was obliged to keep her charges in a separate cradle to prevent overlaying. A striking exception to the employment of a wet nurse in France was the Queen, Blanche of Castile; when she found out that her son had been fed by another lady at court, she thrust her fingers into the back of his throat to make him vomit, so sure was she that the milk of another would be dangerous to him.

A French approach to infant feeding, which appears to us now to have been bizarre in the extreme, was the direct suckling of the infant by asses. Infants were put to the teats of asses at *L'Hôpital des Enfants Assistés* in Paris, a practice which continued into the last century.

In the choice of the wet nurse to Queen Charlotte it seems likely that Augusta, the Dowager Princess of Wales, was involved, just as we will see in the next chapter Queen Charlotte herself would be involved in choosing one for her daughter-in-law, Caroline of Brunswick. Precisely what criteria were used in the selection we do not know for certain, but if we are to judge by Charlotte's first wet nurse, Mrs Margaret Scott, fecundity and lineage were regarded as important.

Margaret Scott was the wife of Edward Scott of Scott's Hall, Kent, a descendant of the Buccleuch family, and she had not long before been delivered of her twelfth child. Olwen Hedley recorded that Mrs Scott's friends took a delight in forecasting that her position in the royal household would prove as nourishing to her own family as her milk would for the Prince. This for a time it did; Mrs Scott remained in a position of some influence for a year or so after the Prince was weaned, though she was always more favoured by the King than the Queen who was not sorry to see her go. Mrs Scott, proud of her ancestry, adopted a superior manner in all nursery disputes, which may well have influenced Queen Charlotte against choosing subsequent wet nurses who were quite so aristocratically connected. Respectable ecclesiastical ladies gained favour. The wet nurse for her son, the Duke of York, was Mrs Griffiths, wife of the Reverend Mr Griffiths of Chiswick, and Edward Duke of Kent was fed by Mrs Anne Percy, wife of Dr Thomas Percy who was later to be Dean of Carlisle and Bishop of Dromore.

It is sad to record, however, that George and Charlotte had far less pleasure from their large family than they might have hoped. While the children were small all went well, but as they grew up relationships became more strained, and the boys, in particular, wounded their parents by their behaviour; 'the damndest mill stone ever hung around the neck of any government' was how the Princes were described by the Duke of Wellington. The Prince of Wales in particular hurt his parents by his extravagant behaviour, his profligacy, and also by his extraordinary marriage.

6

Caroline, Princess of Wales

The disastrous marriage between George, Prince of Wales, and Caroline of Brunswick in 1795 had but one redeeming feature – the birth of Princess Charlotte. When we consider the couple's hatred of each other and the brief duration of their conjugal life together, it is remarkable that she was born at all.

For years the Prince of Wales had been accumulating debts and by 1794 they had reached £500,000 – a staggering sum in the the eighteenth century. He was quite unable to pay them but one course seemed open to him – to agree to marry and produce an heir to the throne, in which case Parliament would grant the sum required to rescue him from his creditors.

The Prince, however, had no wish to marry. Indeed he was in no position to do so for, without the consent or knowledge of either his father or Parliament almost ten years earlier he had married his mistress, Maria Fitzherbert, a woman some years older than himself who was not merely a commoner but a Roman Catholic. Their wedding had taken place at dusk on 15 December 1785 and the ceremony had been performed by the Reverend John Burt, a young curate with pressing financial problems to which the sum of £500, promised for his services, provided a solution. Apart from the bride and groom, and the priest, the only others present were Henry Errington, Mrs Fitzherbert's uncle, and John Smythe, her brother. After the ceremony the Prince himself wrote a certificate of marriage, which he and his wife and the two witnesses signed before it was given to Maria for safe keeping.

Few beyond those present knew for certain that the wedding had taken place. Hibbert, the Prince's biographer, names only three – the Duke and Duchess of Cumberland and Sir James Harris, later Lord Malmesbury, who was the British minister at The Hague; Harris had been active in the negotiations with Parliament over the

Prince's debts and was to reappear in the preliminaries to the Prince's later marriage to Caroline. Others suspected that there had been a marriage but did not know for certain.

The Princes of the royal blood were forbidden to marry without the King's consent, and since 1701 anyone marrying a Catholic was debarred from the succession, as indeed they are still. Since the marriage therefore contravened two Acts of Parliament it remained a secret, and George and Maria lived in separate establishments. Over the next ten years their lives alternated between elation and despair, quarrels and reconciliations. But the debts continued to mount, until ultimately the Prince had no escape. In the summer of 1894 he visited the King, who was on holiday at Weymouth, to tell him that he had broken completely with Mrs Fitzherbert, and, disregarding his former marriage of which his father knew nothing, that it was his intention to choose a bride.

Caroline, Princess of Brunswick was an unlikely choice. It was almost as if the Prince, having no real wish to marry at all, had out of pique picked the most unsuitable candidate. Caroline was his first cousin, and George III did not approve of marriages where kinship was so close. Moreover, she was unattractive physically, being short, thickly set and awkward; her redeeming features were her eyes and hair, but they could do little to offset her general air of gracelessness. Her behaviour was coarse and, although she was often friendly and gay, her conversation was usually inappropriate, if not tasteless. Worst of all, she was slovenly in her dress, even dirty! Lord Malmesbury, who was entrusted with the difficult task of conducting negotiations, and coaching Caroline how she should behave when she arrived at the Court in England, was obliged to urge her to wash more often; through the intermediary of one of her ladies-in-waiting he also suggested more frequent changes of underclothes! To complete this unattractive picture there were rumours of a love affair with a commoner to which Caroline was liable to make indiscreet references and it was said that she had difficulty in controlling herself whenever there was a man around. Queen Charlotte had been told that Caroline 'was not to be allowed to go from one room to another without her Governess and that when she dances, this lady is obliged to follow her for the whole of the dance to prevent her from making an exhibition of herself by indecent conversations with

men'. A less appealing bride for George, the first gentleman of
Europe, it is hard to imagine.

Caroline's first meeting with the Prince was chilly in the extreme.
She attempted to kneel to him, as Lord Malmesbury had taught
her, but the Prince stopped her doing so, raised her upright and
embraced her. This physical contact proved too much for him.
Retiring immediately to the far corner of the room, where the odour
of his bride-to-be could not permeate, he said to Malmesbury,
'Harris I am not well. Pray get me a glass of brandy.' Lord Malmesbury, feeling this inappropriate, suggested the Prince should have
water instead. George swore in reply, and intimated that he was
going straight to the Queen, and left the room, He had spent only
a few minutes in the presence of his fiancée who was understandably
put out, declaring that he was not as handsome as his portraits and
far fatter. That evening, at dinner with the royal family, Caroline
was at her worst, talking incessantly and making snide remarks
about the Prince and one of his mistresses, Lady Jersey, who was
present.

It was an appalling prelude to a life together. By this time the
Prince had realized, only too well, the awful error he had made in
his selection of a wife who was totally abhorrent to him. He was
fastidious and elegant, a man of delicate taste and supreme artistic
refinement, even if he had other less favourable characteristics. She
was coarse and vulgar. Caroline's reaction to the Prince, although
unfavourable, was not extreme, and with her insensitive nature and
natural affability on her side a tolerable relationship might have been
possible. George's dislike for her, however, was instantaneous and
the prospect of marriage and its consummation with such a creature
barely supportable.

During the marriage service, in the Chapel Royal of St James's
Palace on 8 April 1795, the bride was cheerful, the groom silent
and morose. He was more than a little drunk on arrival and seemed
stunned by the proceedings. At one point he unaccountably stood
up during a prayer; after a pause the King spoke to him quietly
and he knelt down again. The Archbishop of Canterbury, plainly
uneasy, stopped and laid down his prayer book and looked hard
at the Prince and the King when he reached that part of the

ceremony when it became necessary to enquire if anyone knew of any impediment to lawful marriage.

At the drawing-room which followed Caroline continued to be gay and effusive. George at first recovered some of his composure but as the night approached his only solace was drink. So intoxicated was he by the time he entered the matrimonial chamber, that he collapsed dead drunk in front of the fire place, where the Princess sensibly left him until the following morning. Only then had he sufficient strength to get into bed beside her.

We do not of course know how long he and she lived together as man and wife, but is possible that they cohabited only on that single occasion, on the morning of 9 April. Their daughter Princess Charlotte was to be born on 7 January the following year and since she was not premature, the calculation of the likely date of conception leads us to early April.

There was nothing to suggest that there was ever a time, even during the early days of their marriage, which could be remotely described as happy, although Hibbert suggests that the first few months of marriage were 'not quite so unpleasant' as this disastrous beginning led people to expect, and as the biographers have suggested. But 'not quite so unpleasant' hardly suggests wedded bliss. It is scarcely to be imagined that the Prince would seek Caroline's favours more often than was absolutely necessary. There may well have been a few occasions when they had intercourse together during the early weeks, since the sooner Caroline became pregnant the sooner would end the need for any continuation of their physical relationship. It seems highly likely that she did not have a menstrual period after her marriage, so the duration of their conjugal life needed only to be brief.

In this graceless fashion was Princess Charlotte conceived. By the time she was born the relationship between her parents was one of open hostility. Mutual dislike had become hatred.

During Caroline's pregnancy the royal family tried hard to create the impression that all was well with the marriage. They made constant reference to her state of health, hoped that she was not becoming too fatigued, and they sent repeated good wishes. They remarked with pleasure that her character showed this feature or that, which they could approve, as if persuading themselves that, after all, she was perhaps not so bad as, inwardly, they feared. Nowhere in their correspondence, however, is there any expression of affection, only polite, carefully chosen phrases of conventional sentiment.

The first reference to her pregnancy is in a letter from the Prince of Wales to the Queen on 26 June. The Prince and Princess were at Brighton, with which 'she is extremely delighted'. She was, he said, 'in the best health and spirits possible, excepting at moments a little degree of sickness, which is necessarily attendant upon her situation'. The Queen replied courteously that she was 'extremely glad to hear that the sea air agrees so well with the Princess, and that she goes on so well in her present situation. I beg my compliments to her, and hope she will take all possible care of herself.' By this time Caroline would have been only some twelve weeks pregnant.

It seems possible that Caroline developed a particular liking for special food, as women not uncommonly do during pregnancy. There is an enchanting letter from Queen Charlotte to her son, dated 5 August, with the intriguing lines, 'I look upon your commission to send some pigs to the Princess sufficiently great as to write you a letter to announce their departure this morning *alive* directed to *Mrs Willis in town* who is to forward them immediately to Brighton. They are to be refreshed upon the road with milk so that they will be fit for killing immediately and I hope they will prove to the Princess's taste.' It may be that the Princess's request had not been merely for young pigs but for very special young pigs, since the Queen goes on, 'My little black lady would not vouchsafe to acoucher sooner than ten weeks to come and Sir George Howard has been so good as to give these up to me and are the same breed as mine.'

With George and Caroline in Brighton, it appears that the Queen assumed some responsibility for the selection, or at least approval, of those who were to attend Caroline in her labour and lying-in period. In the same letter of 5 August, she told her son that she hoped to see Dr Underwood the following Wednesday at Kew, and added, 'I have not yet heard of any recommendations for a nurse.'

Dr Michael Underwood was a surgeon who came to the practice

of midwifery at a comparatively late stage in his career. He was a student at St George's Hospital, where he studied under Mr Caesar Hawkins, the royal surgeon to King George III and Queen Charlotte. He was clearly a man of wide medical interests, publishing articles on ulcers of the legs and a book on diseases of children, which went to many editions. Not until he was forty-eight, however, was he admitted as a licenciate in midwifery of the College of Physicians, after which he practised almost entirely as an accoucheur. He was almost sixty at the time of his attendance on the Princess of Wales.

He was a busy man. Charlotte's next letter to her son on 16 August mentions that not until the day before had she been able to see him; the meeting 'was impossible to be done sooner as he had so much business all the other days'. She and the doctor had a long conversation, agreeing 'on almost every point relating to the qualities requisite for a good nurse'. No one had then applied for the post but the Queen and Dr Underwood had agreed on what they were looking for; he was to keep her informed, and she, in turn, would pass on everything to the Prince of Wales.

It is also evident from this same letter that Dr Underwood had not been a pupil of Mr Caesar Hawkins for nothing: 'He is of the oppinion', Queen Charlotte wrote (spelling not being her strongest point), 'that in case the Princess should feel too full that a bleeding would be beneficial to her.' And bled of course she was. The Prince's letter of 25 August, although relegating his wife to a postscript, reported, 'The Princess continues perfectly well and finds the advantage of having been blooded.'

Caroline's pregnancy continued its uncomplicated course. By November the couple were still in Brighton, but the Queen was writing to say that Dr Underwood urged them to return to London sooner than they intended. 'If any little uneasy feelings should alarm the Princess, at a place where she has not those about her who she wishes to employ, it might perhaps occasion a great deal of unnecessary fright.' Having expressed her own views for the first time, however, Queen Charlotte was very anxious to assure the Prince that, 'I do not mean to meddle' and that she was merely passing on the doctor's advice.

As a mother of immense experience herself, however, the Queen naturally paid a lot of attention to the domestic details of the confinement, such as the choice of a wet nurse and the kind of cradle. There were several contenders for the post of wet nurse. A Mrs Bower was under consideration, as well as a Mrs Smith. There was a chemist's wife, who came of very good parents, and was 'a very proper person for the honour she aspires to'. Mrs Smith, although personable, presented a problem, since her own confinement was not expected until the middle of December; 'Should it happen, as it frequently does', wrote Charlotte, 'that she should go beyond her time, about ten days or a fortnight, she may in all likelihood not be fit to come when she is wanted.' The Queen offered the very sensible advice that Mrs Smith should be engaged if she was delivered in time; if not, whichever of the others was the more suitable should be asked to keep herself in readiness. 'This is exactly what I did', she remarked, 'when the Duke of York was born.'

On the important matter of the cradle the Queen expressed the hope that Lord Cholmondeley, the Chamberlain to the Prince, had ordered it. 'Tell him', she added, 'I, as an experienced woman in such matters, say it should be without rockers to it.'

By early January the royal family were on tenterhooks. Princess Elizabeth was 'in expectation of good news' whenever the door opened, and kept rushing to the window when the bell rang, in the hope of being the first to bring the good news to her mother. She imagined her brother 'upon the high figits walking about the room pulling your fingers and very anxious'. Indeed, anxious he clearly was, since he reported a sleepless night not only on the night of his wife's labour, but on the one preceding it as well.

Caroline's labour began during the evening of 6 January, 1796. She was then at Carlton House, the Prince's residence in town, under the care of Dr Underwood.

The Archbishop of Canterbury, the Chancellor, the Lord President and the Duke of Gloucester attended as officers of State, and the Duke of Leeds, the Duke of Devonshire and Lord Thurlow at the special invitation of the Prince. The Prince of Wales was reported by the Duke of Leeds to have been much agitated all night waiting for news.

Eventually it came, the following morning when Caroline gave birth to a daughter at 'twenty minutes after nine', as recorded in Lord

Colchester's Diary. If we are to judge by the Prince's letter to his mother, the labour had not been easy. 'The Princess', George wrote to Queen Charlotte at 9.45 a.m., 'after a terrible hard labour for above 12 hours is this instant brought to bed of an *immense* girl.' Relieved though the Prince undoubtedly was that an heir had finally been born, he would have preferred a son, but accepted a daughter 'with all the affection possible'.

The news was carried instantly to Windsor by Lord Jersey, husband of the Prince's mistress and master of his horses. The King was out hunting, but on his return expressed himself delighted, and said that he 'always wished it should be of that sex', perhaps feeling that such enthusiasm would offset any disappointment his son might feel. In a note to the Prince the King, with more optimism than he or anyone else in the royal family can really have felt, wrote, 'You are both young and I trust will have many children.'

It was a vain hope, for the Prince and Princess never lived together again. Their relationship went from bad to worse, and later that year the Prince requested a formal separation which the King refused. Their antipathy was well known, however, and they lived apart, vilifying each other at every opportunity.

Three days after Princess Charlotte's birth the Prince of Wales made a will. In it he bequeathed everything to Maria Fitzherbert, 'who is my wife in the eyes of God and who is and ever will be such in mine'. 'To her who is called Princess of Wales', wrote the Prince, 'I leave one shilling.'

7

An Obstetric Tragedy:
The Death of Princess Charlotte

The enmity between the Prince and Princess of Wales was so bitter that it is scarcely surprising that their daughter, the Princess Charlotte, had an unhappy childhood. She was a bone of contention between her parents. The Prince strove to limit her contact with the Princess, for whom Charlotte had a considerable affection, despite her mother's outlandish behaviour. Although undeniably fond of his daughter he did not pay her much attention, and governesses and tutors shaped, or attempted to shape, her character.

Her most recent biographer, Thea Holme, describes Charlotte in early childhood as abounding in good health and brilliant high spirits. The King and Queen were very fond of her, the former especially being captivated whenever she visited them. She was often, apparently, the centre of attraction, dancing and singing 'God Save the King' and 'Hearts of Oak' to admiring drawing-rooms. As an older child she retained much of her early charm, with her bright blue eyes, blond curly hair and pale skin, although the latter was unfortunately badly pitted by smallpox. She was undoubtedly gay and affectionate, but, like her mother, self-willed and excitable as well, and subject to fits of temper.

To the public at large, though, she was a dream princess who personified youth, beauty and vivacity, and she quickly became the darling of the nation. The King could see no wrong in her, and wished her to spend more time in his company. He sought to keep her with him at Windsor all the time, to which her father, fearing that the Princess of Wales would thereby be able to exert too great an influence upon her, would not consent. Eventually agreement was reached that she would live at Windsor from June to January, and spend the rest of the year in London at Warwick House, close to the Prince's home, Carlton House. Her mother would be allowed to see her from time to time, but only as a visitor.

As Charlotte grew older her wilful nature asserted itself more and more. She objected to governesses who were appointed to look after her, and strove to persuade her father to give her an establishment of her own. This he refused to do until she was married.

In 1814, when she was eighteen years old, her possible marriage became an important matter for discussion. Charlotte was clearly attracted by men, and had earlier been censored by her father for a mild if unwise flirtation with a Lieutenant Charles Hesse. A marriage was duly arranged, therefore, and she became engaged to the Prince of Orange despite his unattractive appearance and personality.

It seems probable that the lure of having her own establishment was greater than that of the man who would go with it, and in fact Charlotte found that she disliked the Prince of Orange so much that she abruptly broke off her engagement. Her father was furious, and soundly berated her. The Princess's reply was forthright and typical. The moment he left Warwick House she left too, and drove in a hackney carriage to her mother's house in Connaught Square. Only the persuasion of her favourite uncle, the Duke of Sussex, succeeded in getting her back to her home, where for some time afterwards she was kept in strict seclusion.

The Regent, as her father now was, made repeated attempts to urge her to marry the Prince of Orange, but Charlotte was equally determined that she would not. Moreover Leopold, Prince of Saxe-Coburg, whom she had met briefly earlier in the year, had now taken her fancy. Towards the end of 1815 an approach was made formally from Saxe-Coburg to the Regent. Initially this met with little favour, but eventually, in the face of repeated refusals from his daughter to reconsider the Prince of Orange, the marriage to Leopold was arranged.

Charlotte and Leopold were married at Carlton House in the Crimson Room at 8.00 p.m. on 2 May 1816. Bride and groom were hailed by ecstatic crowds wherever they went, and national pride reached bursting point. The couple spent their honeymoon at Oatlands near Weybridge, home of the Duke and Duchess of York, who had moved out to allow them the seclusion they so much needed.

It seems probable that they were happy together, once they

learned to know each other better. For the next few months they moved into Camelford House in Oxford Street, whilst the necessary arrangements could be made for the purchase of their permanent home at Claremont near Esher.

During the summer Charlotte may have suffered a miscarriage although there is no certainty of this. Thomas Green, writing in 1818, recorded that she had been taken ill at the opera on 6 July, and was attended by Dr Baillie, who prescribed rest and quiet. 'At length', Green wrote, 'it was announced that Her Royal Highness's indisposition arose ... from her having then been in a state which gave hopes that she would in a few months have had the greatest happiness of giving birth to a royal heir.' Miss Cornelia Knight, who had relinquished her post as reader to Queen Charlotte for a place in the Princess's household, recorded in her diary for 12 July after visiting the Princess that 'not having been very well she is not going to the grand ball given by the Regent this evening'. Miss Knight saw Charlotte again on 25 July but was unable to do so during a later visit on 30 July, because 'Prince Leopold was suffering from a pain in his face'.

There is nothing in Miss Knight's account to suggest pregnancy therefore. Nevertheless Green reported that 'the hopes which the nation had ... were ... disappointed on the 30th of July when it became publicly known that Her Royal Highness had experienced a miscarriage'. Perhaps Green was quoting a newspaper report, which I have not been able to trace. It seems unlikely that he was quoting any official announcement concerning either the pregnancy or the miscarriage: it is a characteristic of his book that official announcements are reproduced in lengthy detail and since he included no such announcement concerning a pregnancy he was probably quoting unofficial – and perhaps unreliable – sources. The phrase 'it became publicly known' that the Princess had miscarried has a distinct element of rumour about it.

Leopold and Charlotte moved into Claremont in August and were delighted by its beauty, peace and seclusion. They were to enjoy it for only fifteen months.

Princess Charlotte did definitely become pregnant, towards the end of the month of January 1817. The precise date of the menstrual period which preceded the conception is not recorded, but several pieces of evidence suggest that it was between 9 and 12 January. The first of these is a letter written by the Princess to her obstetrician, Sir Richard Croft, dated 14 March, in which she says that 'the second period is now safely passed over a week'; if we assume 'over a week' to be eight days or more, the first missed period would have been 6 February and Charlotte's last menstrual period 9 January. The second piece of evidence is in the history of the Princess's labour, written in Croft's hand, in which it is stated that the labour began on 3 November, 'being 42 weeks and one day from her last recovery'; this suggests 'the last recovery' to have been 12 January. However, a corrected draft of the history of labour in an unknown hand states that 3 November was 'two weeks and two days past from Her Royal Highness's earliest reckoning', giving 11 January as the period date. Lastly, Croft, in a letter to his sister Elizabeth on 19 October, gave that date as 'the first day I could by reason expect HRH to be put to bed'. If we equate this with the expected date of confinement, we can calculate her last menstrual period as 12 January again. Clearly her labour began well after its expected date, but by how much we cannot say.

There were three doctors responsible for the Princess's care during pregnancy and labour – Matthew Baillie, Richard Croft and John Sims. Baillie and Croft had close links with each other, having married the twin daughters of Dr Thomas Denman, who had been the leading figure in British obstetrics at the end of the eighteenth and the beginning of the nineteenth centuries. Baillie was also the nephew of William Hunter, royal obstetrician to Queen Charlotte, and was therefore well connected in the highest medical circles. His initial career was in morbid anatomy, and his reputation principally rests upon his book on *The Morbid Anatomy of Some of the Most Important Parts of the Human Body* which he published in 1795. He had many interests in clinical medicine too, and his practice eventually became so large that he resigned his membership of the staff of St George's Hospital to attend to it. It was through Baillie that the famous gold-headed cane, the status emblem of the Royal College of Physicians, came into that College's possession, presented by Baillie's widow.

Sir Richard Croft, at the time of his appointment as accoucheur to Princess Charlotte, was also a figure of some importance in the obstetrical world. He was fifty-five years old, and carried on a large fashionable obstetric practice in London, which he had inherited from his father-in-law Thomas Denman. Nevertheless, Croft was probably not a man of stature and he may well have attained his position more through his association with Denman than through personal merit. It is certain that Denman's influence over Croft's approach to obstetrics was great, and may significantly have affected the fatal outcome of the Princess's labour, since, as we shall see, Croft adhered rigidly to what his father-in-law had been teaching for the previous twenty years. Sir Eardley Holland, one of the leading obstetricians of this century, whose brilliant analysis of Croft's papers did so much to clarify the events of Charlotte's labour, believed him to have been a diffident man lacking in self-confidence, and not the ideal person to deal resourcefully with any crisis.

Dr John Sims was Sir Eardley's 'mystery man of the confinement'. He is described as a botanist and physician, and it is clear that his interests and skills rested more with the former. *The Dictionary of National Biography* records his writings on such botanical subjects as 'the expansion of Mesembryanthemum under the influence of moisture' and 'a description of Amomum exscapum' but mentions none on medical nor obstetrical matters. We find him editing Curtis's *Botanical Magazine* for more than twenty-five years, and acting as co-editor of the *Annals of Botany*, and there is much other evidence of his interest in that subject. Yet there is nothing to suggest he was specially skilful in midwifery. He was, moreover, sixty-eight years old at the time of Princess Charlotte's labour.

One other doctor who was involved, though not professionally, was Christian Frederick Stockmar, Prince Leopold's personal physician. He had no practical obstetrical knowledge, having distinguished himself as a military surgeon during the Napoleonic Wars when he met the Prince. He declined to have any responsibility for the Princess's confinement, probably wisely in view of his inexperience; he believed, moreover, that if anything were to go wrong he, as a foreigner, would be blamed.

The doctors were supported by Mrs Griffiths, the midwife. Who the other nursing attendants were we do not know. Two ladies, a Mrs Jans and a Mrs Winchester, are named in letters from the Princess to Croft and were probably candidates for the post of wet nurse. We do not know if either was appointed, although the Princess wrote of liking Mrs Winchester's appearance, but of thinking Mrs Jans not very strong nor so advanced in pregnancy as she said she was.

The events of the Princess's pregnancy are known from nine letters which she wrote to Sir Richard Croft. The record is unhappily incomplete, since it is certain that there were several other letters which have been destroyed. We know too the advice on diet, exercise and general conduct given to Charlotte following a consultation between Croft and Baillie. These documents, reports concerning the labour and other later correspondence, have recently been published by Professor Franco Crainz, who has made a lifetime's study of the event. From Professor Crainz we learn that Charlotte was advised:

to rise at nine o'clock every morning;
to take breakfast before ten o'clock;
to eat a little cold meat or some fruit and bread about two o'clock
  for lunch;
to dine on food plainly cooked and easy to digest;
to have no more than two glasses of wine at and after dinner;
to take gentle exercise either on horseback or on foot every day
  that the weather was suitable;
to take a shower every second day, the water being tepid at first;
to have the loins sponged with cold water each day.

This is, in general, sound advice for a pregnant woman, although the diet is perhaps less sustaining than is desirable. Thea Holme says that the Princess had a hearty appetite, and if so the regime set out above may at times have left her hungry. The importance of maintaining a sufficient quantity of iron in the diet was not realized at that time, and no iron supplements in the form of medication were available. Iron is principally contained in meat and vegetables, and the diet advised was not rich in this respect. Moreover, if as seems likely, a degree of anaemia did arise, it would have been aggravated by bleeding.

We cannot be sure how often Charlotte was bled during her pregnancy, but we know it certainly happened once. Writing to Croft on 10 August she says, 'I am certainly much better for the bleeding.' It has been widely believed since that she was bled much more often, and this may indeed have been so. The newspapers of 22 October contained reference to the necessity at various times to extract blood, to relieve her headaches. It is alleged that the procedure was more than usually difficult since the veins of her arm were so deep, that those of the hand were used instead. Mr Neville, the surgeon and apothecary at Claremont, is credited by the Court newsman with having performed this bleeding several times with great relief to the Princess, although we have no reliable information about how often it was done. Bearing this in mind, in association with a more frugal diet than Charlotte was used to, it seems probable that the Princess became anaemic as pregnancy advanced. Nevertheless by the standards of that time this part of her management cannot be criticized.

Judging from those letters from Charlotte to Croft which have been preserved, her pregnancy was attended by the usual minor discomforts which, with one exception, did not give rise to concern. In her letter of 14 March, in which she recorded having missed her second period, she described other symptoms of early pregnancy as well – nausea and sickness, 'pain in my breasts' and a little pain passing urine. 'Faintness and sickness' was referred to in the letter of 9 July but its duration was brief and a 'pale yellow sort of discharge that comes on every now and then' is mentioned in a later letter. Though these were not matters of great moment they were correctly related by the patient to her doctor.

The symptom which was at least potentially serious is described in the Princess's letter which is undated but simply headed 'Friday, Claremont', and appears in the collected correspondence later than one dated 29 August. Here she reports 'a Show of *fresh blood* wh has this Mg occurred attended too With pain in My legs, back and lower Stomach'. The pain was sufficient to prompt Charlotte to take ten drops of laudanum that night and again the following morning. Not unnaturally she was anxious and rested on the sofa. There was 'as Yet no quantity of blood' and she had not put on 'Any additional clothing but it is quite *fresh* not like the former discharge at different times'.

Bleeding such as this is an alarming sign, especially later in pregnancy. It suggests the possibility that the placenta (afterbirth) may be lying below the baby's head (placenta praevia) or, regardless of position, may have partly separated from the wall of the uterus (placental abruption). The latter is usually accompanied by pain and the former is not, and Charlotte may have had a small abruption. From the continued normal growth of the child, and the absence of any placenta praevia when the Princess was examined by the vaginal route during labour, it seems certain that neither of these events actually occurred; the appearance of such a blood loss would now be taken quite seriously, and there would be doubt about the continued safety of the child.

As October wore on public interest became anxiety. Mrs Griffiths moved into Claremont on 1 October, and Sir Richard Croft went into residence there before the middle of the month, so that he had been waiting for almost three weeks before the labour began. Daily bulletins were issued from 21 October, but not until 4 November did the newspapers report that labour had begun the previous evening.

The principle events which occurred during the Princess Charlotte's labour are not now in doubt, since the discovery in the middle of this century at Fanhams Hall, Ware, Hertfordshire, where descendants of Sir Richard Croft were living, of a series of documents pertaining to the event. These were brilliantly analysed by Sir Eardley Holland in 1951, and the more important were published in full by Professor Franco Crainz a leading Rome gynaecologist in 1977. The doubts which remain concern the constructions which may be put on certain phrases used, or the nuances of one phrase later substituted for a somewhat different one in an earlier draft.

Labour began at 7 o'clock in the evening of Monday, 3 November when the waters broke. Pains followed, which were described by Croft as 'sharp, acute and distressing' and coming at intervals of about eight minutes but 'little advancing the labour'. He suspected that the uterus might be contracting spasmodically and not in the smooth, coordinated manner of normal labour. He made an examination per vaginam at 11.00 p.m. and found that the neck of the womb (the cervix) was open to about the size of a halfpenny. The complete opening or dilation of the cervix constitutes the first stage of labour. It is commonly somewhat slow at first, becoming quicker later in what is now called the active phase of labour. Before the child can be born this part of the uterus must be fully dilated, and when this is accomplished the distance from the thin portion of the cervix on one side to that on the other is some ten centimetres. A halfpenny in those days measured $2\frac{1}{2}$ centimetres across, so little had then been achieved.

About 3.00 a.m. Charlotte felt sick and vomited, and Croft, believing that this might expedite the course of labour, sent for the officers of State* and Dr Baillie, all of whom arrived between 5.30 and 8.00 a.m.

They were to have a long wait. The pains remained 'very insufficient' and an examination at 11.00 a.m. on Wednesday, 4 November showed that the cervix to be open only to the size of a half crown – $3\frac{1}{2}$ centimetres. Sir Richard must have been somewhat apprehensive and yet undecided, since he wrote a letter to Sims but held back sending it. By 6.00 p.m., however, there was more progress and on vaginal examination Croft could feel the cervix only in front and by 9.00 p.m. he could not feel it at all; the cervix was evidently now fully dilated and the first stage of labour was over. It had lasted twenty-six hours, not an inordinate length of time in those days, and not unusual as recently as fifteen years ago.

The second stage of labour begins at full dilation of the cervix and ends with the expulsion of the child. Surprisingly, at this point, just when things seemed to be going more smoothly, Sir Richard decided to send Sims the letter written ten hours previously. His reason was that 'it had occurred to me that the pains might never become sufficiently strong and powerful and that assistance might ultimately become necessary and I thought it improper to afford that assistance by the use of instrument without a consultation'. Dr Sims arrived at 1.00 a.m. – a late hour for an aged botanist. He did not consider it necessary to see Charlotte, and neither did Baillie, although Croft wished him to do so. Since he was not to see her, it was decided there was no purpose in telling her Sims had arrived, thus possibly alarming her.

* The officers of State present were: Charles Manners Sutton, the Archbishop of Canterbury; William Howley, Bishop of London; John Scott, first Baron Eldon, the Lord Chancellor; Nicholas Vansittart, Chancellor of the Exchequer; Henry, Third Earl Bathurst, Minister for War and Colonies and Henry Addington, First Viscount Sidmouth, Home Secretary.

Little is known about the next ten to twelve hours except that pains remained 'less considerable than they generally were at that ... stage of labour'. Croft insisted that 'labour continued progressive' but 'unusually slow'. At twelve noon on Wednesday, 5 November Charlotte began to pass dark green material through her vagina suggesting that the child might be dead; this material is meconium, which is contained in the fetal intestine, and although such a sign is not entirely reliable it usually denotes distress of the fetus, if not death. With our modern knowledge and sophisticated electronic fetal heart monitoring, the immediate reaction to such a discharge is to check the fetal heart sounds. But the fetal heart sounds had not been heard in 1817. They were only reported for the first time in 1818 by Dr Mayor of Geneva, and this method of assessing danger was not available to Charlotte's attendants. When the fetus is in distress its heart rate may become unusually quick, or slow, or irregular, and we now know that if this occurs there is a danger of fetal death.

By three to four o'clock in the afternoon the child's head was so low that it was pressing upon the perineum. At 9.00 p.m. a large male child was born dead and had evidently been dead for several hours; 'The naval string was very small and of a dark green or black colour', wrote Croft. Every known effort to animate it was nonetheless made; 'brandy was put into the child's mouth and its lungs were inflated before the navel string was cut and after everything possible was attempted from the aid of warm bath, inflation and rubbing with salt and mustard.'

The third stage of labour – the expulsion of the placenta – now began. Croft realized that the uterus was acting irregularly, and that 'the afterbirth or the greatest part of it was retained in its upper part'. Croft informed Sims of this about fifteen minutes after the birth whilst the latter was still employed trying to produce some sign of life from the infant. Then, or soon afterwards, Croft, Sims and Baillie all agreed that the placenta should be removed manually.

Sir Richard describes this in detail:

In passing my hand I met with some blood in the uterus but no difficulty, until I got to the contracted part (of the uterus) and, though it was contracted so as only to admit the points of three fingers and had a portion of placenta embraced by it, it readily gave way so as to allow my hand to pass with tolerable ease and I afterwards peeled off near two thirds of the adhering placenta with considerable facility.

When the afterbirth was separated the Princess complained of a sharp pain as the uterus contracted strongly.

Croft , in accordance with his practice, left the placenta lying in the vagina. The Princess found this painful and inconvenient and it was shortly removed. There had been some bleeding during the process of separation of the placenta from the uterine wall and there was more during its removal from the vagina. The amounts are variously described. Croft's original account says that the procedure was done 'before much blood appeared to be lost'. A corrected draft gives 'a very moderate discharge of fluid or coagulated blood'. Sir Richard's more detailed account of the manual removal speaks of 'a very little of fluid blood or coagulum'.

The Princess's pulse rate was less than a hundred at the conclusion of the third stage and she seemed as well as might be expected after her ordeal. 'Her Royal Highness continued as well as ladies usually are . . . talked cheerfully and took frequently of mild nourishment.' By a quarter to twelve, however, it was clear that she was less well. She complained of nausea and had singing noises in her head. Fifteen minutes later she was sick. More mild nourishment was given; 'frequently' was the word used in the original draft to describe how often this nourishment was administered, but later this word was deleted. Between 12.30 and 12.45 she manifested 'extreme restlessness and great difficulty of breathing'; to this phrase was added the words 'with spasmodic affection of the chest' in Sir Richard Croft's handwriting. Her pulse was rapid, feeble and irregular; she was given 'cordials, nourishment, anti-spasmodic and opiate medicines' at short intervals but to no avail. She died at 2.30 a.m.

This official account of the Princess's last few hours of life has been elaborated in other descriptions, but none adds anything of significance to the tale. She was dying and there was little that could then be done to prevent it. Stockmar, summoned by Baillie, found her 'in a state of great suffering ' and showing the restlessness and agitation the official accounts described. One phrase, quoted from a book by

Green written the year after Charlotte's death, cannot be confirmed from the reports of Croft, Sims and Baillie. Green describes the Princess clasping her hands over her abdomen and crying out, 'Oh what a pain! It is all here!' None of the doctors makes reference to such a pain; the only comment approaching it is inserted in Sir Richard Croft's handwriting and quoted above – 'suddenly attacked by a spasmodic affection of the chest'. Precisely what Croft meant we cannot know for certain. A sudden pain in the chest may have arisen from a clot or other substance lodging in the lungs (pulmonary embolus) as described below; or Croft may have been referring to the onset of difficulty in breathing, which often in these extreme circumstances manifests itself as gasping respiration, which might easily have been described as a 'spasmodic affection of the chest'.

Charlotte's last hours, as described by the doctors who were with her, do not suggest to me any sudden catastrophic event occurring after delivery, but a more gradual deterioration in a patient who was probably less well than was believed after a punishing ordeal. The realization of this, shortly before midnight, was followed by a decline which a medical attendant in those times could do little to halt.

The post mortem examination bears this out. Sir David Dundas and Sir Everard Home record 'The Appearances which were observed on inspecting the body of her late Royal Highness the Princess Charlotte of Wales, the 7th November 1817.' Sir David Dundas had been appointed Sergeant Surgeon to the King in 1793. He was prominent in the affairs of the Royal College of Surgeons and was Master of that college in 1804 and 1811. Sir Everard Home was a Fellow of the Royal Society. He too had been Master of the Royal College of Surgeons in 1813 and was to be its President in 1821. His appointment as Sergeant Surgeon to the King was in 1818. He was closely connected with Baillie since Home's sister had married Baillie's uncle, John Hunter. The embalming of bodies of deceased members of the royal family was one of the duties of the Sergeant Surgeon and during the procedure the removal of the various organs permitted their close scrutiny so constituting an autopsy as we know it today.

Several facts of possible significance were disclosed during the examination. (The report of the post mortem examination is

printed in full in the Appendix.) The uterus contained 'a considerable quantity of coagulated blood and extended as high as the navel
and the hour glass contraction was still very apparent'. The pericardium (the sac within which the heart lies) contained two ounces
of red coloured fluid but the heart and lungs themselves showed no
fault. The stomach contained nearly three pints of liquid. The colon
was distended with air. It is of considerable interest, but in no sense
connected with the Princess's death, that a cyst was found replacing
the right ovary 'the size of a hen's egg distended with serum and
a mass of sebaceous matter'. 'Sebaceous matter' is a secretion produced by certain glands of the skin and the finding of this material
in the ovarian cyst indicates that the cyst was of the variety
commonly called a dermoid. Such a cyst often contains not only
sebaceous material but hair, cartilage, teeth and sometimes other
recognizable tissues. Despite this alarming description it is a benign
tumour which nowadays would be removed without difficulty.

What then caused Princess Charlotte's death? This matter has been
debated by obstetricians and others ever since. Only since the publication of the official records of the events by Holland in 1951, however, has there been sufficient information for close analysis. The
possible causes of her death may be summarized as follows:

1. Bleeding either from within the uterus at the site of the
   attachment of the placenta, or from some injury such as a tear
   in the uterus itself.
2. An inversion of the uterus (the organ being turned inside out).
3. A pulmonary embolus (a clot of blood lodging in the lungs).
4. Acute dilatation of the stomach.
5. Porphyria.
6. Haemorrhage into the adrenal gland – a suggestion, not so far
   as I am aware, previously put forward.

All six deserve closer examination.
    The opinion expressed by Sir Eardley Holland, after his initial
perusal of the facts, was, 'It seems hardly possible to doubt that
Charlotte died of post partum haemorrhage.' He points out that
blood loss is recorded on four occasions – before the placenta was
removed, during its removal, when it was taken from the vagina,

and bleeding into the uterine cavity occurred later, which was recognized at the post mortem examination. Holland emphasized that none was severe but 'their cumulative effect must have been considerable.'

It is interesting to note that another of Sir Eardley's comments is almost identical with that expressed in a paragraph added to the corrected draft of the report of the Princess's labour and subsequently deleted. Sir Eardley wrote, 'Charlotte's symptoms, from near midnight to her death two and a half hours later, were typical of blood loss slowly mounting, the lethal phase being a slow leak into the uterus'. The deleted paragraph in the corrected draft of the report on the labour reads, as follows:

The symptoms were such as precede death from haemorrhage, but the quantity of blood loss was scarcely sufficient to create any alarm, being less than usual on such occasions, yet added to about a pound of blood found in the cavity of the uterus might have been sufficient to produce the unfavourable symptoms in so very excitable a constitution.

It is certainly my view, after a careful consideration of all the evidence, that death was more likely to have been due to the effects of several haemorrhages of moderate size, to which was then added the continued loss into the uterine cavity, than to any other cause. As I have already said, I believe that the Princess was probably anaemic by the end of her pregnancy. Bleeding, such as is referred to in the reports, on top of pre-existing anaemia, in a patient exhausted by long labour, and in particular by the protracted second stage of labour, would have been sufficient to cause her death.

If this is so, could her death have been avoided? Only in two respects can the management of her labour be criticized – instruments should have been used sooner to shorten her suffering in the second stage of labour – and the slow collection of blood within the uterus following delivery could perhaps have been prevented.

Croft made only one comment which referred to the condition of the uterus after the final removal of the placenta from the vagina, but it is a very significant one. He wrote that removal of the placenta from the vagina was followed 'by very little of either fluid blood or coagulum', and then went on to say 'at this time, *as well as I could determine, from feeling the abdomen through the bandage*, the uterus appeared moderately contracted' (my italics).

It seems possible that a fundamental error may have been committed here. The fact that only a small loss of blood followed the final removal of the placenta might indeed have been because the uterine muscle was strongly contracted, thus squeezing the blood vessels to the placental site and stopping bleeding as described in Chapter 5. Alternatively the slight loss may have been due to the fact that the uterus was not tightly contracted, and blood was slowly collecting *within it but was not being expelled.*

We know from the post mortem examination that this was actually the case; the uterus was contracted in an hour-glass fashion – that is to say a ring of muscle around the middle of the organ was tightly contracted, but the muscle above and below this was less contracted or even relaxed so that blood was oozing into the cavity. It is an important point of management during the third stage of labour to ensure that this is not happening, and Sir Richard, after taking the placenta from the vagina and finding only a slight loss, should have made certain that there was no internal bleeding in progress. It is evident from his account that he attempted this, but was prevented from doing it properly by the presence of a bandage around the lower abdomen – a method of management not now employed. The phrase 'as well as I could determine through the bandage' really means 'I couldn't be sure'. The comment that the uterus 'appeared moderately contracted' is far from reassuring, and should certainly have led to further examination at intervals, to check for internal bleeding.

But to concern oneself about blood collecting in the uterus in this way was not Sir Thomas Denman's teaching, and, as already indicated, Denman's teaching had a profound effect upon Croft's practice; Croft followed his father-in-law's advice rigidly. Denman, writing about the possibility of blood collecting in the uterus in this fashion and the need to expel it, wrote, 'I have never practised it; nor even troubled myself with the state of the uterus ... but have left whatever coagulum it contained to be expelled by its own action.'

No one now holds this view, and it is recognized that such slow bleeding into the uterine cavity can not only prevent the uterine muscle contracting, so leading to even more bleeding, but can cause shock in the patient out of all proportion to the quantity of blood lost. Even in those days not everyone accepted Denman's view. Sir Eardley Holland referred to a case report by Merriman in 1820; his patient became cold and blanched after delivery, in a manner similar to that of an 'illustrious lady' (Charlotte) who had died only three weeks before. Merriman found the uterus larger than it should be, inserted his hand and brought out twelve ounces of clot; the uterus contracted and the patient recovered.

One of several criticisms which were voiced concerning the post mortem examination, was that the quantity of blood in the uterus was not accurately measured. Another was that none of the doctors concerned in the delivery was present. This was especially surprising in the case of Matthew Baillie, who was the leading morbid anatomist of his day. Croft was deeply distressed, as letters to and from him, afterwards, show, but it is remarkable that he was not present to satisfy himself that he had not overlooked something important.

What are the other possible causes of death?

Two of these were excluded by the findings at the post mortem examination – there was no uterine rupture and the uterus was not inverted. Both are important causes of death following delivery but they are easily recognized at autopsy and they were not the reason for Charlotte's death.

No blood clot (embolus) was found in the lungs. It is likely that if a substantial one had been present it would have been recognized. Moreover such an embolus has to originate in a thrombosis elsewhere; there was no suggestion in the history of the labour that such a thrombus formed and none was found on post mortem examination. One form of embolus does remain a possibility, however, and it is one which was unknown at that time – an embolus of amniotic fluid. Rarely, and usually during a period of very strong uterine contraction shortly before delivery, some of the amniotic fluid surrounding the fetus is forced into the maternal blood vessels. This passes to the lungs and may cause death within a few minutes from asphyxia. If it does not, the amniotic fluid possesses a constituent which prevents blood clotting and causes marked haemorrhage, not only from the uterus but elsewhere in the body also. The circumstances of the onset of Charlotte's decline do not fit this pattern. She had been thought to be fairly well during delivery, and no sudden collapse occurred later such as would arise from an embolus. Moreover, the blood which was discharged from the vagina from time to time was found formed into 'a coagulum', whilst that found in the uterus after death was clotted. It is characteristic of the presence of amniotic fluid in the mother's blood vessels that her blood does not clot. This cause we can exclude.

Acute dilatation of the stomach is a very rare condition which can indeed cause death. Professor Crainz, in his note, seems to view it as a distinct possibility, although I do not agree. It is common during labour for there to be great delay in gastric emptying, both food and fluid ingested remaining in the stomach for twelve or even twenty-four hours. Many medicaments, cordials and draughts were given 'frequently' to Charlotte during the few hours following delivery and she was given broth and gruel too. Little of this would have been expelled from the stomach into the next part of the small intestine, and the accumulation of fluid could have been considerable. Moreover the general lack of strength of her muscles, including those of the stomach wall, may well have become exacerbated as she deteriorated. As a cause of death this seems highly unlikely.

For acute porphyria there is no direct evidence. The suggestion itself is based upon the supposed porphyria of George III, Charlotte's grandfather. It is a rare metabolic fault which I have met only once in my obstetric career when it was associated with a safe uncomplicated delivery. That this disorder caused George III's attacks of 'madness' is neither proved nor disproved, and although Dr MacAlpine and Dr Hunter, the champions of this theory, have provided arguments in its favour, others have provided equally strong arguments against it. There is some circumstantial evidence, based upon comments made by those close to the Princess which from time to time has been interpreted as compatible with this diagnosis, but I would require stronger evidence than that available so far for me to be at all convinced that such a rare condition was present. Lastly there remains the possibility of haemorrhage into the adrenal glands. This is another rare condition and again there is no direct evidence to support this diagnosis. The adrenal glands lie on each side of the body immediately above each kidney. Their proper function is vital to survival, although their importance was not recognized in 1817, and the post mortem examination contains no reference to them. They produce steroids such as cortisol as well as adrenalin and related substances. Destruction of the gland by haemorrhage can occur rapidly, and gives a picture similar in some respects to Charlotte's last illness. In particular, the few cases I have seen show features similar to those caused by bleeding, but with a profound restlessness such as she exhibited. This rare cause is mentioned merely as a possibility; there is no direct evidence either to support it or refute it.

One remaining medical point must be discussed – should instruments have been used earlier in the second stage of labour?

The era in which Sir Richard Croft practised was one of great conservatism in obstetric management, and the person mainly responsible for this extreme policy was his father-in-law, Thomas Denman. Denman had written that forceps should be used 'to supply the total want or deficiency of the natural pains of labour'; they should not be used 'for any motives of eligibility' (i.e. choice, election or expediency). Denman stressed the 'possible mistakes and lack of skill in younger practitioners, and the instances of presumption of those who, by their experience, have acquired dexterity'. The forceps were not to be used therefore whilst progress, however slow, was being made. This, without doubt, was a view rigidly applied by Croft during the Princess's labour.

Rigid rules must of course be broken in exceptional circumstances, but Croft was not the man to break them. Royal obstetricians should be leaders of their profession, and not bound by rules annunciated for the guidance of 'younger practitioners', but Sir Richard was no leader. The extreme view, promulgated by Denman and applied by Croft, was every bit as wrong as that which led to frequent traumatic use of forceps in an earlier era. What Denman was saying was: 'Use forceps only as a last resort.'

Others, however, held different views. It is interesting to speculate what might have happened if another of Denman's protégés and one of Sir Richard's colleagues on the staff of the Royal Maternity Charity – David Daniel Davis – had been at the Princess Charlotte's confinement and not, as he was three years later, at the birth of Queen Victoria.

David Daniel Davis (born David Davies but subsequently alter-
ing his surname and adding his father's christian name to his own)
was the son of humble parents from Carmarthenshire. He was
active as a lay preacher and physician in Sheffield, before moving
to London where he was befriended by Thomas Denman himself.
Davis had become physician accoucheur to Queen Charlotte's
Lying-in Hospital in 1813, just three years after the old Queen had
given her name to it. In 1816 he was appointed physician accoucheur
to the Royal Maternity Charity on the testimony of three physicians,
two of whom were Sir Richard Croft and Dr John Sims.

Davis was one of the minority of man-midwives at that time who
favoured the selective use of instruments to expedite delivery. He
had been directly concerned with improvements in the design of
the instruments, to permit them to be used with greater safety to
mother and child. Obstetric instruments were in fact used at the
birth of his own child in 1807, and injuries had been inflicted, from
which the child later died in infancy; no doubt this sad episode influenced Davis, not only in the choice of his career, but also in the
interest he took in the obstetric forceps. He enlarged the blades and
altered the curve, so as to reduce their compression effect on the
head of the fetus, whilst at the same time improving their purchase
and efficiency. These and other innovations were published later,
in 1825, under the title *Elements of Operative Midwifery; Compris-
ing a Description of New and Improved Powers of Assisting Difficult
and Dangerous Labours*. Not only did Davis depart from the obstetric practice of the day, in so far as operative intervention was concerned, but he did so in other areas too, notably childbed fever. This
he correctly deduced to be contagious and insisted on his pupils
changing their clothes after attending such a case. It is hard to
believe that such a man would have rigidly adhered to Denman's
teaching and stood idly by, whilst the second stage of the Princess
Charlotte's labour went on and on.

Twenty-four hours of the second stage of labour is an inordinate
length of time. For many years it has been considered prolonged
if it exceeds two hours and forceps will then be used. The circumstances were perfectly favourable for the use of instruments during
this time in Charlotte's labour. There was no reason to suppose that
the position of the child's head was abnormal, and the head was

certainly low, and could probably have been delivered without difficulty. Despite the enormous influence of Thomas Denman's teaching, one feels that a true leader of the profession would have intervened earlier, and delivered the Princess many hours sooner, and possibly saved the child's life.

Whether he would at the same time have saved the life of the mother is another matter. The problems which arose during the third stage of labour might still have arisen, and unless greater attention had been paid to the uterus after delivery, the outcome may have been the same. It is possible that shortening the Princess's suffering during the second stage might have preserved her strength sufficiently and permitted her to survive. I think it might well have done so.

One further uncertainty remains, and it concerns an aspect of a patient's response to illness of which all doctors are aware – the will to live. Without the will to live, sick people may die, despite excellent care, when by all the rules they should survive; others can fight their illness strongly and survive against all odds. What was Charlotte's frame of mind?

On 10 October Princess Charlotte wrote, or is believed to have written, a long letter to her mother, who was in Italy. It is a sad, emotional, maudlin letter, and it reveals a morbid preoccupation with death, which a doctor would find disturbing in a patient approaching labour. It laments her mother's absence, her own loneliness, and talks of fate and providence in a manner which suggests resignation to God's will, whatever it may be, but without determination to make a personal effort to survive. Charlotte wrote:

I have determined, should Providence please to bless me with offspring, so to regulate its early reason & to direct its infant energies, that the lessons I have received from you and the wisdom which time and observation have confirmed may be handed down to my child with a view to the perpetuation of the great principal, that the legitimate end of all Government is the welfare of society & that political & private virtue is the sure foundation & the best bulwarks to a Throne.

But, oh my mother! when my timid imagination revolves upon the uncertainty which veils futurity – when I look to the dark probabilities which may put a period to the claim of hope, even shadows shake my courage, and I feel myself the victim of terrors which reason would almost demonstrate absurd, at such a trying moment. Surrounded by strangers, with a single exception, my heart feels itself alone, & should the protection of Heaven leave me and I fall, the presence of a mother would assuredly impart a serenity and resignation to the mind which would soothe the pillow of her dying head.

Should it be the pleasure of Providence that I survive the hour of approaching danger, I may at some future period be endued with power to restore you to that situation you were formed to embellish. But if an allwise decree should summon me from this sphere of anxious apprehension, not for myself but for my mother a pang of terror shoots across my bewilder'd brain, even then however my last prayers would be to Heaven to gift you with that sublime feeling of pious resignation which would teach you to bow submissively to the chastening stroke of our common Father and to console your afflicted heart with the anticipation of our reunion in a world where felicity is unimpaired & where malice is unadmissable. Believe me, my adored mother, I fear less to die than to live. Death, would obliterate no image of delight from my heart, save that which, in the portrait of a beloved mother, nature has still left to the hoping, doubting, yet fearing Charlotte.

Thea Holme does not believe that Charlotte wrote this letter, since it is written in a self-pitying, sentimental style foreign to her. Yet commenting on Charlotte's frame of mind when she learned of her baby's death, she seems to echo similar thoughts: 'The spell was on Charlotte; she received the news that her son was dead as if she had always known it would be so. She did not shed a tear, and tried to console the weeping Mrs Griffiths by repeating it was the will of God.'

We shall never know if the will to fight for her life had left her and, if so, what influence this had on the outcome. Although I have echoed Sir Eardley Holland's opinion that there was enough bleeding to account for her death, the amount was not overwhelming, and she ought to have survived. Did she wish to do so?

The news of the birth of a stillborn son brought deep sadness to Prince Leopold. But the husband's first thought is nearly always for his wife, and she was not then thought to be in danger. He wrote almost at once to the Regent, telling him of the sad event, and soon afterwards fell into a deep sleep of exhaustion. He could scarcely be roused by Stockmar, who came to awaken him as Charlotte lay dying.

Thea Holme paints an ineffably forlorn picture of him afterwards, mourning 'prodigiously, agonisingly' for his dead wife – a sadness from which he never seemed fully to recover. No doubt the depths of his anguish explains the fact that not until 23 November was a letter written in his name by Sir Robert Gardiner, his principal equerry, to Croft assuring him of Leopold's recognition of the earnest endeavour he made in his professional duties. Despite the late dispatch of this acknowledgement – the Regent, Dr Stockmar, Dr Baillie, Sir David Dundas and Sir William Knightly, physician to the Regent, and no doubt many others, had all written in similar terms within a few days of the event – there is no hint of insincerity or doubt about the sentiments expressed on Prince Leopold's behalf.

The Prince Regent was in ignorance of the slow progress of his daughter's labour. He had spent the ten days before her death at Sudbourne Hall in Suffolk, almost a hundred miles from London. News of the onset of labour did not reach him until after midnight on the night of 4 November. At once he set off for London, missing, during the night, other messengers carrying further news. Not until 3.00 a.m. on 6 November when the Princess was already dead did he reach Carlton House, and before he could set off again for Clare-mont the news arrived. Forty-eight hours later, on 8 November, Sir Richard Bloomfield, his private secretary conveyed to Croft, 'His Royal Highness's acknowledgement of the zealous care and in-defatigable attention manifested by Sir Richard towards his beloved daughter ... and to express His Royal Highness's entire confidence in the medical skill and ability which he displayed.'

Charlotte's mother was in Italy on the shore of the Adriatic, where she would perhaps only shortly before have received the sad letter, with its fears and forebodings, written by her daughter on 10 October. No one it seems had afforded her the courtesy of a detailed letter of explanation, and she was obliged to write on 2 December to Baillie, 'the only true friend I have left in England', to 'pray for heavens sake send me a most exact account of all what concerned this dreadful event and I am much afraid that some mistake must have occurred'. The poor unfortunate woman would have to wait in a fever of anxiety for such small comforts as Baillie could provide, for not until Christmas Eve was he able to answer her letter.

Queen Charlotte, who had been ill for some time, was at Bath; the news of the birth of a stillborn son reached her at 1.00 p.m. on 6 November, as she was preparing to receive a deputation from the Mayor and Corporation. A civic banquet had been planned that evening in honour of the Duke of Clarence, and Queen Charlotte, to whom duty was something that should be done, however unpalatable or disturbing, decided that it should be held. At 6.00 p.m. as the company was sitting down to the meal her Private Secretary, General Taylor, was called out; his face, on his return, was enough to tell the Queen what had happened.

The King, a sad demented old man confined in Windsor Castle, was never told.

The officers of State had left after the confinement and messengers had to be sent to them all. Once it was certain that Charlotte's son was dead, his body was shown to them for authorization; 'a noble infant it was', wrote Lord Chancellor Eldon in his diary 'as like the Royal Family as possible.' The ministers took their leave and returned to their homes, but 'before six a messenger arrived to let us know the Princess was dead'.

The country was stunned by the news. Lord Brougham wrote that it was 'as if every household throughout Great Britain had lost a favourite child'. There was a national sense of the deepest sorrow and disappointment; in Brougham's words, 'It is difficult for persons not living at the time to believe how universal and how genuine those feelings were.' Everyone regardless of rank and station wore signs of mourning. Shops, theatres, law courts, gambling houses, the royal exchange, the docks, everywhere was closed. The golden prospect for the future suddenly vanished.

After the initial feelings of anguish and disbelief by the public came an angry reaction that the truth was not being disclosed, and mistakes were being hushed up. Pamphlets, letters and newspaper articles called for more information, or the need for a public enquiry. Part of the trouble was that little official information had been released by the doctors, and the newspaper accounts, which had been written by the correspondents at Claremont, had been to some degree inaccurate.

The three bulletins which had been issued had given no hint of danger, despite the slowness of the labour; at 8.00 a.m. on Wednesday, 5 November the bulletin stated that labour was progressing slowly but favourably; at 5.30 p.m. it described considerable advance in the last few hours and hoped for a conclusion soon, and at 10.00 p.m. the third bulletin merely reported that Her Royal Highness had been delivered of a stillborn child, but was doing extremely well. No further official bulletin was issued. In part this was no doubt due to the shock and horror of the attendants, and in part to the fact that they had no satisfactory explanation to offer.

The brunt of the attacks naturally fell upon Sir Richard Croft, who was alleged to have retired to bed, with his two colleagues, leaving Charlotte solely in Mrs Griffiths's care; it was said he prevented Sims from attending her which, as we have already seen, he did not. The bleedings during pregnancy, it was also alleged, had been much too frequent.

The report that the doctors had retired to bed appeared in the newspapers of 7 November. The same statement is made even now. Thea Holme writes, 'Soon after this [Charlotte beginning to take nourishment following the completion of the third stage] ... Baillie and Sims went to bed and so did Stockmar. Croft, whose room opened out of Charlotte's, lay down, but without undressing'. Thomas Green's account went even further. He not only recorded that Baillie and Sims were in bed and Croft lying down but still dressed, but that Mrs Griffiths had gone to have her supper, leaving Prince Leopold 'reclining on the bed by the side of his beloved Consort'. It was Leopold who, according to Green, came to Mrs Griffiths '10 minutes later' and said, 'the Princess did not seem quite so well'.

The reports of the doctors themselves do not confirm any of this apart from the retirement of Baillie. John Sims, writing to Joseph Clarke of Dublin on 15 November, states: 'It has been said we were all gone to bed but that is not a fact. Croft did not leave the room. Dr Baillie retired about 11 and I went to my own bed chamber and lay down in my clothes at 12'. If Sims is prepared to admit that Baillie had gone to bed and he himself lay down fully dressed about the time of the awareness of Charlotte's decline, and to assert that Croft was still with the Princess, there seems little reason to accept what was, after all, merely a newspaper account that all the doctors were in bed.

The criticism that Sims did not see the Princess often enough does, nonetheless, have some substance to it. He did not see her at all until she was in danger after midnight. When the bleeding first occurred, during the third stage of labour, he was busy attempting to make the child breathe. He was, as he put it, 'perfectly satisfied with Sir Richard Croft's representation and quite agreed with him in the propriety of removing it' (the placenta). He went on: 'Introduction of a stranger at that moment to the royal patient, as it seemed to me, was probably objectionable'.

Perhaps 'a stranger' would have been alarming at that time, but Sims had been at Claremont since 2.00 a.m. the previous morning, and was 'in the adjoining room the greatest part of the day and was continually informed of the state of progress'. With progress so snail-like, however, few in his position would have been prepared to remain in the background without satisfying themselves that what they were being told was really so. Even if Croft did not request it (which seems unlikely since he had wished to introduce Sims on his arrival), Sims himself should have asked to see the Princess. It seems probable that he provided less support than Croft needed, the latter being left to a too-prolonged too-lonely ordeal for which he was ill-equipped.

There was still one final tragedy to come. Three months later Sir Richard Croft, unable to bear the criticism any longer, shot himself whilst conducting another confinement. (The report of the inquest on Sir Richard Croft's death is printed in the Appendix.) Mother, child and obstetrician all died. It was, in Sir Eardley Holland's words, a triple obstetric tragedy.

8

The Great Succession Stakes

The death of Princess Charlotte in giving birth to her stillborn son destroyed at a stroke two generations of heirs to the throne of Britain. In Queen Charlotte's fifty-seventh year as Queen Consort there was not a single legitimate grandchild from the fifteen children she had borne to George III, though there were at least twelve illegitimate ones. Unless one of her sons or daughters produced a legitimate child, the crown would pass to the Duke of Brunswick, a young cousin of George III's, living in Hanover.

The chances, by 1817, of any of Queen Charlotte's large family producing offspring did not seem strong, although twelve of them were still alive. Of her daughters, the eldest, Charlotte Augusta, was fifty-one and Queen of Württemburg. She had borne one stillborn child many years earlier and had never become pregnant again. Augusta Sophia was forty-eight and unmarried. Elizabeth, at forty-six, was Landgravine of Hesse-Homberg and had never been pregnant. Mary was forty and had recently married her simple-minded cousin, William, Duke of Gloucester – known as 'Silly Billy'. It was widely expected that their marriage would prove barren, as indeed it did. Sophia, always ailing, was thirty-nine and unmarried, although rumour had credited her with an illegitimate child some years earlier. Amelia had died of tuberculosis at the age of twenty-seven.

Turning to Queen Charlotte's sons, four of the Princes were married but had failed to produce an heir. The Prince of Wales at fifty-five was, as we know, still tied to Caroline but had lived apart from her for many years and had no children other than the unfortunate Princess Charlotte. The Duke of York was fifty-four and childless despite many years of marriage to an admirable and respectable woman and many liaisons with women far from admirable and anything but respectable. The Duke of Cumberland, who was forty-six, was heartily disliked by most of the royal family and for that matter by many others as well. He had still further incurred his parents' displeasure by marrying, in 1815, the already twice-married Princess of Solms-Braunfel, who had jilted his younger brother, the Duke of Cambridge, a few years earlier. It was rumoured that she had expedited the Prince of Solms's death and considerable scandal surrounded her name. So incensed was the old Queen Charlotte that she vowed she would never receive the Duchess of Cumberland at Court, and she never did. The Duchess had borne a stillborn daughter in 1817 and seemed unlikely to have another child. The Duke of Sussex, aged forty-four, had some years earlier married Lady Augusta Murray without the King's consent, thereby contravening the Royal Marriage Act. The union was declared unlawful and their two children, a son and a daughter, were debarred from the succession.

Three of the Princes, the Duke of Clarence, the Duke of Kent and the Duke of Cambridge, though middle-aged, were still unmarried and it was clearly in the interests of the succession for them to find suitable spouses and produce an heir if at all possible. So the three of them set about the task of finding acceptable wives although, especially in the Duke of Clarence's case, not without some difficulty.

William, Duke of Clarence, was fifty-two and, although unmarried, anything but childless for ten little FitzClarences had been born as a result of his long liaison with an actress called Mrs Jordan. When their association began, Mrs Jordan was the foremost comedy actress of her day and a truly remarkable woman. Her liaison with the Duke started in about 1790 and during the twenty years that it lasted she bore him ten children, all named after members of the royal family. Their association eventually foundered on financial rocks. William was always in financial difficulty; he was ever in debt, and was obliged to pay about a quarter of his income merely to meet the interest on the money he owed. From time to time, when his money problems were particularly acute, Mrs Jordan would return to the stage and tour the country to bolster up the family finances. As the years went by, she departed on these excursions with increasing reluctance, and wrote gloomy letters to the Duke, complaining of the lack of artistic appreciation of the audiences, and threatening retirement. Indeed the possibility of her retirement, and with it the loss of her financial contributions, was certainly a factor, although probably not the only one, in William's decision to sever his connection with her. He decided that only marriage with a rich woman could save him, and he set about finding one. With his customary enthusiasm and optimism he anticipated no real difficulty in being accepted.

His eye fell on Miss Tylney Long. She was twenty-five years his junior, but he was captivated by her youth and beauty, and not least by the £40,000 a year that would come with her. Perhaps she even contemplated marriage with the ageing Duke, but finally the lure of the royal connection lost its appeal and, to the Duke's chagrin, she announced her engagement to a nephew of the Duke of Wellington. Over the next year or two William proposed to several other women. The precise number is uncertain but four are usually mentioned – the Dowager Lady Downshire, Lady Barclay, the widow of ten years' standing of an Irish landowner, Lady Lindsay, and Miss Elphinstone, who was the friend and confidante of his niece, Charlotte. None of them would have him.

Next he turned his attentions abroad, and confidently expected to be accepted by Grand-Duchess Catherine of Oldenburg, the sister of the Tsar. She not only found him quite objectionable, but disliked all the other members of the royal family as well, so the death of the Princess Charlotte found the Duke of Clarence still unmarried.

In 1817, with the need of an heir now so great, the Duke redoubled his efforts. He persuaded Parliament that he would propose to the Princess Royal of Denmark, if they would make it worth his while. So urgent was the position that they agreed to grant him an increase in his allowance from £18,000 to £40,000 a year, to pay his debts of £17,000, to grant a marriage allowance of £22,000 and to carry out repairs to Bushy Park. The Princess of Denmark refused him!

Next on the scene was a Miss Wyckham whose Christian name is not recorded, but who, for obvious reasons, was known by the wags as High Wyckham. The Duke had lowered his sights by this time; she was less attractive than Miss Tylney Long, and worth only £16,000 a year. But she accepted him, only for Parliament to refuse him permission to marry a commoner.

By this time the other members of the royal family were also engaged in the search for a wife for him. Adolphus, Duke of Cambridge, who was surveying the field in Europe on his brother's behalf, discovered someone who would be in every way suitable in Princess Augusta of Hesse-Cassel. There was only one snag. Adolphus decided he wanted to marry her himself. Unable to restrain his feelings, he wrote about her to William in such glowing terms that William realized immediately the true state of affairs. 'By heaven!' he exclaimed on reading the letter, 'he's in love with her himself. I will write and tell him to take her himself, bless him.'

The Duke of Cambridge did 'take her himself', but happily almost at once came across another candidate, who suited his brother's book admirably. She was the Princess Adelaide of Saxe-Meiningen, who was in her middle twenties and said to be quiet, reserved and well brought up. So suitable was she thought to be that the royal family, having ample evidence by this time of the mess William could make of things if left to himself, insisted that all the arrangements should be made through the Duke of Cambridge. A proxy proposal was made and accepted. The Duke no doubt heaved a sigh of relief – he was to be married at last.

He was hopeful, moreover, of a similar financial arrangement to that proposed when he agreed to approach the Princess of Denmark. This time he was less fortunate and was voted a much reduced sum. He was so furious that he declined the offer and elected, after his marriage, to live in Hanover.

On 3 July 1818 Adelaide came to England, where she met the Duke, somewhat surprisingly, at Grillon's Hotel, Albermarle Street. They got on famously, and arrangements were quickly concluded. The honeymoon of the Duke and Duchess of Clarence was far from the conventional one. It was realized after the ceremony that no one had invited the Dowager Duchess of Saxe-Meiningen, Adelaide's mother, to stay, and she could hardly go back alone to Grillon's Hotel. Nothing abashed, the Duke took his mother-in-law to St James's Palace to join them.

But worse was to follow, and William, a figure of fun for some years, was to reach a high spot of farce. The next day, George, William's elder son by Mrs Jordan, broke his leg, whereupon the Duke, again taking such set-backs in his stride, borrowed the Prince

Regent's bed carriage – an ambulance-like vehicle – hastened round to where George had been taken, and brought him back to St James's Palace as well. After several years of trying to find a suitable woman to accept him in marriage, the Duke can hardly have expected to spend his honeymoon in the company of his mother-in-law and his eldest illegitimate son!

Meanwhile the Duke's younger brothers had been seeking brides of their own. The Duke of Clarence was not alone in looking for a wife as a solution to his financial problems, as for a year or so before the death of Princess Charlotte, the Duke of Kent had been doing the same, despite his undoubted affection for, and happiness with, Madame de St Laurent. Edward had been heavily in debt for many years. Of his income of £27,000 a year at that time, £11,000 was all that could be made available to him for his own living expenses, the remaining £16,000 going to pay his creditors. As a result he was living in Brussels, which was much less expensive than London.

In 1816 he formed the notion that Princess Katherine Amelia of Baden might be a suitable wife for him; if approved by the Prince Regent, Edward hoped for a much improved financial settlement. As sister to the Tsarina of Russia and to the Queen of Bavaria, Amelia had an impeccable family background. Moreover, the Duke himself was clearly considered to be suitable on her side, since the Tsar lent him a thousand guineas to make the journey to Baden to meet her. In the event, he found her odious, undesirable and forty-one years old; she was the only one of six sisters still unmarried, a state of affairs the Duke was not prepared to disturb!

But another possible wife was immediately on hand – Mary, the Dowager Princess of Leiningen. She had formerly been Princess of Saxe-Coburg, and it was her brother Leopold who, after some opposition, had married poor Princess Charlotte. During this opposition period the Duke of Kent, Charlotte's favourite uncle, had pressed her cause repeatedly. Charlotte and her sister-in-law began corresponding happily together, and Charlotte was clearly in favour of the match between her uncle and Mary. It was at Charlotte's suggestion, and with her recommendation as a suitor, that the Duke,

during his visit to Germany, also attended the widowed Princess
of Leiningen at their home on Amorbach.

The Princess had been widowed for two years, and was left with
a son Charles aged twelve and a daughter Theodora aged ten.
Edward was dashing in his attentions – perhaps too much so – and
on that occasion, when he poured out his feelings of admiration and
affection and offered his hand in marriage, he was rejected. Later,
however, following Princess Charlotte's tragic death, correspondence and negotiations were re-opened. The Prince Regent, anxious
for the match, may well have swayed the balance by indicating that
the Princess's children, Charles and Theodora, would be under his
protection; since their future, in the event of their mother's remar-
riage, was in question, the Regent's intervention settled any
anxieties there might be. The Princess gladly accepted the offer of
marriage, which in truth had had a considerable attraction for her
since the Duke had first made it two years earlier.

They were married on 29 May 1818 at Coburg in the Hall of
Giants in the Schloss Ehrenburg and, subsequently, were remarried, in the same ceremony as William Duke of Clarence and
Adelaide of Saxe-Meiningen, in the drawing-room at Kew in the
presence of Queen Charlotte.

Mary was described as inclined to plumpness, but otherwise of
good figure, with a good complexion and fine brown eyes and hair.
Cecil Woodham-Smith's sympathetic portrait of her mentions her
to have been 'altogether most charming and attractive . . . with warm
feelings, and she was naturally truthful, affectionate and friendly,
unselfish, full of sympathy and generous'. Moreover, as a woman
of only thirty-one and of proved fertility, she was clearly to be a
strong contender in the competition for the succession. More than
that, she and Edward were to prove very well suited to each other,
although for far too short a time.

Before his meeting with Augusta of Hesse-Cassel the Duke of Cambridge had shown little interest in marriage. He had, it is true, been
engaged a number of years earlier, when arrangements had been
made for him to marry Frederica, widow of a Prince of Prussia.
King George III had given his consent to the wedding, and the
public announcements had been made. Without any ceremony

whatever, though, Frederica had jilted him, and married instead the Prince of Solms-Braunfel. She had sons by both her previous husbands when, as we have seen, Solms-Braunfel died and, amid royal displeasure in Great Britain, in 1815 she married the Duke of Cumberland.

The Duke of Cambridge had lived an enjoyable bachelor existence. He kept no mistresses, so far as it is known, and was not in debt – cause and effect no doubt. His life-style was not extravagant, unlike his brothers', and he lived cheaply in apartments in St James's Palace. In Hanover, where in 1814 he became Governor-General, he had a more flourishing establishment, and altogether led a comfortable existence even having sufficient funds to lend money from time to time to his brothers. He was artistic, musical, and very respectable. He was a mere forty-three when he proposed to the twenty-year-old Augusta and they were plainly favourites in the great succession stakes. Who would be the first Princess to the post?

The three couples left the starting gate so close together that none had any clear advantage. In any event, although the notion of these matrimonial events as a race to produce an heir is irresistible, time was not really important. Any offspring of the Duke of Clarence (the King's third son) would take precedence as heir over any children of the Duke of Kent (the fourth son) who would, in turn, precede those of the Duke of Cambridge (the ninth son). A bird in the hand was not quite worth two in the bush on this occasion, but who was to say whether those with a prior claim would prove fertile. The first child would be the heir until the child of a senior Duke came along – if one did.

The Duchess of Cambridge was the first of the wives to become pregnant, followed by the almost simultaneous conceptions of the remaining two and also, somewhat surprisingly, of the Duchess of Cumberland, at the age of forty. Suddenly, there were four pregnant Duchesses, doing their best to produce a Hanoverian heir.

None of the couples was at that time in England, where news was eagerly awaited, but were all in Germany. The Clarences had joined the Cambridges in Hanover, where the Cumberlands were also residing, while the Kents were at the Duchess's old home in

Amorbach, which was the only place where the Duke could afford
to live.

Although the other three Dukes made no plans for their wives
to return to Britain, to allow their children to be born there, Edward,
the Duke of Kent, was most anxious for this to happen. He informed
the Prince Regent of the Duchess's pregnancy in November 1818.
It was his intention, he stated, to begin the journey to England in
early April. For this he would need financial help, and he petitioned
the Prince Regent not only for money for the journey, but also for
a yacht in which to make it, and apartments at Kensington Palace
for the confinement. The Prince Regent was unsympathetic. He
made it clear that money would not be forthcoming, and he urged
Edward to emulate his brothers William and Adolphus, who were
preparing for their own wives' confinements in Hanover. Not only
would this save expense, the Regent pointed out, but it would spare
the Duchess of Kent the very difficult, and possibly dangerous,
journey at a late stage in her pregnancy.

Taken somewhat aback, Edward wrote again, pressing the total
unsuitability of the house at Amorbach for any confinement, especially one so important as this. Not only was it an old and dilapidated
building, but it was fifty miles from a town of any size, from which
a doctor might need to be summoned, should any obstetric assistance be needed. This brought no better response from the Prince
Regent. The Duke was not without supporters, however, who felt
as he did that the child should be born in England, and who continued to urge him to bring his wife over. The Duke very naturally
replied that he had no money, and there he felt matters would rest.
His friends, however, convinced of the importance of having the
confinement in England, because of the national support for Edward
that this would engender, compared with a birth on foreign soil,
set about raising money to make the Duke a loan. Alderman Wood
and Lord Darnley put up £10,000 whilst two others, Lord Dundas
and Earl Fitzwilliam, advanced £5,000 between them.

Fortified by the confidence of his friends, and no less by their
money, Edward announced his intentions to depart from Cassel in
time to reach Calais by 18 April, when his wife would be just six
weeks away from the expected date of her confinement. His renewed
request for a royal yacht to bring them across the Channel was on

this occasion granted by the Regent, who, it seemed, accepted the inevitable, since he also agreed to make the apartments at Kensington Palace available for the confinement. Despite his acquiescence, however, he none the less expressed his regret that, at such an advanced stage of pregnancy, the Duchess was to be subjected to such a punishing journey.

There can be no doubt that the Prince Regent was right. It was more than four hundred miles from Amorbach to Calais, and the roads of that period would scarcely permit the Duchess to travel in any comfort. The continual swaying, jolting and pitching of the coach might well have disturbed the poor woman enough to induce premature labour; even if the motion of the vehicle and the additional activity of the journey were not actually to bring on labour, it might easily have started spontaneously during the journey. The Duchess was, after all, only two months away from the due date of her confinement, and the journey by coach alone was to take a few weeks. The Channel crossing was likely to be uncomfortable, if not dangerous, and a further coach journey awaited them on arrival in England. All in all, it was a foolish enterprise to embark upon with such a precious cargo as the yet unborn Victoria.

It is true that one member of the very large entourage which travelled the road to Kensington Palace from Amorbach was a well-known obstetrician, Madame Siebold. But skilful though she undoubtedly was, the lack of suitable facilities, should the labour begin at some point along the road, would have been a considerable handicap. She was scarcely in such an unenviable position as the valet-cum-man-midwife Vreid, in the coach with the Princess of Wales on her headlong dash in strong labour to St James's palace in 1735. But any complication occurring on the road, or any significant delay to the journey, might have had serious, even fatal, results for the child.

At the very moment that the Duke and Duchess were preparing to leave Amorbach, stirring events were occurring in Hanover. Augusta, Duchess of Cambridge, had reached the end of her pregnancy, and Adelaide, Duchess of Clarence, still had eight weeks to go. When Augusta started to have pains during the night of 25–26 March the Duke of Clarence and two other gentlemen attended her in her apartments. The presence of the Duke of Clarence at the Duchess of Cambridge's confinement is surprising since the Duchess of Clarence was far from well at the time and his presence was not considered essential. Lord Liverpool, writing to Lord Chancellor Eldon in August 1818, said,

It appears to me by no means necessary that the Duchess of Cambridge should return to England for her confinement. It would be a most severe burthen on the Royal Family in general to oblige them not only to come over to England to be remarried but to be compelled to return here on every occasion of the nature referred to; and as to the latter case there is no law whatever upon the question.

I think at the same time if it can be done without inconvenience it would be advisable that some British subject should be in the house at the time of the delivery in order to ensure testimony of the fact.... It would be as well that it should be a person in the service of the Crown and I conceive that one of the ministers or secretaries of legation resident at any of the neighbouring German courts might be directed to attend who could be most conveniently spared at the time for the purpose.

Despite this somewhat loose instruction William, Duke of Clarence, elected to attend. He and his companions, the Earl of Mayo and the Right Honourable George Henry Rose, the minister at the Court of Berlin, sealed the doors, and took up their positions in an adjoining room, where they could see sufficient of the events to authenticate the birth of a possible heir apparent and ensure that no one could enter the birth chamber without being seen by them. 'That sharp labour', they recorded in a letter to Lord Castelreagh, the Foreign Secretary, 'continued until ten minutes past 2 o'clock of the morning aforesaid when Her Royal Highness the Duchess of Cambridge was safely delivered of a male child whose sex we determined by actual inspection' – which, all things considered, is as good a way of doing it as any! At long last a grandson had been born to the King of England. The boy was christened George, and he was, for a short time only, first in line to inherit the crown.

Meanwhile the Duchess of Clarence was suffering from the effects of a chill which she had caught while walking in the garden a few days earlier. It had developed into a more extensive upper respiratory infection with fever and a cough, indicating a form of pneumonia. She was bled by her medical adviser, Dr Andrew Halliday, an army surgeon who had distinguished himself at the Battle of Waterloo – where opportunities to display his skill as an accoucheur must have been few and far between! The chest infection, or the bleeding, or both, precipitated premature labour, and at 6.30 a.m. on Saturday morning, 27 March, she gave birth to a premature female child, who was christened Charlotte Augusta Louisa. An infant born two months prematurely at that time had little chance of survival, and she lived only a few hours, dying at 1.30 p.m. the same day.

The Times for Wednesday, 7 April 1819 published a brief announcement headed 'Accouchements of the Duchess of Clarence and the Duchess of Cambridge'. The account said that 'Yesterday morning at three o'clock Lieutenant Colonel Prott, the Duke of Cambridge's equerry, and Lieutenant Colonel Edward Hall RN, arrived at Lord Castelreagh's house in St James's Square with dispatches from Mr Rose, the British Minister in Berlin, announcing the accouchements of the Duchess of Clarence and that of the Duchess of Cambridge at Hanover'.

They afterwards waited on the Prince Regent at Carlton House, with letters from the Royal Duke to their brother. The dispatches stated that the Duchess of Cambridge had at 'the principal palace at Hanover' on Friday morning, 26 March, at three o'clock been 'safely delivered of a fine boy by Dr Keine'. The Duchess of Clarence who had been attended by Dr Andrew Halliday had been 'attacked with an indisposition on Monday, 22nd March for which it was deemed necessary to bleed her several times; this caused a premature accouchement', and on Saturday morning 27 March at 6.30 she gave birth to a female child. 'The infant lived till 1 o'clock and then expired.' The Duchess was 'very unwell after the birth and in that state continued several hours to such a degree that considerable danger was apprehended'. Being pronounced better by four o'clock Lieutenant Hall set off to England with the news.

It was twenty-three years since the birth of the previous heir to the throne, the Princess Charlotte. Now, within twenty-nine hours of each other, two other legitimate grandchildren had been born to Queen Charlotte. George, the infant son of the Duke and Duchess of Cambridge had been heir apparent for these twenty-nine hours, then superseded for seven hours by the premature Charlotte, to become, on her death, heir again. He was heir apparent, moreover, not only to the throne of Great Britain, but to that of Hanover as well. He was, however, not to remain so for very long.

The day following these momentous events, on 28 March, the Duke and Duchess of Kent departed from Amorbach bound for Calais. They had allowed themselves three weeks to cover more than four hundred miles. Journeys were to be limited to twenty-five miles a day, and a day's rest was to be taken after every three days of travel. The entourage was large. The Duke and Duchess were accompanied by her two children and their attendants, the Duchess's ladies-in-waiting, the Duke's valet and other attendants, cooks, additional coachmen and servants and two doctors – Madame Siebold, the obstetrician who was to conduct the confinement in London and to supervise the health of the Duchess *en route*, and Dr Wilson.

Charlotte Heiland, known as von Siebold, had studied initially in Göttingen and later in Darmstadt. After passing the examination of a medical college she was given permission to practise midwifery and soon earned for herself a great reputation as a midwife and an aristocratic clientele. In 1817 she was awarded a degree in Giessen and distinguished with the title of 'Doctor of Midwifery'. In 1818 she had delivered the Duchess of Coburg and it is not surprising that she was asked to attend the Duchess of Kent. Dr Wilson had formerly been a naval surgeon aboard His Majesty's ship *Hussar* and had acted as the Duke's personal physician. It appears that he had undertaken some of the necessary care of the Duchess during the early stages of pregnancy.

The impedimenta necessary for such a large party was increased still further by the Duchess's bed and bedding; should her labour begin before journey's end, she would at least have enjoyed some comfort!

They encountered no serious difficulties, however, on this section of their journey, and they arrived at Calais on schedule. Here there was a delay due to unfavourable winds. They were obliged to wait almost a week, until 24 April, when a favourable wind appeared which blew them across the Channel in under three hours. The seas were running high, however, and the Duchess was very sick during the crossing. Their arrival in the capital was to be just a month before the child would be born.

The arrangements for Mary's confinement are well described by Cecil Woodham-Smith who corrects a number of previous inaccuracies. The apartments which the Duke and Duchess were to occupy had been empty for nearly five years, and renovation was only slowly accomplished. The rooms were nonetheless ideally suited to such an important occasion. The windows overlooked the park, where a delightful stretch of water, splendid trees and majestic lawns made an altogether magnificent vista. Kensington Palace was in the country at that time, and quiet and secluded.

The Duchess had comfortable time to settle in, to get her effects in order, and to prepare herself for her confinement. But frustrating delays to the refurbishing of the apartments, especially to the Duke's dressing-room, in which the Duchess was to be confined, may have disturbed her composure to some degree. The room was in fact only completely ready on 23 May, the day on which the Duchess's labour began.

Her pains started during the late evening of that day – a Sunday. At 10.30 p.m. that night, the Duke sent an urgent letter to General Wetherall, the Comptroller of his Household, informing him that labour had begun, and bidding him present himself at the apartments at once to receive the officers of State, who were to attend the confinement, to whom messages had already been sent.

They assembled in the room adjoining that in which the Duchess was lying-in: the Duke of Wellington, the Archbishop of Canterbury, the Bishop of London, the Marquis of Lansdowne, the Right Honourable George Canning, the Right Honourable Nicholas Vansittart, Chancellor of the Exchequer, Earl Bathurst, the Duke of Sussex, the younger brother of the Duke of Kent, and Lieutenant General Wetherall had gathered for what was to be an historic event.

It was fortunately an event which proceeded smoothly and without complication, contrary to early beliefs. The infant Victoria was born at 4.15 a.m. on Monday, 24 May 1819 after a labour of little more than six hours. The Duchess had of course borne two previous children, and a smooth confinement of this kind was to be expected.

As Cecil Woodham-Smith points out, however, it had previously been stated that labour was far more difficult and the delivery perilous. *Victoria from Birth to Bridal*, written in 1840 by Agnes Strickland, described lengthy suffering and great danger to the mother, before the future Queen was safely born. It had been rumoured also that Dr David Daniel Davis, one of Wales's greatest obstetricians, saved the day by taking over from Madame Siebold, who had despaired of achieving a successful outcome.

There is no likelihood whatever that any complications, such as are implied, arose during the Duchess of Kent's confinement. Queen Victoria's own comment, in the margin of Miss Strickland's book against the sentence referred to above, is 'not true'. The Duchess's mother was informed that everything had gone smoothly, and there is no reason to believe otherwise. Two previous labours, without complication, such as the Duchess had had, reduce the risk to the mother and child during the third confinement to its lowest, all things being equal. So indeed it proved. Madame Siebold not only supervised the birth of Queen Victoria with complete success but, five months later, in August the same year, was to conduct an equally safe birth of Prince Albert to the Duchess of Coburg, wife of the reigning Duke, and the Duchess of Kent's brother.

David Daniel Davis was indeed in attendance at Queen Victoria's birth, but there is no evidence that he was required to take any active part. He was a flourishing society obstetrician of his time, and was no doubt there, as Cecil Woodham-Smith suggests, as the British medical representative, at the confinement which was being conducted by a foreign doctor – and a foreign female doctor at that – whom the country would undoubtedly view with suspicion, however great the faith the Kents might have in her ability. As we have seen, he was a pioneer in the design and use of the obstetric forceps, but at the birth of Queen Victoria he was probably little more than a spectator. When natural processes go smoothly there is little that a doctor need do, save to allow them to continue. Such is the pattern of normal labour, and it is unlikely that Madame Siebold was to any extent troubled by the Duchess of Kent's confinement. Well enough was left alone, and the outcome was dramatically successful. The child was destined to be one of the greatest monarch's this country has ever had, and the crisis of succession was over.

Within a space of two months, therefore, three heirs to the throne had been born. One – the infant Charlotte – had been too premature to survive and had died a few hours later. Victoria had superseded George, son of the Duke and Duchess of Cambridge, as heir apparent, but George remained heir to the throne of Hanover, which was subject to Salic law, and which a woman could not inherit. By another remarkable coincidence, in this curious history of coincidences, he did so for only three days. On 27 May, seventy-two hours after the birth of Victoria, the Duchess of Cumberland was delivered of a son, also christened George, who was subsequently blinded in a riding accident as a boy, and became George, the Blind King of Hanover.

Although the succession was safe, the story was not quite over. If the Duke and Duchess of Clarence succeeded in having a child, that child would inherit the throne, despite the prior birth of Victoria.

In August 1819 William was writing to the Prime Minister, Lord Liverpool, to tell him that the Duchess was pregnant. 'It is now a fortnight since Halliday and myself had our suspicions; but within the last 3 days the symptoms that attended the Duchess in her last pregnancy have so fully appeared, that Halliday thinks it his duty to write by tomorrow's post to Sir Henry Halford on this most important event.' The Duke goes on, 'My anxiety to see the Duchess safe landed in England must be and is very great.'

He was right to stress 'safe landed' as events turned out. The Duke continued his letter with the significant sentence, 'I lament we cannot leave this place till the 15th instant and with the two visits I cannot put off to my two sisters, and with the week I have promised the Duchess to spend with her sister at Ghent, it will not be in our power to reach Calais before the 5th or 6th September.'

He was contemplating a journey similar to that undertaken by the Duchess of Kent in April, but it was to prove too much for Adelaide. On the way to the coast they visited the recently widowed Queen of Wurttemberg, the Duke's eldest sister, then his third sister, the Landgravine of Hesse-Homberg, and finally they stayed in

Ghent with Adelaide's sister, Ida, Duchess of Saxe-Weimar. On arrival at Calais, Adelaide collapsed and miscarried. Judging from her husband's 'suspicions' on 2 August, which presumably arose about mid-July, some weeks after her first missed period, the Duchess was probably about three months pregnant. This is the commonest time for a miscarriage, and it cannot be asserted with any confidence that the journey she undertook was responsible. However, considering the importance of the pregnancy to the Clarences and to the country, it was an injudicious journey to make at such a time. Moreover, the Duke of Clarence's experience of pregnancy was founded upon Mrs Jordan's ten successful ones. No doubt he was quite unaware that to undertake this journey to England as he did, might not be wise. Indeed his medical advisor, Dr Andrew Halliday, does not appear seriously to have demurred. The comparison of the Duchess of Kent's journey is so close, however, that is easy to appreciate how her pregnancy too might have come to grief, and altered the whole history of our country.

Surprisingly the Duke and Duchess of Clarence remained only a few days in Calais after her miscarriage, when 'seeing how Clarence disliked the French' they embarked and set sail for England. The sea was very rough, and the poor Duchess was obliged to spend some weeks in bed on her return to the country before she was well again.

They were not deterred, however, and Adelaide was again pregnant early in the following year. All seemed to be going well until she was two months away from the expected date of her confinement, when she was suddenly taken ill in a manner similar to her indisposition before the birth of her first child. Dr Halliday was sent for, and the following morning he summoned Sir Henry Halford and Sir William Knightly, the King's confidential medical advisor. The Regent, who had by now become George IV, and was hoping against hope that the Clarences would have a child, to put an end to the Kents' right to succession, sent to enquire about the health of the Duchess every day. The Duke of Clarence, too, was most attentive, and everyone hoped the indisposition would pass.

Premature labour threatened, however, although every effort was made to prevent it. The knockers on all the doors were muffled; straw was put down to deaden the sound of carriage wheels, but to no avail. At 5.30 p.m. on 10 December 1820 a female child was born. The official bulletin signed by Sir Henry Halford, Sir William Knightly and Dr Andrew Halliday stated, 'Her Royal Highness is as well as can be expected. The infant was born before its time about 6 weeks.'

The only Cabinet Minister present at the birth was Lord Chancellor Eldon who recorded in a letter that the child was 'a very small one at present; but the doctors seem to think it will thrive: and to the ears of your humble servant it appears to be noisy enough to show it has great strength'. Sir Henry Halford, however, was less confident: Henry Edward Fox recorded in his journal that Sir Henry 'will not answer for the safety of the little Princess Elizabeth 6 weeks from her proper time of being born'. But for a time she thrived and was christened Elizabeth Georgina Adelaide. 'It is to be a future Queen Elizabeth', recorded Lady Jerningham, 'but I trust less sanguinary.' The King was delighted that the Kents' nose was, after all, put out of joint, and agreed to the infant having the family name Elizabeth, a privilege which he had denied the Duke and Duchess of Kent on the christening of Victoria.

But Lady Jerningham's prediction was not to be. On 1 March, when three months old, the child was suddenly taken ill, and treatment was of no avail. She began to convulse, and died on Sunday, 3 March at 1 a.m. The press reported that 'Her Royal Highness the Duchess of Clarence has endured the great affliction of losing her infant child. The young Princess expired yesterday morning at 1 o'clock in a convulsive fit. She was taken ill on Thursday; it appears that the cause of death was an entanglement in the bowels.'

Yet another threat to the succession to the throne of the baby Victoria had been removed. One more was to come and go. On 8 April, 1822, the Duchess of Clarence had a further miscarriage, this time of twins. Thereafter although there were a number of reports of pregnancies, none was confirmed. Princess Victoria remained heir and in 1837 was to ascend the throne to reign as Queen for longer than any other monarch in our country's history.

9

Rumours of Royal Confinements

Before we leave the Hanoverian era, there are three rumours of royal intrigues leading to clandestine pregnancies that I should like to look at. The first involves George III himself and a beautiful Quakeress called Hannah Lightfoot.

There are a number of versions of this story, which is not surprising since the allegation of liaison between Hannah and the King did not appear until after his death in 1820. It is, let me say at the outset, quite without foundation, although Hannah and a number of others named in the story were real people who did live in London in the middle of the eighteenth century. Some of the events which are supposed, according to the story, to have involved the King, did actually take place, but George had nothing to do with them.

William J. Thoms, in a humorous account of the genesis of the story, which he published in 1867, says that he could trace no allusion to it in any historical, political or satirical work published in the King's lifetime. He adds the convincing comment that Walpole, 'whose industry in collecting gossip equalled the delight with which he disseminated it', was clearly totally ignorant of any such scandal, since he 'could never have known and kept a secret'.

The story, as it unfolded from several publications in the early nineteenth century, ran as follows: The *Monthly Magazine* of April 1821 published a letter from 'B'. 'All the world', it stated, 'is acquainted with the attachment of the late King to a beautiful Quakeress of the name of Wheeler. The lady disappeared, on the royal marriage, in a way that has always been interesting, because unexplained and mysterious.' In 'B's opinion the publication of further information in the magazine would 'doubtless be agreeable to many of your readers'.

A reply in the July number of the magazine by 'Warminsteriensis' reported that the lady was not called Wheeler at all but Hannah

Lightfoot, who had lived with her parents in a linen draper's shop at the corner of St James's market. She was often noticed by the Prince of Wales, as George then was, whilst he passed from Leicester House to St James's. The royal family became alarmed, and arranged to marry Hannah to Isaac Axford, an assistant to Barton, a grocer on Ludgate Hill, who saw Hannah when she came into the shop to buy groceries. Miss Chudleigh, later Duchess of Kingston, offered Isaac a considerable sum of money to undertake the marriage. They were together for only a short time when Hannah was 'taken off in a carriage and Isaac never saw her more'. He lived for many years as a respectable grocer in Warminster, where he related to 'Warminsteriensis' that he had presented a petition at St James's which had been ignored.

September brought a communication from another correspondent who denied that Isaac and Hannah ever cohabited, and alleged that 'she was taken away from the church doors the same day they were married and he never heard of her afterwards'. Moreover, the writer continued, Isaac was assistant to a grocer called Bolton, not Barton, and the sum of money he received was only a small one. Furthermore the King saw Hannah at his shop door when he was going to and from Parliament. Most dramatic of all, Isaac's petition had been presented to the King 'in the park on his knees' but without success.

'An enquirer', writing in October, agreed that the King had indeed been going to and from Parliament when he noticed Hannah. The marriage to Axford had been in Keith's Chapel in Curzon Street in 1754 after an elopement with him, but the 'general belief of her friends was that she was taken into keeping by Prince George' directly after the ceremony. 'Enquirer' had lately seen a half-pay cavalry officer from India, who knew a gentleman of the name of Dalton, who married a daughter of this Hannah Lightfoot by the King.

July 1822 brought a flood of details from 'TGH', in the course of which the beautiful Quakeress became Miss Wheeler again. TGH had the story 'from my relatives who were her father's neighbours' and therefore 'had peculiar means of knowing the facts'. The Prince saw Hannah on his way to the opera, which the royal family entered by a private door in Market Lane, and so passed by the Wheelers'

shop. Anyone who suggested he saw her as he went to Parliament
House and back, TGH indignantly asserted, obviously knew nothing
of that part of London. Through two mysterious agents of the
Prince, Jack M—— and Mrs H——, 'interviews were thus obtained
between the parties; and, on elopement, it was found that her
clothes and trinkets had been clandestinely removed'. TGH then
became less certain of his ground. 'It was generally reported' that
Hannah was kept at Lambeth, 'or some other village on the south
of the Thames', he wrote, but he had 'heard it said' that she lived
at Knightsbridge on a farm which 'supplied the royal family with
ass's milk' and which being away from the road and 'less than a
mile from the Palaces was well adapted for the purpose of private
visits'. He even had an ingenious explanation for the Wheeler/
Lightfoot confusion. 'Was not Mrs H——'s maiden name Lightfoot?' he asked and, since he clearly had no idea whether it was
or not, added, 'This might probably be ascertained by the register
of St Martin in the Fields; thus had some confusion arisen between
the two females in the elopement.'

But this simple solution to the problem of names would not do
for 'Warminsteriensis' who returned to the fray in September. 'It
is certain that the fair Quaker was Hannah Lightfoot, not Wheeler',
he wrote, and it was Axford's own niece who told him so. She also
told him a number of other things of great interest. After Hannah
and Isaac were married 'they cohabited for a fortnight or three
weeks, when she was one day called out from dinner and put into
a chaise and four and taken off'. According to the niece, 'it was
reported' that the Prince had several children by Hannah, 'one or
two of whom became generals in the army'.

But the stories of the supposed children of the union with the
King are no more in agreement than those of the weddings, abduc-
tions or liaisons which preceded them. 'Curiosus, Clapham', in the
Monthly Magazine of December 1822, stated that he had dealt with
Axford the grocer at the corner of the Old Bailey for nearly half
a century. There were 'a few children' he reported – one of whom
was in the army but never became a general officer.

A pamphlet published in 1824 reported that Hannah had been
taken under the protection of Prince George under an assumed
name, and was said to have had a daughter, who later married a

man called Dalton with an appointment in the East India Company. This 1824 pamphlet was entitled *An Historical Fragment Relative to Her Late Majesty Queen Caroline* and was appropriately anonymous. It went further than any account had done previously, by affirming Caroline's belief that the King and Hannah had been married, prior to his marriage to Queen Charlotte in 1761. It further alleged that Hannah did not die until after Queen Charlotte's first two children were born – thus effectively disinheriting the present King, George IV, and the Duke of York, and making the Duke of Clarence the rightful heir.

The pot was kept well and truly boiling with the publication in 1831 and 1832 of two scandalous accounts of alleged Court life, *Anonymous Authentic Records of the Court of England (1831–2)* and *The Secret History of the Court of England from the Accession of George III to the Death of George IV*. These were frankly imaginary libellous accounts of unsavoury Court activities, and the first included the statement that George III, as Prince of Wales, had married Hannah in the Curzon Street Chapel in 1759. (It had in reality been closed in 1754 and its records transferred to St George's, Hanover Square.) The sequence of events after the marriage was now reversed: the King's ministers induced Axford to go through a later ceremony of marriage with Hannah, and to take her off where the King, despite his efforts, could never find her. 'The King', the Authentic Recorder recorded, 'was greatly distressed to ascertain the fate of his much-loved and legally-married wife the Quakeress; and he entrusted Lord Chatham to go in disguise and endeavour to trace her abode.' The King was not the only distressed member of the royal family either! According to the Authentic Recorder Charlotte learnt his secret, and in 1765 insisted on being married again; Dr Wilmott, it was said, performed the ceremony by the King's order at Kew.

With Dr Wilmott coming into the story we learn at last what was behind this astonishing attack on the late King's integrity; a remarkable and very complex story it proved to be, admirably described by Patricia Storrar, in her book *George Rex* as 'one of the most extraordinary stories of *folie de grandeur* on record'.

The details concerned the George–Hannah relationship only obliquely, being directly involved with an attempt by Mrs Olivia

Wilmott Serres to prove that she was the daughter of the late Duke of Cumberland. Mrs Serres was in reality the daughter of Robert Wilmott and his wife Anna Maria. Robert Wilmott's brother was the Rev. J. Wilmott, Vicar of Barton-on-the-Heath in Warwickshire. He was, as far as is known, a blameless bachelor, but Olivia claimed that she was not his niece but his granddaughter. It was alleged that the Reverend Wilmott had married a beautiful Polish princess called Poniatowski, sister-in-law of the King of Poland. Their daughter, Olivia's mother, had captivated the Duke of Cumberland, who had married her secretly in 1767. Their elder daughter, Lavinia, carried on a desperate battle for recognition of her royal status and went around calling herself Princess of Cumberland and Duchess of Lancaster.

Dr Wilmott was the clergyman who was alleged to have remarried George III and Queen Charlotte at Kew in 1765. But not only that! It was later asserted, with the production of so-called documentary evidence, that he had solemnized the marriage of the Prince of Wales to Hannah in 1759. Unfortunately, one certificate 'authenticating' the wedding said that it had taken place at Kew on 17 April, and a further certificate that it had occurred at Peckham on 27 May. These documents were but a small part of a mass of forged 'evidence', produced in support of this preposterous claim that Olivia Serres and her daughter were of royal blood.

There was one unusual result, however. Since the 'evidence' of Lavinia's own aristocratic birth could not be substantiated, she attempted to provide proof of her other allegations, believing that if they were proved her own would be more favourably received. Accordingly she published a public appeal for information on the liaison between the late King and Hannah. She received an answer at the end of 1866 from a Mrs C. Nelson living in Knysna in the Cape of Good Hope, which contained the phrase 'I am the daughter of George Rex, the son of Hannah Lightfoot.'

Mrs Nelson was only repeating a belief which had existed in that part of Southern Africa for many years, and which probably persists still, despite an admirable refutation of it by Patricia Storrar in 1974. It was widely and strongly held that Mr George Rex, who lived for over forty years in the Cape, was the banished son of George III. Rex's biography by Sanni Metelerkamp, published in Cape

Town in 1955, purported to give the authentic story. The King was supposed to have given his son a number of keepsakes to take with him, to remind him of his heritage – a large watch, a gold seal bearing a cornelian, a gold locket containing a lock of His Majesty's hair, a Wedgwood medallion with the King's portrait on it, and a signet ring bearing the initials GR. The book contained an account of the supposed last interview between the father and son, at which the King told George Rex the truth of his birth but affirmed, nonetheless, his intention to banish him forever.

It became in the end a long tangled story perhaps best summed up in the words of William J. Thoms:

Once upon a time there was a fair Quaker whose name was Hannah Lightfoot. No, Anna Eleanor Lightfoot. No, Whitefoot. No, Wheeler.

Well, never mind what her name was; her father was a shoemaker who lived near Execution Dock, Wapping. No, he was a linen draper and lived at St James's market. No, that was her uncle.

But these are mere trifles. No doubt she had a name and lived somewhere.

Well, the Prince saw her as he went from Leicester House to St James's. No, that's wrong; it was as he went to the opera. No, you are both wrong; it was as he went to Parliament House!

Never mind where he saw her: he did see her and fell in love with her; and as neither his mother, the Princess Dowager, nor Lord Bute looked after him, and as he was then nearly 16 years old, he married her in 1754! No, that's not right, it was in 1759. But it does not matter when he married; he did marry her, at Keith's Chapel in Mayfair. No, it was at Peckham. No, it was at Kew.

No, that is all a mistake. Her royal lover never married her. Isaac Axford married her and left her at the chapel door, and never saw her after that. Yes, he did; they lived together for three or four weeks, and then she was carried away secretly, in a carriage and four but he never saw her after that.

Wrong again, it was the King from whom she was so strangely spirited away, and he was distracted; and sent Lord Chatham in disguise to hunt for her, and he could never find her.

No, that's all wrong. It was Axford who couldn't find her, who petitioned the King to give him back his wife at St James's. No, that was at Weymouth. No, it was on his knees in St James's Park as directed.

As Mr Thoms said, it became a waste of time to continue to repeat the contradictions. The legend is no longer believed, even George Rex, its last remnant, having had his real and humbler origin uncovered by Mrs Storrar. Indeed in her delightful book she separates fact from fiction admirably. Hannah Lightfoot, as she points out, was no myth, but was born on 12 October 1730 at Wapping-in-the-east. Her father died when she was five. Her mother was a Miss Wheeler whose brother, Henry Wheeler, had a linen draper's shop in Market Lane, near the Opera House. Hannah married Isaac Axford without the consent of her mother, and the marriage did take place in Keith's Chapel, Curzon Street on 11 December 1753. By marrying without her mother's consent, and being married by a priest, Hannah the Quakeress had infringed the rules of the Society of Friends, who disowned her in a Testament of Denial in January 1756. Hannah left Isaac soon after their wedding, and neither he nor her relations ever saw her again. Patricia Storrar believes it likely that she was indeed taken under the protection of an influential person, but nothing is known for certain. Isaac married again in 1759.

It is easy to see how, with a true story as its basis, the legend of the King's involvement might have begun, but it is astonishing that it blossomed as it did, long after his death.

George Rex, the so-called banished son, was in reality the son of John Rex, who was the third husband of his wife Sarah. Many of their antecedents are known. George became a notary public, and emigrated to the Cape in his thirties to find fame and fortune. He did so, becoming an influential and successful man, but one who never at any time claimed for himself royal blood.

The second rumoured confinement concerns Princess Sophia, the eleventh child of King George III and Queen Charlotte. As a child and young woman she was often unwell, although the precise nature of her illness or illnesses has not been determined. She certainly had periodic attacks of pain – 'spasms' was the word applied to them – but in addition to any physical disability she suffered, it seems probable that there was a psychological element too, for she enjoyed the status of a semi-invalid and the additional attention which this afforded her.

In common with her unmarried sisters, Sophia led an unusually

restricted life within the very rigid confines of the Court. Her opportunities for meeting young people of her own age were very few
indeed, and those she did meet were female. It is natural, therefore,
that she and her sisters would focus their interests on older men,
including their elder brothers. Each sister had a favourite brother
with whom she regarded herself as being 'very close'; in Sophia's
case her favourite was the Duke of Kent.

In the early 1800s the story began to be put about that Sophia
had become pregnant and had been delivered of a child. The delivery was said to have occurred at Weymouth in August, where the
court was spending its usual summer visit. The supposed father was
Major-General Thomas Garth, who was the King's favourite
equerry.

A less likely person to be the object of a susceptible young girl's
passion it would be difficult to imagine. Garth was short in stature,
and his face was disfigured by a large purple birth mark on his forehead and over one eye. Charles Greville called him 'a hideous old
devil, old enough to be her father, with a great claret mark on his
face'; but Greville did not regard this as any disqualification as the
supposed father of Sophia's child since, in his words, 'women fall
in love with anything'. The General had been in the King's service
for several years, and had known the Princess since she was eleven
years old. At the time of the alleged birth she was twenty-two, he
fifty-five.

The evidence that the Princess was infatuated with Garth is anything but strong. Morris Marples, the Princess's biographer,
quotes one of her ladies-in-waiting as saying of Sophia 'she could
not contain herself in his presence'. There is a veiled reference to
him in a letter from Princess Mary to the Prince of Wales in 1798:
'As for General Garth the purple light of love *toujours la même*', she
wrote. This can clearly mean anything and, as it stands, it cannot
be linked to Sophia.

Prior to the supposed confinement that is all we know. The next
hint comes in a letter to the Prince of Wales from Princess Amelia,
then aged seventeen, written in Weymouth and dated 8 August
1800. She wrote about 'the prospect of seeing our dear Sophia
restored to health very shortly' and went on to add, 'She is going
on well. Pray sweet love don't answer this, and when you come here

take no notice to high or lowe of having heard from me.' Marples considers that 'this secrecy, and Amelia's guarded language, would not have been necessary if Sophia's had been an ordinary illness'.

This is certainly one construction which can be put upon the phrase, although others can be surmised. Amelia may just have been forbidden to write to her brother, but could not refrain from doing so to tell him the news of his sister's improvement from an ordinary illness; or if there was any truth in Sophia's obsession with Garth, she, in her already invalid-prone state, may have been deeply disturbed emotionally by being forbidden to see him, from which episode she was now recovering. The letter is very slender evidence upon which to assert the birth of an illegitimate baby.

Several other references to the event appear in the writings of Sylvester Douglas, Lord Glenbervie. In 1801 he was writing in his diary about Sophia's 'extraordinary illness at Weymouth last Autumn' when 'she was attended by Sir Francis Milman'. Sir Francis was at the time Physician Extraordinary to the King's household, and was created a baronet that year. He was an influential, if in no sense distinguished, physician but he was not an accoucheur, and there can be no special significance attached to the fact that it was he who attended the Princess.

Glenbervie obtained his information from a variety of sources. One source was Lady Bath, who told him that the Mistress of the Robes had told her that the Princess had been 'brought to bed' nine months after having been left with Garth in the Upper Lodge at Windsor.

Christopher Hibbert, George IV's biographer, reporting this event, suggests that Sophia had been ill for a while, and had been moved from her normal house, the Lower Lodge at Windsor, to the Queen's Lodge. Here, since the King and Queen were in town, she found herself alone with Garth 'one summer's evening'. There is something imprecise in time about these accounts, however. If it had indeed been on a summer evening that Sophia and Garth were together, she would have been delivered well before the following August; moreover, if she had been delivered in early August, this does not correspond with Glenbervie referring to an extraordinary illness at Weymouth 'last Autumn'.

Another of Glenbervie's informants was the Princess of Wales, an unreliable witness if ever there was one. She said that the Princess Sophia was so ignorant as not to know that she was with child until the last moment – an unlikely thing in a twenty-two-year-old woman, who had brothers with numerous mistresses and children. Glenbervie asked Caroline if Sophia 'did not perceive anything had passed and if she could think it a matter of indifference and as unlikely to have consequences as blowing her nose'. That a twenty-two-year-old girl could not have been aware of the nature of the act and its possible consequences seems inconceivable, if such is the correct word!

The Princess of Wales's conversation with Lord Glenbervie then took an even less savoury turn. 'The Duke of Kent tells the Princess that the father is not Garth, but the Duke of Cumberland,' reported Glenbervie and added piously, 'How horrid.' The Duke of Kent, as we have seen already, was the favourite brother of Sophia, and it is most unlikely that he would have gossiped in this fashion to such an unreliable person as the Princess of Wales, with her delight in spreading rumour. Indeed Glenbervie, in his next paragraph, reported Caroline as saying that Princess Elizabeth also had had a child by Mr Carpenter, son of General Carpenter.

The story was told to the Princess by Miss Hayman 'who had it from the midwife'. It was a highly melodramatic account of a midwife being visited secretly by two accoucheurs in a closed carriage. For £500 she agreed to undertake a secret delivery, and was taken to an unknown house in a closed sedan chair. Her labouring patient was heavily veiled, but, whilst she was asleep, the midwife could not restrain herself from lifting the veil and looking at her face. The midwife went to St James's on the next King's birthday, scrutinized every face she saw, and recognized the Princess Elizabeth 'without a possibility of doubt or hesitation'. This preposterous story indicates, as well as anything could, what little reliance could be placed on Princess Caroline's word.

Others later repeated the assertion that a child had been born to Sophia, but none produced evidence of it. Many years later when the scandal erupted Greville wrote that there was no doubt that Garth was the father. 'The King never knew it,' wrote Greville. 'The court was at Weymouth when she was big with child. She was said to be dropsical and suddenly recovered. They told the old King that she had been cured by roast beef and this he swallowed' – the story, it is to be presumed, not the beef!

Among this repetitive hearsay evidence, however, there is one curious letter of Sophia's which has not yet been satisfactorily explained, nor indeed has any innocent construction ever been advanced for it.

In December 1800 Sophia wrote to Lady Harcourt, promising to be prudent in her conduct in the future, and thanking her for kindness and consideration during her troubles. She wrote, too, that however unjust 'the reports' she had 'partially myself to thank for them'. She went on to say what a serious thing it was that 'a little trifle will slur a woman's character forever'.

What could Sophia possibly have meant by that? She could not in all conscience have been referring to a baby as 'a little trifle'. She might, however, have meant that a girlish infatuation with Garth was the 'little trifle', which led to 'reports' of a pregnancy and labour, which she was powerless to refute. Her language, when we study it carefully, is unusual. She does not say that she has herself to blame, but to 'thank', suggesting foolishness not guilt. This could easily be construed as meaning that the public exhibition she had made of herself, in her obsession with Garth, had led to the unjust 'reports' of her pregnancy, not, it will be noticed, to its reality. Had Lady Harcourt known of the pregnancy and delivery, as she must if she was being thanked for her help at that difficult time, Sophia would not have referred to 'reports, however unjust they are' in this way. In the event, she had been a very foolish young lady over a far older man, and the 'reports' which resulted she was obliged to put up with since, as a member of the royal family, she could not openly defend herself. One certain statement which the letter contains, which has received scarcely any comment, is that the stories going round were untrue.

Not the least strange aspect of the whole affair, if the stories were true, is the subsequent treatment of Major-General Garth by the royal family, and his relationship to a young protégé called Thomas Garth. The General remained *persona grata* with the King and Queen and royal family throughout his whole life. He was promoted at the proper time to Lieutenant-General and then to General. He was appointed to the household of the Princess Charlotte, the heir

apparent, which would surely not have been a likely thing to happen
had he seduced Sophia. The Princess Amelia stayed in his home
near Weymouth during her last illness, and was very kindly received. On retirement, he was specially commended by George III
for his exemplary conduct.

These facts are very hard to explain. Marples suggests that he
and Sophia were secretly married, but this would not excuse his
conduct in the eyes of the court. If he were an acceptable suitor,
there was no need for secrecy; if he were not, he had grossly
offended the King and Queen by leading their daughter astray.

A possible explanation which has been advanced is that the Princess did have a child, and, although Garth was not the father, he
allowed it to be believed that he was. Such a supposition is more
in keeping with his remaining in favour at court than any other –
except of course the simple explanation that there never had been
a baby. It would explain, in part, his continued interest in young
Thomas Garth. There was such a boy who joined the army in 1816,
eventually rising to the rank of Captain. He saw the General regularly, and is reported to have seen the Princess Sophia regularly too,
on occasions when she sent away all the servants. If all the servants
indeed were sent away this too was assumption. The General took
quite an interest in the boy's career, and on one occasion wrote
to the Duke of Kent, commanding the army in Ireland, to request
that 'his protégé' as he called him, who was ill in Sligo, might be
granted leave, as soon as he was well enough to travel.

The scandal blew up in March 1829, when Thomas Garth filed
an affidavit, which, in effect, said that in return for valuable documents which had recently come into his possession, General Taylor
(the late Queen's private secretary) had agreed to pay his debts
and settle upon him an annuity for life. General Taylor denied any
agreement, however, and refused to pay. For a while there was much
unpleasantness, and the old story of the Duke of Cumberland being
the father was resurrected. Eventually it blew over, and Thomas
Garth vanished to avoid his creditors.

The story pursued General Garth to his death-bed. Charles
Greenwood, a friend of General Herbert Taylor, wrote to the
General on 18 November 1829 to tell him of General Garth's death
'last night' in his 'son's' house in Grosvenor Place. According to

Greenwood, Garth embraced his 'son' and told him he had left him all he had. 'This intelligence', Greenwood wrote, 'comes to me from a person who was present at the scene.' But the house in Grosvenor Place was the General's, not Thomas's, and he did not leave the boy all his money either; this was divided equally between his nephew Captain Garth, RN, and his 'son', with a small annuity to his sister, and bequests to servants.

On reviewing the evidence, the explanation which satisfies all its contradictions best is this. Princess Sophia cherished a hopeless love for Garth, and in the phraseology of the time 'went into a decline' as a result; her illness at Weymouth in the Summer of 1800 followed. She did not have a child by Garth, however. On the other hand, he did have an illegitimate son, whom he was unable to acknowledge perhaps because of his position in the royal household. This accounts for the letters Princess Amelia and Princess Mary wrote to the Prince of Wales, and Sophia's own letter to Lady Harcourt, for the royal family's continued approval of the General, and his continued interest in Thomas Garth. It ignores, of course, the assertions of the Princess of Wales, but these remain statements without foundation from a lady renowned for her love of spreading scandal about the royal family – a very dubious witness.

Princess Sophia was, however, not the only member of the royal family, in the reign of George III, against whom the charge of giving birth to an illegitimate baby was levelled. The other was Caroline, Princess of Wales, and in this case the charge was formally investigated by a Royal Commission, an event generally referred to as The Delicate Investigation.

In 1801 Caroline moved to Montague House, Blackheath, where she entertained a curious collection of guests in her own outlandish manner. Sir Walter Scott, Sir Thomas Lawrence, the artist who was painting her portrait, George Canning, Lord Hood and several of the royal duke's, contrasted strangely with sea captains and others of humble origins. To all she adopted a bold, flirtatious, familiar manner, which naturally led to a good deal of gossip. She was indiscreet, displaying a brash vulgarity and a complete disregard for convention or good manners. She delighted in making the most outspoken remarks, whether true or false, purely for their effect; though her fantasy world was so bizarre, that she may at times have believed that what she said was true.

To her more cultured guests her behaviour was disgraceful or offensive. Lady Hester Stanhope called her a nasty, vulgar, impudent woman. Others believed her to be insane, and her behaviour on occasions bordered on the deranged. Lady Hester, who was clearly exasperated and repelled by her, wrote, 'Oh what an impudent woman was that P——ss W; she was a down right ...... She had a Chinese figure in one of her rooms at Blackheath that was wound up like a clock and used to perform the most extraordinary movements.' And it was not only the Chinese figure that performed extraordinary movements. 'How the sea captains used to colour up when she danced about exposing herself like an opera girl ... she was so low, so vulgar,' said Lady Hester, whilst Lady Charlotte Campbell described her behaviour as 'gross ribaldry'.

Caroline also caused much gossip by her habit of taking one of the men off with her alone to the blue room, and remaining with him for hours at a time. It caused her not the slightest concern that such a practice could be thoroughly misunderstood, and lead to much scandal.

A curious habit, which was to lead directly to the investigation of her conduct, was that of adopting abandoned or orphaned babies, and putting them in the custody of foster parents nearby. One of these children was William Austin. Caroline made many conflicting statements about the origins of William Austin, the most likely being that he was the son of Samuel and Sophia Austin, a country couple who had come to London to find employment. Samuel's health was indifferent, however, and he could not keep a job for any length of time. Sophia came to Montague House with the boy, looking for charity, and the footman whom she met there suggested that Her Royal Highness would probably be prepared to adopt the boy, if his mother would permit it. When the Princess saw the child, a short time later, she was captivated by him and, with his mother's agreement, he went to live with her. He grew up an unpleasant, extremely spoilt boy, whom Lady Hester Stanhope described as 'a little nasty vulgar brat', 'a little urchin' and 'so ugly'.

The Princess afterwards invented different stories of his origin, insisting that he was not William Austin at all, but someone else, whose identity would remain secret and die with her. Later she embroidered this account, and said that he was the natural child of Prince Louis Ferdinand of Prussia, and had been brought to this country and substituted for another child of the same age, whom she had contrived to obtain.

Into this remarkable ménage were introduced Rear Admiral Sir Sidney Smith, the hero of the siege of Acre, and Sir John and Lady Douglas, his close friends. Sir John had been a colonel of marines, and had served at Acre with Sir Sidney, and at the period in question all three lived together in the same house. The Douglases were 'persons of low origin and coarse habits', according to the historian Greenwood's description of them, but they soon became extremely friendly with the Princess. They and Sir Sidney were frequent and regular visitors for a year or more, and their relationship with Caroline was a close one.

The attraction of the Douglases ultimately began to fade, but they so persisted in their attention to the Princess that it became necessary to ask them to stop calling at Montague House. Lady Douglas, in high dudgeon, began spreading scandalous stories about the Princess, and in turn began to receive anonymous, insulting letters, which she believed Caroline had sent to her; one contained an obscene drawing of Lady Douglas and Sir Sidney.

Towards the end of 1805 Sir John and his wife laid serious allegations against the Princess before the Duke of Sussex, who passed them on to the Prince of Wales. Eventually, after much consultation, it was decided that the whole matter of her conduct should be the subject of enquiry by Lords Grenville, Ellenburgh, Erskine and Spencer, with the Solicitor-General, Sir Samuel Romilly, to advise them. In the early summer of 1806 the commission began its work.

The charges placed before them were that Her Royal Highness was the mother of William Austin, and had been intimate with a number of men, including Rear-Admiral Sir Sidney Smith and a Captain Manby, RN.

The commission questioned a large number of witnesses, including nearly all the Princess's servants, and several prominent persons who were regular visitors at Montague House. Lady Douglas gave evidence that Caroline had told her that she slept with men whenever she felt like it, and could not understand why Lady Douglas did not do the same. Caroline had become pregnant, Lady Douglas said, and had decided on the pretext of taking babies into her home, so that no one would be surprised when her own was born and another appeared. Lady Douglas believed that the Rear-Admiral was the father of the Princess's child but was not certain. Lady Douglas was herself pregnant at the time, and the Princess had shown the greatest interest in the approaching confinement, and had asked if she could be present at the birth, since she had never seen a child born. Her notion of the events during a confinement seemed strange, since she promised Lady Douglas that she would bring with her a tambourine and a bottle of port to encourage her during the labour!

Other evidence pointing to the Princess having been pregnant and later confined was given by Sir John Douglas and several of the servants; much of it, however, was of a very flimsy nature. According to Sir John 'she appeared to us to be with child'. Frances Lloyd, a coffee-room woman in the Princess's household, reported that when a doctor had visited her, whilst she was in bed with a cold, he had asked if the Prince ever came to the house, because he had noticed that the Princess was pregnant. William Cole, one of two servants who came to the Princess's service after a long period with the Prince of Wales, presumably to spy on her and report to the Prince, said that Her Royal Highness was very big during the summer of 1802, but was later her usual shape again.

Many statements were made about men having been seen in the house very early in the morning or very late at night. The Douglas's servant, Mrs Lampert, gave evidence that Sir Sidney Smith used to walk in the garden late at night with Her Royal Highness; sometimes Sir Sidney would creep out of the Douglas's house after they had gone to bed, and his bed would not have been slept in the following morning. William Cole had surprised Caroline and Sir Sidney sitting close together on a sofa in a compromising position. Cole had noticed both Sir Thomas Lawrence and Captain Manby also with the Princess a great deal. Robert Bidgood, who, like Cole, had spent years working for the Prince of Wales before entering the Princess's service, confirmed that Sir Sidney had been seen in the house very early in the morning, before anyone had been admitted by the footman. Bidgood believed that Captain Manby often slept in the house, and he had once seen him kissing the Princess.

Much other evidence, from less suspicious sources, appeared to refute some of these accusations. The Hon. Mrs Lyle, Bedchamber Woman to Her Royal Highness, said emphatically that she did not believe that the Princess had been pregnant. She admitted, however, that Caroline had a highly flirtatious manner, and said, in particular, that her behaviour in public with Captain Manby was not appropriate for a married woman. Although the Princess had spent several hours alone with a number of gentlemen, this type of behaviour was in her nature.

The doctor, who was supposed to have told Frances Lloyd that the Princess was pregnant, denied that he had ever said anything of the kind. Sir Francis Milman, the royal physician, said that he had noticed no evidence that Caroline was pregnant. Sir Sidney Smith and Captain Manby indignantly denied any impropriety. Sir Thomas Lawrence admitted that during his work on the Princess's portrait he had slept in the house, but never had he been alone with her behind locked doors. Several servants, who had been in the Princess's service for years, had noticed no conduct of the kind that the Douglases, Cole and Bidgood alleged.

The commission reported to the King on 14 July 1806 in these terms:

We are happy to declare that there is no foundation whatever for believing that the child (William Austin) is the child of Her Royal Highness ... a fact so fully contradicted and by so many witnesses ... that we cannot think it entitled to the smallest credit.

The Commission went on to declare, however, that the evidence they had considered contained:

Other particulars concerning the conduct of Her Royal Highness such as must especially, considering her exalted rank and station, necessarily give occasion to very unfavourable interpretations ... particularly the examinations of Robert Bidgood, William Cole, Frances Lloyd and Mrs Lyle ... witnesses who cannot, in our judgement, be suspected of any unfavourable bias, and whose veracity in this respect we have seen no grounds to question.... We think the circumstances to which we now refer, particularly those stated to have passed between Her Royal

Highness and Captain Manby, must be credited until they receive decisive contradiction, and if true are justly entitled to the most serious consideration.

The Prince of Wales's obsession to have his marriage to Caroline dissolved was so well known that it seems strange that Bidgood and Cole, who had been in his service for so many years, prior to joining her household, should have been described as without suspicion of any unfavourable bias. Similarly it is odd that Frances Lloyd, whose testimony concerning the doctor's statement of Caroline's pregnancy he had flatly denied, could be considered one 'whose veracity we have seen no grounds to question'.

Subsequent events in the Princess's lifetime suggest very strongly indeed that, although William Austin was probably not her child, impropriety of the grossest kind almost certainly took place in her home at Blackheath. Later during the years 1814 to 1820, when she was living abroad, her scandalous behaviour, crass bad manners, flagrant disregard of convention, and in particular the disgraceful and open liaison with her majordomo Bartolomeo Pergami led to a further investigation of her conduct by the Milan Commission of 1818, and her trial in the House of Lords in 1820. Neither by the Milan Commission, nor during her trial, however, was a further charge of bearing an illegitimate child made against her.

10

Victoria and Albert

George IV died in 1830, and his brother, the Duke of Clarence, aged sixty-five, succeeded him as William IV. He reigned for only seven years, and when Victoria became Queen upon his death, on 20 June 1837, she was only eighteen years and one month old. Her many confinements were to be free from serious trouble, but they were to have, in the words of the *British Medical Journal*, 'no small degree of medical importance'.

Following her accession, a suitable marriage, whilst in no sense a matter of urgency, was clearly one of importance, which should be arranged before very long. Her mother, the Duchess of Kent, had never been in any doubt who her future husband should be. Albert, Prince of Saxe-Coburg, the Duchess's nephew, had been her choice since he was a child, and Victoria's German uncles, Ernest, Duke of Saxe-Coburg, and Leopold, King of the Belgians, were of the same mind. William IV, however, was not. He had no liking for the Duchess of Kent, the House of Coburg, nor the Belgian King, and strongly favoured a marriage with one of the two sons of the Prince of Orange. When Victoria was seventeen, William had arranged that the Prince and his sons, William and Alexander, should visit England with the firm intention of agreeing a marriage between one of the boys and Victoria. But at the same time, the Duchess of Kent had invited Duke Ernest and his sons, Edward and Albert, with the same idea in mind. King William's request that the Duchess of Kent withdraw her invitation was firmly rejected, and so both parties arrived within a few days of each other.

Victoria's own preference was plainly for the Coburgs, of whom Albert was the favourite, and William and Alexander of Orange appear to have had no attraction for her at all. By the time Albert's visit came to an end, he and she had developed an understanding, and Victoria wrote to her uncle, King Leopold, indicating her acceptance of Albert as a suitable husband.

She was not then in love with Albert, however; that had to wait until their second meeting, three years later. So much had his physical attractions increased when they next met, that the Queen was captivated by his tall, slim, handsome elegance. Only five days after their reunion, she proposed marriage to him and was instantly accepted. They embraced 'over and over again'. 'How I adore him', she wrote in her diary; 'I feel the happiest of human beings.'

Victoria's marriage to Prince Albert took place on 10 February 1840. She did not have to wait long before becoming pregnant. The Queen was ultimately to bear her first child two or three weeks sooner than anticipated, on 22 November that year, and she must therefore have conceived only a month after her wedding.

The prospect of childbearing had not been pleasant for Victoria. She had described it in her diary as 'the only thing I dread', and the possibility of having to endure it many times was something which she found particularly disturbing. Her demeanour during the early months of her first pregnancy, however, suggested that she had overcome her distaste, at least for a while. She was clearly in high spirits, and was not prepared to restrict her activity any more than was necessary. She gave a large ball and danced so often that Lord Holland expressed some concern that 'if he had been a nurse or man-midwife' he would not have approved.

Before her pregnancy was halfway through she had to contend with a complication of an alarming and extraordinary kind – an attempt upon her life.

On 10 June at 6.00 p.m. she and Prince Albert had driven out of Buckingham Palace and were proceeding up Constitution Hill in a small open carriage; they had barely travelled a hundred yards, when a man standing on the footpath on the side of the carriage where the Prince was seated, raised a gun and fired. The Prince had actually noticed him waiting there and had seen him raise his arm, but was not able to distinguish what was in his hand nor what his intention was. The shot deafened the royal couple, for it had been fired from a distance of only a few yards. The carriage stopped.

The Prince turned instantly to his wife to make sure that she was all right and to calm her. The man raised his pistol and fired again. This time the Queen saw his intention and ducked down in the carriage as passers-by, realizing at last what was happening, set upon the assailant.

Unhurt, and with great presence of mind, but not without considerable alarm, the Queen and the Prince drove on to the Duchess of Kent's residence at Ingestre House; later they continued through the Park, 'to show the public ... we had not lost confidence in them' and to give Victoria some air.

The Prince's main anxiety, of course, was that fright should not precipitate premature labour, or 'prove injurious to Victoria in her present state'. Fortunately a pregnancy of eighteen weeks duration is not easily disturbed. So far from being incommoded, the Queen received an upsurge of popular feeling, and was received with great enthusiasm by a large crowd which had gathered as the news spread. Public demonstrations of sympathy and loyalty continued for many weeks thereafter.

Victoria's pregnancy gave no further cause for anxiety, although she and her attendants must many times have remembered that it had been in the same month of November, twenty-three years earlier, that the Princess Charlotte had died in childbirth and her son with her. Elizabeth Longford records that, after the funeral of the aged Princess Augusta, the Queen's aunt, Prince Albert went with his wife to Claremont to take her mind off such gloomy events. A startling rumour arose that Victoria was expecting to die in childbirth. It was said that she was refurnishing the room, in which Charlotte had been delivered, exactly as it had been on her death in 1817, and that once this had been accomplished, Victoria too would follow her to the grave.

A morbid preoccupation with death can indeed be a serious matter for a pregnant woman. But her medical advisors did not allow any concern she might have felt to go beyond reasonable bounds. She was reassured in a most wholesome, down-to-earth fashion that her cousin had died because her resistance was undermined by constant blood-letting, a starvation diet and lack of exercise! As we have seen, there is some evidence to support the view that Charlotte suffered from injudicious bleeding, whilst her diet was more restrictive than it need have been. Lord Melbourne insisted that the Hanoverians needed a lot to eat and plenty of wine to drink, and Victoria evidently had no difficulty in conforming to these instructions.

Those who had the responsibility for the Queen's care during her confinement were Sir James Clark, her Physician in Ordinary, and Dr Locock, her first Physician Accoucheur, who was assisted by Dr Ferguson and Mr Bagden, with Mrs Lilly as the monthly nurse.

Sir James Clark was a Scot from Banffshire, who had originally embarked upon a career in law, which he had practised for a while. Not finding this profession very much to his liking, he abandoned it and began to study medicine. His medical career was to be eventful and successful, to say the least. After becoming a member of the College of Surgeons of Edinburgh in 1809, he joined the navy, only to have his first two ships sink beneath him. Later, in 1817, he obtained his degree of MD at Edinburgh University, and for some years thereafter practised as a physician in Rome. Whilst making a study of the effects of climate on disease, he met Prince Leopold, afterwards King of the Belgians, who not only made him his physician, but also obtained for him the appointment as physician to the Duchess of Kent. When Victoria became Queen, he was made Physician in Ordinary, and became a baronet in 1837. Despite the important supervisory role he was to enjoy at her confinement, midwifery was not, it seems, his strong point. He was guilty of an initial error of diagnosis when called upon to give an opinion on Lady Flora Hastings, a young unmarried lady at court, who had developed a large abdominal tumour from which she was later to die. The lump had caused some gossip that she was pregnant, which Clark at first confirmed, although he was later to state correctly that she was not. His mistake, and his unsympathetic handling of an innocent young patient, gained him a great deal of unpopularity, although he remained in favour with Victoria.

Charles Locock, later to be Sir Charles, came from Northampton. He obtained the degree of MD, also in Edinburgh, in 1821, and thereafter devoted himself to the study of midwifery. He quickly built up a large and successful private practice, and gave lectures at St Bartholomew's Hospital. Later he was made a Fellow of the Royal College of Physicians and became a member of the staff of the

Westminster Lying-in Hospital, He was principally a practical man, whose knowledge of his subject was thorough and complete, and he was therefore an admirable choice for such an awesome responsibility. No Queen of England had been confined for more than fifty-seven years, since Queen Charlotte had been delivered of her last child in August 1783.

Robert Ferguson, who supported Dr Locock, was a Scot who received his schooling and some of his medical training in London. After holding several medical posts of a varied nature at home and abroad he devoted himself to the practice of obstetrics, and was also appointed to the staff of the Westminster Lying-in Hospital, and was made Professor of Obstetrics at King's College, which had been founded in 1831. He received his royal appointment as Physician Accoucheur to Queen Victoria in 1840, and was to assist Dr Locock at the births of all Victoria's children.

Surprisingly little is known about Mrs Lilly: even her Christian name seems to have eluded the nursing historians. After attending all Victoria's confinements she enjoyed a long retirement, and she was eighty-eight when she last saw the Queen. She died in Camberwell, aged ninety-two, on 26 April 1882, and was buried in Highgate Cemetery.

However eminent and skilful doctors and midwives might have been at that time, they were almost wholly dependent on nature. In particular, they were dependent upon the uterus working efficiently during the first stage of labour, so that the delivery could be accomplished within a reasonable time, and before the mother or the child could suffer. If this stage became prolonged, there were no safe means, such as we now possess, by which anyone could expedite it. In the event, Queen Victoria's first labour was as straightforward as anyone could have hoped.

She awoke in some discomfort during the night of 21 November 1840. The expected date of her confinement was not for a further fortnight or more, but such a date was only an approximation, and it seemed likely that labour had begun. Albert was sound asleep and was wakened only with some difficulty. He at once informed Sir James Clark, who despatched a message for Dr Locock. He in turn arrived by 4.00 a.m., and confirmed that the Queen was indeed in labour and everything was normal. Ten hours after his arrival, at 1.10 p.m. on 22 November, a daughter was born, later to be christened Victoria and known as Vicky.

Dr Locock, who must have felt that everything was going perfectly, was clearly a little taken aback, and said, 'Oh Madam, it is a princess.' 'Never mind,' was the reply, 'the next will be a prince.'

Of course, Victoria and Albert had hoped for a boy, but such is the rapidity of adjustment on such occasions, that the Prince too was disappointed 'for a moment only'.

The customary practice at the birth of an heir to the throne had been departed from, on the Queen's special request. She had, not surprisingly, displayed some distaste at the number of people who had traditionally been present in the birth chamber. The Prince, Dr Locock and Mrs Lilly were her only attendants in the room itself, although in the adjoining room, the door to which was left ajar, many others were assembled – the Archbishop of Canterbury, the Bishop of London, several cabinet ministers, Sir James Clark and the other doctors. Sir James went into the delivery room at once when the child was born, and as soon as the umbilical cord was divided she was brought out to be inspected by the waiting officials.

There was of course general rejoicing. Despite all the shadows which the spectre of the Princess Charlotte had cast on the event, here at last was a live daughter born of a normal confinement.

The Lancet reported the event for its medical readers in self-satisfied terms:

DELIVERY OF THE QUEEN
and the
BIRTH OF A PRINCESS

We have to congratulate our readers on the safe delivery of HER MAJESTY, without any deviation from nature that could injure either the illustrious mother or her daughter. It appears from official circulars, bulletins and other sources that HER MAJESTY was in perfect health on Friday, that the pains came out early on the morning of the 21st and that the PRINCESS was born at 10 minutes to 2 o'clock p.m. The presentation was natural, and the throes of travail terminated happily in 10 hours.

Victoria's safe delivery was not, according to *The Lancet*, solely due to the collective efforts of the whole medical profession; 'It must be ascribed', the journal wrote, in as nearly an indelicate allusion as would then have been possible, 'partly to her well modelled form ... but in no small degree, we believe, to the recent improvements and progress in medical science.'

So the first of many confinements was safely over. It is a medical axiom that a normal confinement occurs only in retrospect. When it is all over and the child is safely in the cot one may say 'that *was* a normal confinement'. There can be many a slip between the cup of labour and the lip of safe delivery as the tragedy of Princess Charlotte had shown only too well. The Queen's confinement had occurred a little earlier than expected, true (the wet nurse was still at her home in the Isle of Wight and had to be sent for immediately); the child was a girl, to be sure, but the next would be a boy; and the infant was perhaps frail enough to cause concern for a time. But when all was said and done it had been a great success.

The doctors and other attendants were rewarded for their efforts – Dr Locock with £1,000, Dr Ferguson £800, Mr Bagden £500. The wet nurse, a doctor's wife from – appropriately – Cowes, also received £1,000 plus a pension of £300 a year!

The Queen's recovery was rapid and apparently complete. Her fears of child-bearing had in no way been diminished, however, and her biographer, Cecil Woodham-Smith, has suggested that the confinement had in reality been a considerable emotional shock for her. Victoria certainly referred again to her dislike of the prospect of having a large family when she wrote to her uncle, King Leopold, in January 1841. She spoke of what a burden it was to go through pregnancy and labour 'very often', how men were unfeeling in their view of child-bearing, and of her belief that no one could really wish her to be the mother of a large family.

But as many wives have found to their chagrin, it is possible for some of them to become pregnant all too easily. By the spring of 1841 she knew she was pregnant again, and she resented it. She was eventually to be confined in early November, less than a year after her first delivery, so her conception must have dated from the middle of February, which was almost the earliest possible moment.

She was less tolerant of her pregnancy and its discomforts this time, and bouts of depression worried her. Nor was she in good spirits, being out of sorts and wretched in herself, besides being anxious about the health of her daughter, Vicky, who had begun to lose weight. As the Queen's pregnancy advanced, there was concern that labour might begin even more prematurely than the first one. An episode of threatened premature labour did occur in early October, more than four weeks away from her due date, and there was another later in the month. When the Queen saw Dr Locock, on 26 October, he seemed to think that labour might not be far away, but could not be sure. This uncertainty did not make the Queen any happier, and her depression and low spirits continued. By the beginning of November she was so uncomfortable, and so full of foreboding, that she could not say properly whether she thought her labour was beginning or not since she 'had had so many false alarms'.

Early in the morning of 9 November, however, there seemed little doubt. Mrs Lilly sent at once for Dr Locock, and after a labour which, by Victoria's own description, was 'really very severe', she gave birth to a large healthy son at 10.58 a.m. He was christened Albert Edward and was to reign, many years later, as Edward VII.

Perhaps there had still been some uncertainty in Dr Locock's mind as to whether labour was fully established that morning, or perhaps, as some said, the Prince delayed too long in sending out the information about the imminent confinement to the officers of State. At all events several of those who should have been in the ante-room of the birth chamber, including the Lord President of the Council and the Archbishop of Canterbury, did not arrive in time.

The Queen had clearly been very disturbed by this confinement. The distress of a patient in labour is, of course, not easy to assess. It is common knowledge that some people bear pain more easily and less complainingly than others. The intensity of a person's discomfort is something only they can know. Circumstances do moreover infuence pain reactions, and someone who is elated, if only temporarily, by some pleasant event will feel pain sensations less during that time, whereas someone who is downcast and disturbed will often feel the pain unusually severely. Victoria's frame of mind throughout her pregnancy had been one of resentment that she was pregnant at all, and particularly so soon after her first confinement.

She found it barely tolerable that she could not enjoy her youth, her marriage and her adoring husband because of her perpetually pregnant state. It is not surprising that her pains were felt to be worse than before and her labour 'very severe'. The labour was not a long one, but neither had the first one been. But it was as much as she could bear, even to produce a son. Without Prince Albert, who was an enormous comfort and had sustained her during her worst moments, she did not know what she would have done. It is not to be wondered at that her return to normal health was slower than after the birth of her daughter.

But she was a person of resilience, and towards the end of 1842 she was able calmly to accept the realization of her third pregnancy. It was barely eighteen months since her son's birth but she had been able to regain her composure and recover her vitality. She and Albert were intensely happy, which was mainly responsible for her more placid acceptance of yet another child. She had spirit enough, nonetheless, to repeat to Leopold that a child every year was not her wish. With her mental attitude altogether more tranquil, the pregnancy was more tolerable and her labour uncomplicated. On 25 April 1843 a second princess was born, and later christened Alice. The Prince, as always, was there to give his support and comfort.

The Queen's reaction to the pregnant state, however, was never one of tolerant acceptance for long. She was upset by the restriction it put upon her, preventing her indulging in her particular pleasures of dancing and riding. As the sovereign, who was always at the centre of everything, she was the target of speculators wondering if she was pregnant, noticing her increasing girth, discussing when she might be confined, if it would be twins, and many other associations of pregnancy, which gossips find so irresistible. She was quite literally confined by pregnancy, repressed, unable to express her real self and seldom at ease.

Despite all this, there was to be no occasion during the next seven years, when she would be in the non-pregnant state for longer than the one and a half years which had preceded her third confinement. Her fourth child Alfred was born on 6 August 1844, Helena on 25 May, 1846, Louise on 18 March 1848 and Arthur on 1 May 1850. Leopold, her eighth child, was born on 7 April 1853; almost three years had passed since the birth of Arthur, which was easily the

longest interval up to that time between any of the Queen's confinements. Her last child was not to arrive for another four years,
when Beatrice was born on 14 April 1857.

All these confinements were free from abnormality, but the birth
of Prince Leopold in 1853 was in one respect a *cause célèbre*: chloroform was administered for the relief of her discomfort.

Anaesthesia had first been used in medicine only a little more
than ten years earlier, in 1842. Dr Crawford Long, a country practi-
tioner in Georgia in the United States of America, had given ether
successfully to relieve the pain of surgical operations. Two years
later William Morton, a Boston dentist, extracted a tooth under
ether anaesthesia, and later that year Horace Wells, a dentist in
Hertford, Connecticut, had a tooth extraction under nitrous-oxide
gas and was delighted by the experience. Barely a week after the
news of these events reached England, in December 1846, Robert
Liston, the famous surgeon, did a successful operation under ether,
and a Mr Robertson, a dentist, also used it for the painless extraction
of a tooth.

In Edinburgh, Dr James Young Simpson realized the possible
application of these substances to midwifery, although he was uncertain about the effects they might have on the contractions of the
uterus. On 9 January 1847 he administered ether to a patient with
a contracted pelvis, and was able, without pain, to insert his hand
right inside the uterus, grasp the child's leg and pull it into the pelvis
to assist delivery. The ether did not appear to affect contractions
of the uterus, but Simpson realized that as an anaesthetic agent it
was not ideal, on account of the irritation caused to the throat and
air passages during its inhalation and the large amounts of it which
were necessary.

He and his two assistants, Dr Keith and Dr Mathews Duncan,
used a small amount of chloroform on themselves, and were first
reduced to hilarity, then to a soporific state. In November 1847
Simpson used chloroform, to dramatic effect, on a doctor's wife for
a normal confinement, and the day of pain relief in labour had
dawned. It provoked, as we saw in Chapter 1, violent opposition
on moral grounds. The use of anaesthetics for childbirth without
complications was denounced from pulpits, scripture was invoked
by both sides to support their arguments and Simpson was the

target for much invective. Fortunately, he was more than a match for his adversaries, and when his cause received royal support his case was virtually won.

The Queen was in many ways an ideal subject for anaesthesia. The pain which she had suffered so severely and on so many occasions could now be relieved, and Victoria was quick to welcome a means of escape from her recurrent ordeal. Chloroform was used in her eighth labour, being administered by Dr John Snow, who was the most skilful exponent of its use in Britain at that time. The event was clearly worthy of special mention, and *The British Medical Journal* gave it such emphasis in its issue of 15 April.

On Thursday, the 7th instant, at half past one p.m. the Queen was safely delivered of a prince. This announcement has, we feel sure, inspired among all classes feelings of interest and sincere gladness; but there are circumstances connected with the event which have likewise imparted to it no small degree of medical importance. We refer to the employment of chloroform having been sanctioned by Her Majesty's Physician in Ordinary, Sir James Clark, Her Majesty's First Physician Accoucheur Dr Locock, and Her Majesty's other Physician accoucheur Dr Ferguson; to its having been administered by Dr Snow, and to the fact of the Queen and the infant Prince having gone on favourable from the first.

The Court Circular, issued from Buckingham Palace on 7 April, after announcing the Queen's delivery at 'ten minutes past one o'clock', detailed those present* and then continued: 'We understand that chloroform was administered by Dr Snow during the last part of the labour with very satisfactory effects; and that the Queen expressed herself as grateful for the discovery of this means of alleviating and preventing pain.'

In her diary Victoria was more eloquent in its praise. 'The effect was soothing, quieting, and delightful beyond measure', she wrote, and there can be no doubt the experience had been altogether dif-

---

* 'His Royal Highness Prince Albert, Dr Locock, Dr Snow and Mrs Lilly the monthly nurse. in the adjoining apartments besides the other medical attendants (Sir James Clark and Dr Ferguson) were Her Royal Highness the Duchess of Kent, the Lady-in-Waiting on the Queen, and the following Officers of State and Lords of the Privy Council: viz the Earl of Aberdeen, First Lord of the Treasury; Earl Granville, Lord President of Council; the Duke of Norfolk, Lord Steward; the Duke of Wellington, Master of the Horse; the Duke of Newcastle, Secretary of State for the Colonies; the Marquis of Lansdowne; the Marquis of Breadalbane, Lord Chamberlain; the Duke of Argyll, Lord Privy Seal; Viscount Palmerston, Secretary of State for the Home Department; and the Lord Chancellor.'

ferent from those of her previous confinements. The presence of the
two midwives, Mrs Lilly and Mrs Innocent, and the anaesthetist,
Dr Snow, had been symbolic of the unsullied success of the occasion!

Not everyone in the medical profession was so sure that this was
an entirely safe procedure. *The Lancet* produced a leading article
a month later commenting upon 'a very extraordinary report', as
they put it, concerning the Queen's recent confinement.

It has always been understood by the profession that the births of the
Royal Children in all instances have been unattended by any peculiar
or untoward circumstances. Intense astonishment therefore has been
excited throughout the profession by the rumour that Her Majesty during
her last labour was placed under the influence of chloroform, an agent
which has unquestionably caused instantaneous death in a considerable
number of cases. Doubts on this subject cannot exist. In several of the
fatal examples persons in their usual health expired while the process
of inhalation was proceeding, and the deplorable catastrophies were
clearly and indisputably referable to the poisonous action of chloroform
and to that cause alone.
... On enquiry therefore we were not at all surprised to learn that in
her late confinement the Queen was not rendered insensible by chloroform or by any other anaesthetic agent. We state this with feelings of
the highest satisfaction. In no case could it be justifiable to administer
chloroform in perfectly ordinary labour, but the responsibility of advo-
cating such a proceeding in the case of the Sovereign of these realms
would, indeed, be tremendous. Probably some officious meddlers about
the court so far overruled Her Majesty's responsible professional advisers
as to lead to the pretence of administering chloroform but we believe
the Obstetric physicians to whose ability the safety of our Illustrious
Queen is confided do not sanction the use of chloroform in natural labour.

The Lancet was wrong in its view of what Victoria's physicians
sanctioned, but right that death had occurred in patients given
chloroform in various circumstances. The whole science of anaesthesia was only ten years old and knowledge of the risks involved
was still elementary. Chloroform, although in many respects an
ideal anaesthetic agent, and an advance on previous ones, did have
disadvantages which would ultimately be responsible for its replace-
ment many years later by other agents with fewer risks. Comparatively little was known of the circumstances in which chloroform
might be toxic, and to administer it to the Queen was, as *The Lancet*

suggested, a questionable step to take. Had labour been less of an ordeal to her it is doubtful if she would have received it. We do not know to what extent her own wishes influenced her medical attendants, but it seems not unlikely that she might have been the prime mover, having heard of the enormous relief it provided.

The British Medical Journal, feeling that it had been accused of inaccurate reporting by its sister journal, wrote on 27 May, 'As the article in *The* Lancet is calculated to throw discredit upon our statement we think it right to repeat it along with an assurance of its accuracy.' *The British Medical Journal* then repeated its original report and went on:

The Medical Times of May 21st in the reply to *The Lancet* of the 14th repeats and enlarges our statement in the following words: 'Dr Snow administered chloroform to the Queen in the presence of Sir James Clark for the last hour of parturition. A handkerchief on which a small quantity of chloroform had been dropped was held to the face. Her Majesty was never completely insensible; but she expressed herself as satisfied with the anodyne effects produced. Should further information be required we are confident that Dr Snow will, with his usual courtesy, afford it to all such as consider themselves entitled to ask it. . . . We would remind *The* Lancet that anaesthesia may be induced without loss of consciousness. To those accoucheurs who are in the habit of using chloroform in labour we would refer for final decision the question of its being a safe or a dangerous practice. From a careful perusal of most of what has been written on the subject, as well as from some personal experience of the practice, we may in the meantime state as our own humble opinion that the cautious inhalation of the vapour of chloroform during labour is entirely free from danger and calculated to afford merciful relief from pain in one of the most agonizing trials of humanity.'

With such a forthright statement *The British Medical Journal* seemed to have emerged victorious from the fray but the *Lancet* was nearer the truth. Despite *The British Medical Journal's* 'humble opinion', the inhalation of chloroform during labour was not 'entirely free from danger', even when given in such a manner as not to render the subject completely insensible. Sudden deaths had occurred and would continue to occur even though great care was taken to administer the anaesthetic properly. The same medical journals which were reporting the royal event contained in their pages during 1853 several accounts of deaths from its use. Later it became known that chloroform had, in some circumstances, a markedly toxic effect upon the liver, from which fatalities also occurred. Looking back on this royal confinement now it seems a too-bold step to have taken which, had it been attended by complications, would have left the members of the royal team with few supporters.

The Queen was nonetheless so pleased that she had chloroform again for the latter part of labour and delivery in her last confinement. '*Anaesthesia à la Reine*' was the title by which it became known.

Despite the comparatively painless quality of Victoria's last two deliveries, her emotional state had not been improved by pregnancy after pregnancy. Elizabeth Longford records that Sir James Clark had warned the Prince that it might be dangerous for the Queen to have another child. It was not her physical health, which was robust, but her mental state which so concerned him that he spoke to her also on the subject.

How this was to be accomplished was of course another matter. Victoria's distaste for child-bearing at all, and in particular for bearing a large family, is in sharp contrast to the nine children she finally bore. That she loved her husband dearly there is no doubt, although their temperaments were strangely contrasting and their relationship was at times a love–hate one. But, with her passionate nature and the deep physical attraction they felt for each other, she would have had no wish to limit her family by breaking off, or even making infrequent, their sexual relations. It is generally held that her need for, and her enjoyment of, the sexual side of her marriage was great and, although this view is based upon veiled references in her own writings and those of her daughters, it is probably correct.

Of contraceptive methods, however, she would have had little knowledge. Even by declining to feed her children – as had been common practice in royal circles for generations – she was, although she probably did not know it, depriving herself of a period of physiological contraception which lactation affords for a while. Continued lactation for a long period of time is not of course a reliable method of contraception, but a woman who does not feed her child at all is likely to begin to ovulate again much sooner than one who does.

Population studies in various countries have suggested that the interval between births in women not practising contraception may be six to nine months longer in those who breast-feed their infants than in those who do not. But breast-feeding was just another aspect of human reproduction which Victoria found distasteful, and when her daughters were later to have children and breast-feed them she disparagingly referred to them as 'cows'.

There can be no doubt that birth control by *coitus interruptus*, known as onanism from Biblical times, was practised on occasions by many. It was at best a fallible method of contraception which required strength of will rather than scientific knowledge, but by the middle of the nineteenth century comparatively little more of value had been learned. The whole armamentarium of contraception consisted of 'coverings used by males, blocks and injections by the females to complete their shame'. But it was not so much that there were no methods of birth control to use, as that these methods were regarded as repellent practices beneath the notice of decent people. The medical profession ignored the subject, and there was very little scientific work on the mechanism of conception or knowledge of the menstrual cycle. For example, one of the pioneers of contraception, Dr Knowlton, who already in the nineteenth century had advocated the douche as a method of preventing conception, believed that menstruation was the preparation for a pregnancy, rather than an indication that it had not occurred. He also believed the ovum took four weeks to pass down the length of the fallopian tube, which we now know it accomplishes in three days. A French scientist, Pouchet, who did excellent early work on the ovum, was nonetheless wildly out in the view he expressed that the most fertile time in the cycle was during menstruation and twelve days following it. It was to be years before the true relationship of ovulation to menstruation was established, and the practice of limiting intercourse to a 'safe period' became possible.

But the overriding obstacle to birth control was that it was not a subject decent people discussed, let alone practised, and it had no social acceptance. Had it even approached the degree of approval it enjoys now, and had it been put upon a reasonable scientific footing, it is difficult to believe that the Queen would not have wanted to exercise it to space her children further apart and, once her duty to the succession was well and truly done, reduce their number. Of course Victoria's psychology was immensely complex and certainly not least on matters touching the pregnant state and its effect on male–female relationships. David Duff has suggested that one of the reasons why Queen Victoria bore so many children was that she believed that by doing so she tightened her grip on her husband. It is true that during her pregnancy and labour Albert was immensely kind, considerate, attentive and understanding of her tantrums, which could always flare up so easily and unaccountably, whether she was pregnant or not. Victoria was a creature of emotion, Albert of reason, and he was more reasonable when she had more excuse for her outbursts. But it does not seem altogether likely that this would have been enough to overcome her hatred of the pregnant state, or her impatience with the irksome restrictions which it imposed upon her.

But to have restricted her family even to seven children would in one respect have had a very important effect although she could not possibly have known this. For Victoria was a carrier of the disease haemophilia, the effects of which before the birth of her two youngest children, Leopold and Beatrice, were present only in her second daughter Alice. Leopold was to be a sufferer from the disease, and Beatrice a carrier, like her elder sister.

Haemophilia is an inherited disorder of the variety known as a sex-linked recessive. A recessive abnormality is one which must be present on each of a pair of our chromosomes to have a physical effect. Inheritance is carried on our genes, which in turn are carried on our chromosomes which are in the nucleus of every cell in the body. These chromosomes exist as twenty-three pairs, all carrying information which determines our particular physical characteristics. If a recessive abnormal trait exists in only one of a particular pair of chromosomes, the potential ill effect that this might produce will be overcome by the other normal member of the pair, and the individual will show no manifestation of the disease in question. If both chromosomes of the pair have the trait, the disorder becomes clinically evident. The person with the trait on only one of the chromosomes is the carrier of the disease but not a sufferer.

One variety of recessive inheritance is called sex-linked, and to this group haemophilia belongs. What happens here is that the trait is carried on the x chromosome, which is one of the pair of chromosomes which determines our sexual development; if both members of the pair are xs the child is female, but if one is an x and the other y the child is male. The abnormal gene for haemophilia exists on the x, but in the female its effects can be compensated for by the normal genes on the other x; the woman is then a carrier but does not have the disease. If the child is male, however, and the other chromosome is a y, it cannot compensate for the abnormality on the x and a haemophiliac is born.

This disease then is carried by affected males and by females, but only males suffer from it. A woman with the trait on one of her x chromosomes has a fifty per cent chance of passing this gene to her offspring, since half the eggs in her ovary will contain the abnormal chromosome and half will not; half of her daughters will therefore be carriers and half normal; half her sons will be haemophiliacs and half normal. A man with haemophilia cannot pass the disease to his son since that son receives the father's y chromosome; the daughter of a haemophiliac must be a carrier since she must receive her father's x chromosome which is the abnormal one.

Haemophilia is a haemorrhagic disease. Bleeding cannot be stopped by the ordinary clotting mechanisms by which normal individuals control minor haemorrhage. Trivial injuries can cause large bruises, painful effusions of blood into joints, serious blood loss from minor cuts and abrasions, and in those days the unfortunate haemophiliac often became a permanent invalid with a short life expectation. Many advances in the treatment of the disorder have been made in recent times but in the middle of the nineteenth century it was not fully understood and little could be done to ameliorate its effects.

The relationship of Queen Victoria's nine children to haemophilia is as follows:

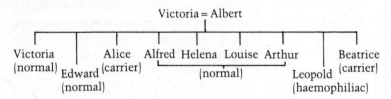

She was indeed lucky. Of four sons who might have been affected, only one was a sufferer; of five daughters who might have been carriers, only two had that misfortune. As things turned out, however, had she borne but seven children there would have been only a single carrier. It is sometimes suggested that her eldest daughter, Vicky, was a carrier but there seems to be no medical evidence to support this. She bore her husband, Frederick III, the German Emperor, four sons – Wilhelm, the Kaiser of the First World War; Henry, Prince of Prussia; Sigismund, who died at the age of two and Waldemar who died at the age of eleven. Neither Sigismund nor Waldemar appears to have been a haemophiliac.

Her second daughter, Alice, was later to marry Louis IV, Grand Duke of Hesse-Darmstadt. She was to bear five daughters, two of whom were carriers, and two sons, one of whom was a haemophiliac. Leopold, Victoria's haemophiliac son, lived until he was thirty-one and his wife bore two children, a carrier girl and a normal boy. Beatrice was the most unfortunate; of her four offspring, there were two haemophiliac sons and a carrier daughter. Queen Victoria's great-grandchildren contain in their number four boys afflicted with the disorder (see the table on p. 186); the carrier status of several of the girls is unknown.

Haemophilia affects some of its sufferers more severely than others. Leopold, her first affected son, had, in the Queen's own words 'been four or five times at death's door' and was hardly ever 'a few months without being laid up'. When he was twenty-nine years old he married Helena of Waldeck; even at that early age he was lame from the episodes of bleeding which had affected his joints. Their first child, Alice – an inevitable carrier – was later to bear one affected son and a second who died in infancy who might also have been affected. Leopold's second child, a normal son, was not born until a few months after his father's death which, ironically, was caused by a brain haemorrhage resulting from a minor blow to the head whilst he was on a visit to Cannes for his health.

The most dramatic effects of the disorder are to be found in the Russian and Spanish royal families. Alix, the second carrier daughter of Alice, married Nicholas II, the Tsar of all the Russias. She gave birth to four daughters and one son, Alexis, the Tsarevitch. All were murdered with their parents in a cellar in Ekaterinburg

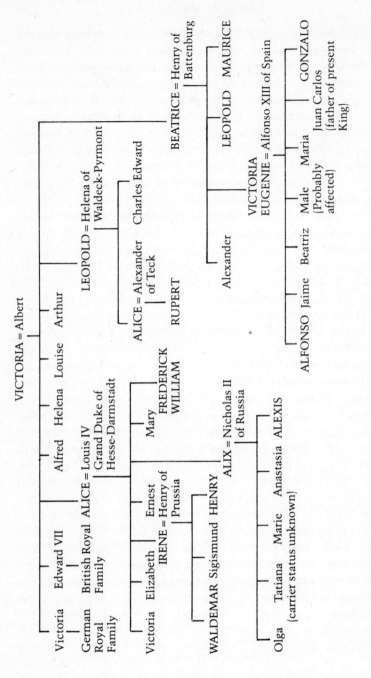

Males in CAPITALS are haemophiliacs, females carriers.

in 1918. Alexis was then fourteen years old but so severe had the
manifestations of the disease been in him that he was little more
than a helpless cripple for most of his short life; his sisters' carrier
status is unknown. Victoria Eugenie, daughter of Beatrice and
Prince Henry of Battenburg (the name later anglicized to Mount-
batten) married Alfonso XIII of Spain. They had five sons of whom
one died at birth and may have been affected, two who were healthy,
and two, Alfonso and Gonzalo, haemophiliacs. Alfonso died aged
thirty-one from haemorrhage resulting from breaking a leg in a car
accident, and Gonzalo at the age of twenty, also from a motor accident although the injuries he received were trivial. The longest
affected member of Queen Victoria's family was Prince Waldemar
of Prussia, grandson of Princess Alice, who survived until he was
fifty-six.

The origin of the haemophiliac gene in Queen Victoria is uncertain. It may have developed as a spontaneous mutation or she
may have inherited it from her parents, the Duke and Duchess of
Kent. It could not have been passed to the children from Prince
Albert since he did not suffer from the disease. His son, Leopold,
who was a haemophiliac, must have had a male arrangement of chromosomes – XY; the Y chromosome had come from his father so Victoria must have provided the X which carries the abnormal genes
as we have seen.

Examination of the Duchess of Kent's family tree does not show
any clear sign that she had inherited the disorder, and the Duke
cannot have inherited it since he would have been affected if he had.
McKusick, on whose excellent study this account is based, says,
'It is clear that the mutation had taken place in the preceeding genera-
tion' (i.e. preceding Queen Victoria) ... 'the mutation had occurred
in one of the germ cells that made her.' The same author speculates
on the possibility of the mutation having occurred in the sperms
of her father, the Duke of Kent, who was fifty-two when she was
born; he suggests that such events are more likely to occur in older
men but, whilst there is evidence to support this in some abnormali-
ties, haemophilia does not show such an age effect. It is more likely
that the mutation occurred in the Duchess of Kent who contributed
an abnormal ovum to the conception of her daughter.

Whether Queen Victoria's abnormal gene has become extinct or not is uncertain. The possible carriers in the four daughters of the Tsar Nicholas II were killed before they had children. The abnormality at any rate in Russia died with them. In Spain the two daughters of Alfonso XIII, Beatriz and Maria, each had a fifty per cent chance of being carriers and in Britain a descendent of the affected Leopold, Lady Mary Abel-Smith, had a similar chance of carrier status. In none of their descendants, however, has the gene become clinically evident and, although it is not certain that it has disappeared for ever, there is every reason to hope that it has.

It is ironic that Beatrice should provide the largest number of Queen Victoria's affected grandchildren and great-grandchildren for she was her last child. Albert, Prince Consort, died in 1861 aged only forty-two. Victoria reigned for forty years more and mourned him agonizingly until her death in 1901.

Not until 103 years after the birth of Princess Beatrice did a British Queen or Queen Consort again bear a child when Queen Elizabeth II gave birth to Prince Andrew on 19 February 1960.

Appendix I

Reports on the Post Mortem Examinations on the Bodies
of His Royal Highness William Henry, Duke Of Gloucester,
and His Mother, Her Majesty Queen Anne

William Henry Duke of Gloucester
(Blenheim M/S FI 16a)

Upon the death of His Highness William, Duke of Gloucester, which happened on Monday, 29th July about midnight, the right honourable the Earl of Marlborough, one of their Excellencies the Lords Justices of England and Governor to his late Highness, was pleased to give order, that the Body should be opened.

Accordingly the surgeons appointed by his Lordship (whose names are subscribed) in the presence of Dr Hannes, who was commanded to assist at the operation, and of several other spectators, made the Dissection; and afterwards jointly with the Dr. gave in the following report on it, on Wed. July 31 1700.

1. On the inspection of the outward surface of the body, the Head, Chest, Abdomen and Arms appeared livid and tainted more than usual, the legs and thighs not much altered from their proper colour.
2. The Abdomen was first opened, and these observations were made upon the parts contained:
The Omentum was found as is natural.
The Gutts from the Rectum inclusively upwards to the Duodenum, had the common appearances: excepting only that a few inflammatory spotts were seen disperse upon the small gutts, and that the plerus glandulares of the same gutts were become florid, and therefore more conspicuous than is usual.

The Duodenum and stomack and gullet were highly inflamed, especially the stomack which had in its cavity wind and a small quantity of liquor.

In the Pancreas, spleen, liver and bladder of gall was nothing remarkable only the spleen and liver were more livid than usual: the substance of the kidneys carried a colour deeper than ordinary: besides which they were not noted to have anything preternatural: as neither had the glandulae renales or the ureters of the urinary bladder of the Urine expressed from the bladder.

3. Next after the abdomen, the Thorax or chest was examined. Here the Pleura was inflamed to the most intense degree.

The Diaphragm and mediastinum and pericardium were thought not to differ from the constitution given them by nature: excepting that the Diaphragm was some thing inflamed.

The Humor of the Pericardium was red: and perhaps not without a mixture of blood: And even the Thorax and abdomen were judged to have more blood in their Cavitys than could well proceed from the mouth of the vessels cut by the knife at the time the respective venters were laid open:

In the Larynx, the membranes that join the cartilages, cricoides and Thyreoides were very dark with inflammation.

The membrane that links the Epiglottis at the root of the tongue was also inflamed insomuch that the glandulae miliares of it which are scarce visible at other times, were much distended and very conspicuous.

4. In the mouth, we found the palate inflamed, as also the uvula: the membrane of which has swelled.

The almonds of the ears were swelled and had in them purulent matter, there being prest out of one of them, as much of it as filled a tea spoon.

5. Last of all, the head was opened, and out of the first and second ventricles of the cerebrum was taken about four ounces and halfe of a lympid humour.

The Heart was extremely flaccid and weak in its texture, the right ventricle had very little blood, and the left ventricle was altogether empty.

The Lungs in both sides were filled with blood to the height of an inflammation.

The neck was swollen and upon dissection the condition of the contained parts appeared such as is observed in bodys strangled. At the place where the jugulares arise above the claviculae, the inflammation approaches very near to a mortification.

The glandula thyreoidea were almost black with the inclosed blood: and being putt into scales were found above five drachms in weight.

The gullet was much inflamed, as was said above.

The windpipe also was affected in the same kind, especially the upper parts of it called the larynx.

In this region nothing besides was found particular or differing from the natural state and disposition of it.

Signed: Edward Hannes M.D.
        Charles Bernard
        Edward Greene
        William Cowper

Queen Anne
The British Medical Journal, 12 November 1910, p. 1530)
At the Council Chamber, St James's, the 3rd August, 1714.

Present:
    Their Excellencys the Lords Justices in Council.
    The Physicians called in and Dr Laurence delivered the following paper, containing an Acct. of what was observed at the opening of her late Maj^{ys}. Body.

                                      Kensington Palace,
                                      2 August, 1714.
Upon opening the Body of her late Majesty of Blessed Memory, We found a small Umbilical hernia Omentalis without any excoriation, a large Omentum well Coloured. No water in the Cavity of the Abdomen. The Stomach thin, and its inward coat too smooth. The Liver not Schirous, but very tender and Flaccid, as were all the rest of the Viscera of the lower belly. The Gall, Bladder, Kidneys, and Urinary bladder without any stone. There was a very small Scorbutic Ulcer on the left leg. We can give no further account, being forbid making any other inspection than what was absolutely necessary for Embalming the Body.

    The Physicians' Report to their Excellencys deliver'd by Dr Lawrence as Principal Physician.

    (Signed)

                                      Jo. Shadwell,
        Thos. Laurence,   Hans Sloane,
        Davd. Hamilton,   Amb. Dickins,
        Jno. Arburthnott,   Rd. Blundell.

A true Copy.
(Signed) EDWARD SOUTHWELL.

Appendix II

Report of the Postmortem Examination on the Body of
Her Royal Highness Princess Charlotte and of the Inquest
on the Death of Sir Richard Croft

Princess Charlotte
(from *An Obstetric Tragedy* by Franco Crainz.
William Heinemann Medical Books Ltd, London 1977).

The appearances which were observed on inspecting the Body of Her
late Royal Highness The Princess Charlotte of Wales the seventh of
November 1817.

The Membranes of the Brain had their natural appearance. The Vessells of the Pia Mater were less distended with Blood than was to be
expected after so severe a Labour. The Ventricles of the Brain contained
very little fluid. The Plexus Choroides was of a pale Colour, and the
substance of the Brain had its natural texture.

The Pericardium contained two ou^ces of red coloured fluid: The Heart
itself and the Lungs were in a natural state. The Stomach contained
nearly three Pints of Liquid. The Colon was distended with Air.

The small Intestines Spleen Pancreas & Kidneys were in a healthy
state. The Uterus contained a considerable quantity of coagulated Blood
and extended as high as the Navel, & the Hour Glass Contraction was
still very apparent. The right Ovarium was formed into a Cyst the size
of a Hen's Egg, distended with Serum, and a Mass of Sebaceous Matter,
the left Ovarium was in a Healthy state.

The Urinary Bladder was empty & in a sound condition.

The Child was well formed and weighed nine pounds – Every part
of its internal Structure was quite sound.

(Signed)   David Dundas
          Everard Home

Sir Richard Croft
(from Green, T., *Memoirs of Her Late Royal Highness Charlotte Augusta*, London, Caxton Press, 1818).

Friday morning, the 13th of February, an inquest was held on the body of Sir R. Croft, who shot himself that morning in Wimpole-street. The Rev. Dr Thackeray, one of His Majesty's Chaplains, stated that, in consequence of his lady being taken ill, Sir R. attended her from Tuesday till Thursday night about eleven o'clock, when, conceiving that he was much fatigued, they prevailed on him to retire to rest; which he did, after many entreaties. Witness retired to bed about the same hour, and Sir R. appeared anxious to get up at any time they might call him. About two o'clock in the morning, witness heard a noise, which he thought was like the falling of a chair, but took no further notice, and went to sleep again; and in about an hour afterwards he was awoke by the servant maid, who told him his wife was in labour. He went immediately to the room the deceased slept in, and opened the door, went in, and found him on the bed, on his back, with a pistol in each hand; the muzzles of both were at either side of his head. He was quite dead. He could have no intention of destroying himself when he went to bed, as he did not close the door of the apartment. Witness observed to the deceased before he went to bed, that he, witness, was in great agitation. Sir Richard answered, 'What is your agitation compared to mine?' and witness supposed at the time that he was suppressing his emotions. The deceased bled at the nose several times during his attendance. – Mr Hollings, surgeon, of Green-street, Grosvenor-square, said that he had observed a considerable alteration in the deceased's state of mind and his manners for some time past; he had frequently seen him so melancholy, that it was quite distressing; his mind was so absorbed, that he would not give answers to questions which were put to him: for the last ten days the deceased had been attending a patient who was in a dangerous state; and on witness conversing with him respecting her, deceased threw himself on the bed, and struck his forehead, as if his brain was very much agitated. He noticed him particularly on Tuesday night, as he was attending a lady; he was so agitated, that Dr. Warren asked him if he was ill? He answered in an incoherent manner, 'No'. Witness is of opinion, that had a person been present when he had the pistol, he could have obtained no control over him; indeed, he should have thought it very dangerous to have left such weapons within his reach. A short time ago, witness was in company with the deceased, when he exclaimed abruptly, 'Good God, what will become of me!' Witness positively believes he was in a state of derangement when he committed the act. (Here one of the jurymen asked Mr

Hollings, whether, in his opinion, the death of the Princess had been the exciting cause of his derangement? or whether he had observed his mind to be diseased previous to that melancholy event? Mr Hollings replied, he had no doubt whatever of the insanity of the deceased having been caused by the unfortunate events at Claremont; that, previous to that time, he had never observed his mind to be disturbed.) – Drs Baillie and Latham, and Mr. Finch, proved that the deceased had, since the death of the Princess Charlotte, laboured under mental distress. He had repeatedly been heard to say, that this lamentable circumstance weighed heavy upon his mind, and he should never get over it. – The Jury then went to view the body, On a table lay the play of 'Love's Labour Lost', which was open at a page in which appeared the words, 'Good God! where is the Princess?' The Jury remarked this as a singular coincidence and returned to the jury-room, where the Coroner summed up the evidence, and the Jury, after a short consultation, returned a verdict of 'Died by his own act, being, at the time he committed it, in a state of mental derangement'.

Select Bibliography

Aspinall, A. (ed.), *Correspondence of George Prince of Wales*, 4 vols. (London 1965–7).

Arkell, R.L., *Caroline of Ansbach* (Oxford 1939).

——*The Letters of the Princess Charlotte, 1811–17* (London 1940).

Aveling, J.H., *English midwives: their history and prospects* (reprinted London 1967 from the 1872 edition by John L. Thornton, FLA).

Edwards, Averyl, *Frederick Lewis Prince of Wales* (London 1947).

Bathurst, Benjamin, *Letters of two queens* (London 1924).

Baxter, Stephen, *William III* (London 1966).

British Medical Journal, 15 April 1853, p. 318; 27 May, p. 450.

——'Some royal deathbeds', 12 November 1910, p. 1, 530.

Brooke, John, *King George III* (London 1172).

Burnet, Bishop, *A history of my own time* (London 1875).

Cambridge, George Duke of, *A memoir*, edited by E. Sheppard (London 1906).

Campbell, *Lives of the Chancellors*, 8 vols. (London 1845–7).

Coke, Lady Mary, *Letters and Journals, 1756–74* (Bath 1970).

Colchester, Lord (ed.), *The Diary and Correspondence of Charles Abbot, Lord Colchester* (London 1861).

Cowper, Lady, *Diary of Mary Countess Cowper, 1714–20* (London 1864).

Craig, William, *Memoirs of Her Majesty Sophia Charlotte of Mecklenburg-Strelitz, Queen of Great Britain* (Liverpool 1818).

Crainz, F., *An obstetric tragedy* (London 1977).

Curtis, Gila, *The life and times of Queen Anne* (London 1972).

Curtis Brown, Beatrice (ed.), *The letters and diplomatic instructions of Queen Anne* (London 1938).

Denman, T., *Aphorisms on the application and use of forceps* (6th edition, London 1817).

——*An introduction to the practice of midwifery*, edited by C. Waller (London, Vol. I 1788; Vol. II 2nd edition 1798; 3rd edition 1830).

Doran, Dr, *Lives of the queens of England* (London 1855).

Duff, David, *Albert and Victoria* (London 1972).

Egmont, 1st Earl of, *Diary, 1730–47*, 3 vols. (London 1920–3).

Fox, Henry Edward, *Journal* (London 1923).

Fulford, Roger, *Royal dukes* (London 1973).

Glenbervie, Lord, *Diary of Sylvester Douglas*, edited by F. Bickley (London 1938).

Green, David, *Queen Anne* (London 1974).

Green, T. (ed.), *Memoirs of Her late Royal Highness Charlotte Augusta of Wales and of Saxe-Coburg* (London 1818):

Greenwood, A.D., *The Hanoverian queens of England* (London 1911).

Greville, F., *The diaries of Colonel the Hon. Fulke Greville*, edited by F. McKno Bladon (London 1970).

Haggard, H.W., *Devils, drugs and doctors* (London 1929).

Hamilton, E., *William's Mary* (London 1972).

Hedley, Olwen, *Queen Charlotte* (London 1975).

Hervey, Lord, *Memoirs*, edited by Romney Sedgwick (London 1952).

Hibbert, Christopher, *George IV Prince of Wales* (London 1972).

Holland, Sir Eardley, 'The Princess Charlotte of Wales: a triple obstetric tragedy', *Journal of Obstetrics and Gynaecology of the British Empire*, 1951, *58*, p. 90.

Holme, Thea, *Prinny's daughter* (London 1976).

Hone Campbell, R., *The Life of Dr John Radcliffe* (London 1950).

Hopkinson, M.R., *Anne of England* (London 1934).

Hopkirk, Mary, *Queen Adelaide* (London 1946).

Hunter, William, *An obstetric diary of 1762–5*, edited by J. Nigel Stark (reprinted from *Glasgow Medical Journal*, 1908).

Jerningham, Lady, *Letters*, 2 vols. (London 1946).

Jones, Glunn R., 'David Daniel Davis', *The Carmarthen Antiquary*, 1972, VIII, p. 91.

Jones, O.V., 'Welsh obstetricians' (reprinted from the *Transations of the Honourable Society of Cymmrodorion*, 1978):

Kaye, J.W., and Hulton, J. (eds.), *Autobiography of Miss Cornelia Knight* (London 1861).

Kemble, James *Idols and invalids* (London 1933).

Kroll, Maria, *Sophia, Electress of Hanover* (London 1970).

Lancet, 'Delivery of the Queen', 28 November 1840, pp. 347, 348.

——14 May 1853, p. 450.

Le Fort, H., *Des maternités* (Paris 1866).

Lewis, Jenkin, *Queen Anne's son: memoirs of William Henry Duke of Gloucester* (reprinted London 1881 from a tract published in 1789).

Livingstone, G. Bancroft, 'Louise de la Vallière and the birth of the man-midwife', *Journal of Obstetrics and Gynaecology of the British Empire*, 1956, *63*, pp. 261–7.

Luttrell, N., *Brief historical relation of state affairs 1678–1714*, 6 vols. (London 1857).

McKisick, Victor A., 'The royal haemophilia', *Scientific American*, Vol. 213, 1965, pp. 88–95.

Marlow, Joyce, *The life and times of George I* (London 1973).

Marples, Morris, *Six royal sisters* (London 1969).

——*Poor Fred and the butcher* (London 1970).

Medical Times, 21 May 1853.

Metelerkamp, Sanni, *George Rex of Knysna: the authentic story* (Cape Town 1955).

Miller, John, *The life and times of William and Mary* (London 1974).

Northumberland, Duchess of, *Extracts from the diary of the first Duchess of Northumberland*, edited by James Grieg (London 1926).

Oman, Carola, *Mary of Modena* (London 1972).

Pound, Reginald, *Albert* (London 1973).

Radcliffe, Walter, *Milestones in midwifery* (Bristol 1967).

Rath, G., 'Die Gottingher Buchausstellung', *Sudhoff's Arch. Gesech. Med.*, 1962 *46*, pp. 182–4.

Russell, Lady Rachel, *Letters* (London 1826).

Sadler, S.H., *Infant feeding by artificial means* (London 1896).

Sandford, Francis, *Genealogical history of the kings and queens of England*, continued by Samuel Stebbing (London 1707).

Sedgwick, Romney (ed.), *Letters of George III to Lord Bute, 1756–66* (London 1939).

——'The marriage of George III' *History Today*, June 1960, p. 371.

Seymour, Lindsay, J., *Iron and brass implements of the English house* (London 1971).

Stanhope, Lady Hester, *Memoirs* (London 1845).

Stanley, Mary F. *The life and times of Queen Adelaide* (London 1840).

Stevenson, R. Scott, *Famous illnesses in history* (London 1962).

Stockmar, Baron von, *Memoirs* edited by his son, E. von Stockmar (London 1872).

Storrar, Patricia, *George Rex: death of a legend* (South Africa 1974).

Strickland, Agnes, *Victoria from birth to bridal* (London 1840).

——*Lives of the queens of England from the Norman Conquest*, 8 vols. (Bath 1972).

Stuart, D.M., *The daughters of George III* (London 1939).

Thoms, William J., *Hannah Lightfoot*, reprinted with some additions from 'Notes and Queries' (London 1867).

Twiss, Horace, *The public and private life of Lord Chancellor Eldon* (London 1844).

Van der Zee, H. and B., *William and Mary* (London 1973).

Vernon, James, *Letters illustrative of the reign of William II*, edited by G.P.R. James (London 1841).

Walpole, Horace, *Correspondence*, edited by W.S. Lewis (London and New Haven 1937).

——*Letters of Horace Walpole to Sir Thomas Mann*, vol. I. (London 1943).

Wickes, Ian G., 'A history of infant feeding', *Archives of Disease in Childhood*, *28*, pp. 151, *252*, 332, 416, 495 (London 1953).

Willoughby, Perceval, *Observations on midwifery*, edited by H. Blenkinsop (Wakefield, Yorks. 1972).

Winwood, Ralph, *Memorials of affairs of state in the reigns of Queen Elizabeth and King James I* (London 1725; facsimile reprint London 1972).

Woodham-Smith, Cecil, *Queen Victoria* (London 1972).

Young, J.H., *The history of Caesarean section* (London 1944).

Ziegler, Philip, *King William IV* (London 1971).

Index